D1451213

CONSUMER HEALTH AND PRODUCT HAZARDS - CHEMICALS, ELECTRONIC
PRODUCTS, RADIATION

The MIT Press
Cambridge, Massachusetts, and London, England

CONSUMER HEALTH AND PRODUCT HAZARDS - CHEMICALS, ELECTRONIC
PRODUCTS, RADIATION

Vol. 1   of THE LEGISLATION OF PRODUCT SAFETY

Samuel S. Epstein and Richard D. Grundy, editors

Dedicated by Samuel S. Epstein to his children:
Mark, Julian, and Emily

This book was typed by Dorothy Linick.
It was printed by Clark-Franklin-Kingston Press
and bound by The Colonial Press, Inc.
in the United States of America.

Library of Congress Cataloging in Publication Data

Epstein, Samuel S.
Consumer Health and Product Hazards - Chemicals, Electronic
Products, Radiation

[The legislation of product safety, v. 1]

   CONTENTS: v. 1. Chemicals, Electronic Products, Radiation
   1. Hazardous substances. 2. Product safety.
T55.3.H3E67   604'.7   74-995
ISBN 0-262-05013-7

# CONTENTS

This book along with its companion, Vol. 2, which deals with regulatory aspects of the problem, confronts the consumer with the problem of how to develop a protective response to the onslaught of toxic materials that are now found in the everyday environment. The books provide the consumer with a useful guide through the maze of substances, effects, standards, and legislative controls which now surrounds the problem. Having confronted this issue and having learned what can be done about it, the reader will be led to another question: How did this problem arise in the first place; why, in the most technologically advanced society known to history, have we managed to develop new technologies which are so threatening to human health and welfare?

In seeking an answer to this question, we have an important clue in the nature of the problems which are taken up in this book. The threats to health which are discussed are almost entirely due to new synthetic chemicals and to radiation. We can ask, then, what there is about synthetics and radioactive materials which tends to generate threats to human health. The answer arises out of an understanding of the relationship between living things and their environment.

During the course of evolution the chemical, physical, and biological properties of the earth's surface gradually achieved a state of dynamic equilibrium, characterized by processes which link together the living and nonliving constituents of the environment. Thus were formed the great, elementary cycles which govern the movement of carbon, oxygen, and nitrogen in the environment, each cycle being elaborately branched to form an intricate fabric of ecological interactions. In this dynamic balance, the chemical capabilities of living things are crucial, for they provide the driving force for the ecological cycles; it is the chemistry of photosynthesis in green plants, for example, which converts the sun's energy to food, fiber, and fuel.

The chemical processes which are mediated by living things are particularly rapid because they are activated by very effective catalysts -- the enzymes. These are specific proteins, often complexed with particular metallic ions or with small organic molecules that participate in the activation process. The events catalyzed by enzymes -- the processes of cellular biochemistry -- are typically cyclical and are intricately branched to form a network in which hundreds of different types of enzymes and many thousands of different organic substances are interconnected.

However, despite their considerable number and variety, the chemical processes which are mediated by the biochemical system

represent an exceedingly small fraction of the reactions that
are <u>possible</u> among the chemical constituents of living cells.
This principle explains the frequency with which synthetic
substances that do not occur in natural biological systems --
such as those which are discussed in this book -- turn out to
be toxic.

It will be useful to provide a simple example of what is
meant by the restriction of possible reactions in a living
system. If tissue from a potato tuber is crushed in the
presence of oxygen, a familiar reaction takes place; there is
formed a reddish pigment and eventually a black precipitate.
The biochemical mechanism is well known; it involves the
enzymatic oxidation of an amino acid, tyrosine, through a
series of colored intermediates, to form the natural black
polymer, melanin. Clearly, the substances present in the
potato cell are capable of undergoing this reaction.
Nevertheless no melanin is formed in an intact, living potato
cell. The production of melanin, although possible, is simply
not realized in the normal, living potato cell.

Some other examples of this principle are the following:
(a) Of the approximately 100 chemical elements which occur in
the materials of the earth's surface, less than 20 appear to
participate in biochemical processes, although some of those
which are excluded, such as mercury or lead, can in fact react
quite readily with natural constituents. (b) Although oxygen
and nitrogen atoms are common in the organic compounds found
in living systems, biochemical constituents which include
chemical groupings in which nitrogen and oxygen atoms are
linked to each other are very rare. (c) Although the numerous
organic compounds which occur in biochemical systems are
readily chlorinated by appropriate artificial reactions, and
the chloride ion is quite common in these systems, chlorinated
derivatives are extremely rare in natural biochemical systems.

The extremely small fraction of the possible reactions which
are actually realized in biological systems is closely related
to the process of evolution, which is basically a process of
natural selection. On the chemical level, this means that as
the present biochemical system evolved numerous opportunities
probably existed for the occurrence, at least once, of many of
the chemical processes which are now <u>missing</u> from the
biochemical system. For it should be recalled that evolution
has spanned several billion years, in which a vast number of
individual organisms and separate cells had an opportunity, in
the course of their development, to give rise to a given
chemical reaction. Thus, we must regard the processes and
constituents which <u>do</u> occur in present living organisms as,

so to speak, survivors of a long period of trial and error
involving a vast opportunity for trials and therefore for
errors. What is meant here by an "error" is simply an
innovative chemical event which is incompatible with the
survival of the rest of the biochemical system, and which is
therefore unable to become perpetuated in the system.

The instances cited above of chemical constituents which
tend to be excluded from biochemical systems are indeed, as
expected, incompatible with these systems: (a) If mercury is
artificially introduced into a living organism, from which it
is normally excluded except at negligible concentrations, the
mercury readily reacts with sulfur-containing groups that
occur in amino acids in proteins. These groups often constitute
the catalytically active site of an enzyme and when they react
with mercury the enzyme is inactivated, with often serious
and sometimes fatal consequences to the living cell. In effect,
biochemical systems, having evolved a system of enzymatic
catalysis in which sulfur-containing groups play a crucial
role, are not able to tolerate the introduction of mercury.
(b) When living organisms are exposed to synthetic nitroso
compounds in which nitrogen and oxygen atoms are linked,these
substances often have very powerful deleterious effects, for
example, as carcinogens and mutagens. In general, nitroso
compounds are not only rare but also appear to be incompatible
with the very subtle array of reactions involved in the orderly
development and inheritance of living cells. (c) As amply
demonstrated in this book, synthetic organo-chlorine compounds
(e.g., DDT, PCB's) are responsible for some of our most serious
environmental hazards; such substances are often acutely toxic,
or produce long-term damage such as carcinogenesis.

These examples suggest that the <u>consistent</u> <u>absence</u> of a
chemical constituent from natural biological systems is an
extraordinarily meaningful fact. It can be regarded as prima
facie evidence that, with a considerable probability, the
substance may be incompatible with the successful operation of
the elaborately evolved, exceedingly complex network of
reactions which constitutes the biochemical systems of living
things. Of course, a substance which is absent from natural
systems is not <u>necessarily</u> toxic or biochemically disruptive.
For example, this may be true of a synthetic polymer such as
nylon (at least in the pure form, free of plasticizers or
stabilizers, many of which are now known to be damaging).
However, on the larger scale of the ecosphere, this very
inertness of nylon and other plastics does constitute a hazard;
since the materials are not degradable by biological systems
they accumulate as trash, or are burned and pollute the air.

It seems to me that a similar argument can be advanced to account for the biological hazard from radioactive substances and X rays. Radioactive substances emit -- and X rays can be characterized as -- highly energetic particles which are likely to disrupt, at random, any molecules with which they collide. The intricate, delicately integrated network of reactions in living cells is particularly susceptible to this kind of energetic, random intrusion and we can anticipate an <u>inherent</u> incompatibility between radioactivity and living things.

What this means is that technologies which propose to work with synthetic organic compounds or with radioactive substances must deal with these materials with the prudence and care that is demanded when a situation is inherently dangerous. This book offers evidence that we have not yet achieved this goal, and suggests what can be done to remedy this grave defect.

Barry Commoner

One is struck by what this book does not say, as much as by
what it does say. While the book admirably accomplishes its
purpose of describing current thought about the regulation of
hazardous chemicals in consumer products, a further message
rings clear. For a great number of chemical substances,
knowledge about the harmful effects of these materials is
imperfect at best or nonexistent at the very worst.

Recent experience with such materials as mercury, the
polychlorinated biphenyls, and asbestos has aroused the public
and their representatives in the Congress. Many people are
haunted by the thought that new "mercuries" are only waiting
to be discovered. We are all being forced into a hard look at
our system for consumer product regulation and control to
determine where it has failed us and allowed the widespread use
of highly toxic chemicals without our full knowledge of what
we are doing to ourselves.

The body of environmental and consumer law continues to
grow. While the lawbooks are filled with means of controlling
the quality of consumer products, and their component
chemicals, we still find gaps in the regulatory framework
which must be closed.

One such gap exists with respect to the environmental
effects of consumer products. As an example, in the past the
nation has been concerned about discharges of industrial
mercury, of industrial pollution, and rightly so. The virtual
elimination of this source is a victory we can all look to
with pride and relief; however, possibly an even greater threat
of mercury pollution exists from consumer products since
mercury from such sources passes through municipal waste
treatment facilities virtually untouched. Testimony before the
Senate Committee on Commerce has shown that there is a good
chance that even more mercury enters our waterways from this
source than from industrial effluents. While part of this
source can and should be eliminated under the Federal
Insecticide, Fungicide, and Rodenticide Act, there are some
products containing mercury which are unregulated. Examples
are home thermometers, electrical switches, barometers,
batteries, some antiseptics, soaps, cosmetics, pharmaceuticals,
and paints. Taken together, these sources amount to a
substantial contribution of mercury to the environment. Thus
the statutory framework contains a flaw that should not exist.

Before too many readers digest this book I would hope that
this loophole in the law is closed. Legislation to fill this
gap, the proposed Toxic Substances Control Act, is making its
way through the Congress. Diversity in the types of hazards,
the number of chemical substances, and the number of products

governed by the legislation has complicated the task of the
Committee on Commerce and the Congress almost beyond belief.
Despite the roadblocks and difficulties, I feel confident that
the Congress will approve the legislation requiring an
assessment of the public health and environmental hazards of
chemical substances prior to their introduction in the
environment, rather than -- as too often is now the case --
determining the facts after the damage is done.

While it would be indeed tragic if the Federal Government
were to rest on the record of past accomplishments, significant
progress has been made in controlling the hazards of consumer
products. Within the last six years, no less than fourteen
measures dealing with such hazards have emerged from the
Committee on Commerce and become law. Not the least of these
is the Consumer Product Safety Act of 1972, which passed in
the waning days of the 92nd Congress. This omnibus measure,
which grew out of studies by the National Commission on Product
Safety, is designed to deal with virtually all direct hazards
to human beings which arise from consumer products. When the
Toxic Substances Control Act passes, one further step will be
made to close the circle of consumer product safety.

With rare exception, the impetus for legislation of the
type that is shaping up now in the Congress begins with a
scientific discovery that a chemical is much more dangerous,
particularly with regard to long-term effects, than we had
thought. The contributions of the scientific community to the
wave of environmental and consumer awareness has been enormous.
I commend the scientists who make these discoveries and the
lawyers, journalists, and others who prod a sometimes unwilling
government into action. Over the years the scientific community
has offered testimony before the Committee on Commerce and its
subcommittees on a myriad of environmental and consumer
protection issues. Without the help of these men and women the
work of the Committee would have been difficult, if not
impossible. So many times, that first hint of danger has only
foretold problems of a much greater significance.

Among the authors and editors of this book are to be found
proponents of this public-interest science. Their problems in
putting together a book of this sort are immense and are not
completely unlike those facing us who must design the
regulatory framework for the control of chemical substances.
I sympathize with them because I can feel the enormity of their
task. I commend them for performing it so well.

Warren G. Magnuson

CONTRIBUTORS

RICHARD A. CARPENTER, Ph.D.
Executive Director Environmental Studies Board, National
Academy of Sciences, National Academy of Engineering,
Washington, D.C.

SAMUEL S. EPSTEIN, M.D.
Swetland Professor of Environmental Health and Human Ecology
and Director of Environmental Health Programs, Case Western
Reserve University Medical School, Cleveland, Ohio

RICHARD D. GRUNDY, M.P.H., E.I.T.
Professional Staff, Senate Committee on Public Works; Executive
Secretary, National Fuels and Energy Policy Study, Senate
Committee on Interior and Insular Affairs, Washington, D.C.

HANNO C. WEISBROD, LL.D.
Former Legislative Assistant, Congressman Peter H.
Frelinghuysen, House of Representatives, Washington, D.C.

CONSUMER HEALTH AND PRODUCT HAZARDS - CHEMICALS, ELECTRONIC
PRODUCTS, RADIATION

# 1

## LEGISLATIVE APPROACHES TO BALANCING RISKS AND BENEFITS IN THE REGULATION OF CHEMICALS

Richard A. Carpenter

CONTENTS

## Introduction

The truism "it's a chemical world" needs to be examined thoughtfully in arriving at a public policy position on the health and environmental hazards of chemicals. Life has evolved in contact with the chemical elements, their salts and solutions, and thousands of different compounds. The survival of the fittest came, among other tests, from the successful resistance of living organisms, including man, to naturally occurring chemicals and the poisonous contents of many plants and animals. Given the leisurely pace of evolution, each chemical threat from nature could be adapted to, if not by one species then by another.

The result is the present diversity of life in the biosphere. Even now, the testing goes on and it is common knowledge that unusual exposure to natural materials is still hazardous. Salt ingested in sufficient quantity is poisonous. Mushrooms and raw fish kill gourmets every year. Sulphurous vapors in volcanic regions can overcome the unwary. Many natural chemical products are known to be carcinogenic. The normal rate of genetic mutation is provided in part by radioactivity in the environment.

However, the advent of chemical technology in the past few decades has radically increased the contact of living things with new chemicals in ways never before encountered. The techniques of chemistry have synthesized new compounds with unique biological activity. Chemical technology can produce novel materials in large quantities. These chemicals are often alien to the environment, persistent, and mobile, interacting with natural products and biological processes in unpredictable ways.

Citizen confidence in the institutions of society has ebbed as the complexity of modern life has grown. The combination of increased population density and intensified technological change has strongly affected the human environment and has made the individual aware of his loss of personal control over his well-being. The total system is suspect; not simply business or government. A strong reaction to the daily evidence of environmental hazards has been directed against applied science and its practictioners. In response, the technical community exposes the case that the only plausible path to an improved quality of life is through greater knowledge in the natural and social sciences and ever more ingenious engineering options to achieve our goals. A steered technology, tuned to human needs over the long term, appears to be necessary -- and possible.

Improvement in social control of applied science is a proper
concern of politics and in particular the legislative branch of
government. The United States Constitution gives (in Section 8)
the Congress the power to regulate commerce among the States.
The courts have interpreted this to apply not only to goods
but to their components. This federal control allows equitable
treatment of manufacturers and consumers of chemicals in the
United States. In fact, the "Commerce Clause" is the basis of
all regulatory legislation. Administrative agencies reduce
these policies to practice. Both consumers and responsible
manufacturers need to be protected by legal safeguards against
operators who are not concerned with undesirable consequences
or side effects of their products or practices. In the United
States the most important decision-making institutions are the
democratic processes of government and the choices of a free
market economy.

The foregoing is a capsule description of the current
operational situation within which we begin to discuss
improving the benefit-to-risk ratio for chemicals as they are
used today. The problem is not new. As recounted by the National
Research Council's Food and Nutrition Board (1), "for more than
2,000 years, the main purpose of coloring foods was to disguise
poor quality and, in many cases, obscure adulteration." Some of
the coloring agents were highly toxic (e.g., copper sulfate,
copper arsenate and lead chromate). For over 500 years
governments have been legislating protection for the public
against adulteration, with varying degrees of success.

The current realities are illustrated more succinctly by
a news article in Science (2), concerning the information
available to make a judgment of safety for a certain
contaminating substance. A harrassed federal official is
quoted as saying, "It's not complete but you've got to go on
what you have. We can't be held accountable for every goddamn
chemical!" Decisions are always made with less than perfect
information; the pace of human activity usually does not slow
to allow for desired additional research. Yet government and
business must be concerned and accountable for the welfare of
citizens in situations where the five senses and conventional
wisdom are not enough protection.

This paper reviews some of the constraints and opportunities
in constructing a system of assessment which goes beyond the
primary cost/benefit balance of short-term, localized
marketplace economics. The Lincolnian limitation of government
to those functions which the individual cannot accomplish for
himself would encompass a great proportion of life in the
western world. The regulation of synthetic chemicals, so

apparently vital to our national economy, is one of the most difficult problems posed by modern technology, largely because the undesired consequences may be subtle and long term. A willingness of the public to accept restrictions, expensive control programs, and substitute materials must in part derive from a growing recognized responsibility to unborn generations and the environment they will inhabit. President Lincoln is also credited with a description of the attitude of all too many people toward this distant future. He said that they ask, "What has posterity ever done for me?" We are dealing with human nature as well as science, economics, and politics when we address the problem of chemicals in the environment.

## The Legislative Process

A Search For Balance  Current events and research in environmental sciences concur in pointing up the immediate need to do a better job of assessing the consequences and impacts of chemicals on man and the human environment. At the same time, the benefits to health, nutrition, and economic well-being of chemical synthesis and formulation must be retained and enhanced. An optimum balance, reached through rational decision-making, is the ideal which society is now expressing. A benign technocratic authority might set up a cost accounting system and the requisite scientific inputs and proceed toward the goal in a systematic way. Those who have been involved in this field for the past twenty years have occasionally longed for such a seemingly straightforward approach. But there are complexities and value judgments involved which defy neat scientific quantification or formulae and few citizens (even few technologists) are willing to abandon the management of the human environment to an elite. The question is not only one of benefits and risks which can be measured; there are many unknowns. "Society must be willing to accept some finite risk as the price of using any carcinogenic material in whatever quantity. The task of selecting a socially acceptable level of human risk rests with society and its political leaders." (3) Therefore, the effort continues to bring information and knowledge to the democratic institutions and open debate which are considered to characterize American government.

Goals and Priorities  The 92nd Congress (1971-1972) can best be viewed as an integrating institution composed of 435 voting Representatives and 100 Senators who are called upon to bring the enormous diversity of America to bear on complex societal

issues in the form (finally) of a simple Yea or Nay vote.
Elected, at least in part, on the basis of their individual
prescription for achieving national goals, these men and women
must search for the best balance at any given time. An added
difficulty is that everything cannot be done at once, even in
a country so rich as the United States. Priorities must be
assigned for the allocation of money, manpower, and natural
resources.

<u>Committee Jurisdiction</u>  The legislative process is made up of
three major activities: the authorization of new or continuing
programs; the appropriation of money to implement the
authorized activities; and overview (oversight) hearings and
investigations by Congressional committees to determine whether
the intent of the Congress is being followed. In each two-year
session about 30,000 bills are considered and about 600 Public
Laws enacted. These laws are expressions by the Congress of
the goals and objectives set in continuing discussion and
debate in committees, on the Senate and House floors, and
ultimately, in House-Senate conferences.
    Although the Congress integrates a great many viewpoints
and bits of factual information, its own Committee organization
tends to fractionate issues to the extent that resulting
legislation may not be coherent. For example, legislation
covering pesticides regulation is under the jurisdiction of
the House and Senate Agriculture Committees; but it also is
of concern to Subcommittees of the House and Senate Commerce,
the House Merchant Marine and Fisheries, and the House and
Senate Government Operations Committees. It must be admitted,
however, that no other organizational format would likely be
better in dealing with the multidisciplinary problems of
today.
    Table 1 summarizes the current jurisdictions of
Congressional Committees over chemicals in the environment.
At least 27 separate subcommittees are involved in the two
bodies in considering some 50 different aspects of the
regulation of chemical products. The major subjects which are
covered by several subcommittees (in addition to the necessary
bicameral duplication) are:
Pesticide regulation
Food inspection
Wildlife conservation
Air pollution
Eutrophication
Consumer protection
Hazardous Substances Transportation

Table 1  Congressional Committee Jurisdiction Over Chemicals
In The Environment

| Committee | Subcommittee(s) | Examples of Current Topics Under Consideration |
|---|---|---|
| **House of Representatives** | | |
| Agriculture | Commodity Operational | Agricultural and industrial chemistry |
| | | Agricultural colleges and experiment stations |
| | | Agricultural economics and research |
| | | Animal industry and diseases of animals |
| | | Dairy industry |
| | | Entomology and plant quarantine |
| | | Forestry in general, and forest reserves other than those created from the public domain |
| | | Human nutrition and home economics |
| | | Inspection of livestock and meat products |
| | | Plant industry, soils, and agricultural engineering |
| | | Regulation of the Dept. of Agriculture |
| | | Insecticides and pesticides |
| | | Laboratory animal welfare |
| | | Migratory Bird Conservation Commission |
| Appropriations | Agriculture Environmental and Consumer Protection | Appropriations for: USDA, EPA, FDA, etc. |

Table 1 (cont.)

| Committee | Subcommittee(s) | Examples of Current Topics Under Consideration |
|---|---|---|
| | Labor, Health, Education, and Welfare | |
| Government Operations | Conservation and Natural Resources | Studying the operation of Government activities at all levels with a view to determining its economy and efficiency |
| | | Overview of air pollution abatement activities |
| | | Eutrophication in lakes |
| Interior and Insular | Environment | Forest reserves and national parks created from the public domain |
| | Irrigation and Reclamation | Irrigation and reclamation |
| | Mines and Mining | Mining interests generally |
| | | Petroleum conservation on the public lands and conservation of radium supply in the United States |
| | | Energy and fuels resources |
| Interstate and Foreign Commerce | Public Health Environment | Interstate and foreign commerce generally |
| | | Public health and quarantine FDA |
| | | Adulteration, misbranding, etc., of foods and drugs |
| | | Air pollution, i.e., the Clean Air Act |
| | | Federal Cigarette Labeling and Advertising Act |
| | | Consumer protection, i.e., Federal Trade Commission Act |

Table 1 (cont.)

| Committee | Subcommittee(s) | Examples of Current Topics Under Consideration |
|-----------|-----------------|------------------------------------------------|
| | | Establishment of a commission to study the use of chemicals in peace and war |
| | | Resource recovery and solid wastes |
| | | Electronic products and medical devices |
| Merchant Marine and Fisheries | Fisheries and Wildlife<br><br>Conservation<br><br>Oceanography | Fisheries and wildlife, including research, restoration, refuges, and conservation |
| | | Transportation of inflammable substances on passenger vessels |
| | | Environmental quality, i.e., National Environmental Policy Act |
| Public Works | Flood Control<br><br>Watershed Development | Flood control and improvements of rivers and harbors |
| | | Oil and other pollution of navigable waters |
| | | Water pollution control, i.e., Federal Water Pollution Control Act |
| Science and Astronautics | Science Research and Development | National Science Foundation Scientific research and development |
| | | Science resources as applied to environmental quality |
| | | Establishment of an Office of Technology Assessment |

Table 1 (cont.)

| Committee | Subcommittee(s) | Examples of Current Topics Under Consideration |
|-----------|-----------------|------------------------------------------------|
| Senate | | |
| Agriculture and Forestry | Agricultural Research and General Legislation<br><br>Soil Conservation and Forestry | Inspection of livestock and meat products<br><br>Animal industry and diseases of animals<br><br>Agricultural and industrial chemistry<br><br>Dairy industry<br><br>Entomology and plant quarantine<br><br>Human nutrition and home economics |
| Appropriations | Environmental Agriculture and Consumer Protection<br><br>Labor and Health Education, and Welfare | Appropriations for EPA, USDA, FDA, etc. |
| Commerce | Consumer<br><br>Energy, Natural Resources, and the Environment | Fisheries and wildlife, including research, restoration, refuges, and conservation<br><br>Interstate and foreign commerce generally<br><br>Oceanography<br><br>Effective criteria for the care and treatment of animals used for research and experiment |

Table 1 (cont.)

| Committee | Subcommittee(s) | Examples of Current Topics Under Consideration |
|---|---|---|
| | | Extension of public health protection with respect to cigarette smoking, and for other purposes |
| | | The Flammable Fabrics Act |
| | | Matters involving product labeling |
| | | Matters involving hazardous substances |
| | | Regulation of trade in drugs |
| | | Matters relating to safety |
| | | Electronic products and medical devices |
| Government Operations | Executive Reorganization and Government Research | Reorganization in the Executive Branch of the Government |
| | | Studying the operation of government activities at all levels with a view to determining its economy and efficiency |
| | | Matters relating to consumer affairs |
| Interior and Insular Affairs | Minerals, Materials and fuels | Forest reserves and national parks created from the public domain |
| | Legislative Oversight | Mining interests generally |
| | | Petroleum conservation |
| | | Environmental quality, i.e., National Environmental Policy Act |

Table 1 (cont.)

| Committee | Subcommittee(s) | Examples of Current Topics Under Consideration |
|---|---|---|
| Labor and Public Welfare | Health | Public health and quarantine<br><br>National Science Foundation<br><br>FDA health research |
| Public Works | Air and Water Pollution | Air pollution control, i.e., Clean Air Act<br><br>Water pollution control, i.e., Federal Water Pollution Control Act<br><br>Oil pollution<br><br>Solid wastes and resource recovery<br><br>Environmental noise |
| Joint Committee on Atomic Energy | Raw materials<br><br>Research, Development, and Radiation | Continuing studies of the activities of the Atomic Energy Commission and of problems relating to the development, use, and control of atomic energy<br><br>Radioactive materials<br><br>Radiation standards |

Hazardous Substances Transportation
Chemical Warfare Agents
Laboratory Animal Welfare
Drug Regulation
Labeling Requirements

An Ethical Base For Political Action  Another difficulty in
formulating laws concerned with social priorities is that the
value system against which decisions and their consequences are
tested is changing. Public attitudes are reflecting a new
social "ethic" of personal responsibility for environmental
quality. This ethic is similar to our belief in free education
or in abiding by the law. It is the only ultimate means of
obtaining the correct individual behavior toward the
environment which will add up to a proper societal behavior

(i.e., preventative rather than remedial). For example, antilitter laws have been generally ineffective and unenforceable, but the impression of individual responsibility in school programs and public information campaigns has gradually led to an ethic under which more and more people voluntarily refrain from the easy course of dumping their refuse along the public roads. Another example is in population control; coercive laws would be abhorrent, but evidence is accumulating that young persons are planning their families according to an ethic of only replacing themselves.

An environmental-quality ethic is still in the early stages of development. The perception of the environment and its amenities is, itself, a growing phenomenon. The association of longer term environmental detriments with lessened human health and longevity is beginning to be accepted without detailed scientific proof. These shifts in public opinion bring about the possibility of political action which would not have been possible a few years ago.

## Information For The Congress

Sources of Assistance  A legislator may discharge his duty and vote on proposed laws with no regard for informed opinion or facts, and of course, many do follow a set pattern or ideology without considering the merits of the case in point. But the Congress has, in recent years, shown a marked interest and receptivity for advice and counsel. The old saying is that the Executive proposes and the Legislative disposes. That is not what the Constitution envisioned in "separation of powers" and "checks and balances." If the Congress is to maintain its proper role in our branches of government, a parity of information resources vis-a-vis the Administration is essential.

A many-faceted scheme of assistance has been constructed to bring timely and accurate information to committees and individual members of the Congress. Sources under the direct control of Congress include the staffs of members and committees, the General Accounting Office (for postaudits and program evaluation), and the Congressional Research Service (CRS) of the Library of Congress. The CRS comprises eight problem-oriented divisions for research and analysis. Their staffs are composed of specialists from many disciplines, who provide bridges between the political process and the various professional fields. Three groups are particularly concerned with chemicals and the human environment: the Environmental Policy Division (pollution, effects on fish and wildlife,

ecological impacts); the Science Policy Research Division
(effects on human health, research on test methods and medical
information); and the Education and Public Welfare Division
(Federal regulatory agencies and programs, and public health).
The other CRS divisions are American Law, Economics, Government
and General Research, Foreign Affairs, and Senior Specialists.

The Congress receives a great amount of information from
the Executive departments and agencies as they advocate their
programs, request funds, and defend or explain their
performance. There is a natural (and healthy) skepticism in
the Legislative Branch toward Administration testimony. When
different political parties control each Branch and especially
when controversy arises, the candor and completeness of
information provided is subject to further question.

The internal staff assistance has been increased
substantially in recent years to give the Congress more
resources responsible only to its needs. The Legislative
Reorganization Acts of 1946 and 1970 implicitly accepted and
approved the pattern of multiple support staffs. The
philosophic assumptions are that the Congress as a separate
and equal branch of the Federal Government is entitled to a
reasonable parity with the Executive Branch in the quality and
variety of its informational and policy analysis resources;
that these units should be capable of supplying objective,
unbiased evaluations of information and proposals received
from any source; that these staffs should enhance the ability
of the Congress to maintain continuous surveillance of the
Executive Branch's operations; and that they should assist the
Congress in developing policy initiatives of its own.

Scientific Information and Advice  Very few legislators are
trained or experienced in science or engineering. In the past
ten years considerable effort has been made from within both
the political institutions and the scientific community to
facilitate the interchange of questions, ideas, opinions, and
facts. A high degree of receptivity on the part of policymakers
is a keystone in erecting the system of effective communication.
The Congressmen must have confidence in their information
sources. Table 2 shows the processing which must take place to
make the results of scientific research useful in decision
making. Four stages can be identified: generation, analysis,
assessment and decision making. The two intermediate steps are
currently under development to create an orderly flow and
transformation.

Scientists work in a variety of research facilities to
generate new understanding of the natural environment (Stage 1).
Over 350 years of development has gone into the scientific

method which establishes facts and extends the boundaries of knowledge. Disciplinary specialists assemble raw data around hypotheses in order that their colleagues may replicate experiments and verify results.

At the next level these reports are combined by equally competent researchers into peer judgments of broader significance. This information analysis (Stage 2) produces the traditional review articles which compare and select the most valid information and synthesize a state-of-the-art report on a particular field. This is an intradisciplinary validation of what is known, what is unknown, and what could be known with more research in a certain time period.

The third stage of information transfer adds more context such as social and economic considerations. The applications of scientific knowledge through engineering innovations and guidelines for human activities are discerned and evaluated. Options and their consequences are investigated. A systems viewpoint is assumed and inputs from other disciplines are integrated. The real-world situation is the matrix in which the scientific facts are embedded for examination. Relevance is a key word.

Finally, the structured, interpreted, validated information is submitted to the political context. This stage must be supported independently to respond to the special purposes of each of many decision-making groups: The Executive departments and agencies, the Congress, the Judiciary, private-sector interest groups, conservation, environmental, and consumer-protection organizations, and so on. Subjective values are included at this point and the alternatives offered by science are tailored to support political objectives.

Some Advice For Scientific Advisers    The role of the public-spirited scientist who undertakes to participate in the formulation of public policy extends over all four stages, but the scientist assumes different roles at each stage. Therefore, it is very important for the lay user of scientific information to establish the level or stage at which he is communicating with his scientific advisor. Is the scientist speaking as a generator of new facts, a validator of disciplinary information, an interpreter of relevance, or an advocate of a particular option?

Extrapolations and "if-then" scenarios are useful in arousing public interest, but they confound those responsible for policy formulation. The decision maker is used to incomplete knowledge -- in fact this is always the case. The scientist is used to hypothesis and experimentation. The tradition of experimental verification, peer review, and synthesis into

Table 2   The Flow of Environmental Science Information

| Stage | Functions and Products | Institutions and Performers |
|---|---|---|
| I. Generation | New facts and knowledge from research, monitoring, surveys, testing. Publication in the scientific literature after peer review and editing. Discussion in meetings of learned societies. | Universities, government laboratories, industrial research operations, independent laboratories and foundations. |
| II. Analysis | Information processing: collection, organization, indexes and bibliographies, storage, retrieval. Critical review: synthesis and comparison of independent studies, evaluation and validation, confidence and error limits, digestion and repackaging. Publication as critical reviews, state-of-the-art reports, compilations, standard reference data. | Specialized information analysis centers. Ad hoc panels from professional societies. Federal agencies, commercial information organizations and publications. Recognized scientific leaders. |

Table 2 (cont.)

| Stage | Functions and Products | Institutions and Performers |
|---|---|---|
| III. Assessment | Economic and social context added. Applications, alternatives and options for engineering innovation. Social indicator and environmental quality indicator concepts. Cost/benefit, risk/benefit analysis. Interdisciplinary systems consideration with long time horizon. Reports and studies may be closely coupled to particular user or may be freely available. | Regulatory agencies, industrial marketing organizations, policy advisory apparatus such as the Council on Environmental Quality. Ad hoc studies, impact assessments. Congressional hearings, including staff studies and with the assistance of the Congressional Research Service. |
| IV. Decision making | Political judgment added, means are related to goals, Management action and implementation in the real world. Integration of all aspects. Timetables and priorities are set. Different decision makers respond to their own constituencies and policy objectives. | The Congress, the Administration and mission agencies. Special-interest groups, consumers, conservationists. Business organizations. Individuals and the collective public make many decisions. |

theory is the time-consuming method of approximating the truth. However, the pace and momentum of current events exert pressure on scientists to shortcut this process and all too often the resulting decisions are based on false or fragmentary knowledge.

I suggest that any answer by scientists to a question from the public affairs arena be composed of four parts:

1. What is known and with what degree of certainty.
2. What is not known and why (difficulty of measurement, incomplete theory, etc.).
3. What could be known given a certain additional time and resources.
4. What should be known in order for society to make a decision with reasonable assurance that important costs and benefits have been considered.

A pro-and-con or adversary format may be useful. Another device is the admitted weighting of evidence (on the basis of peer judgment) in order to make a definitive statement -- with dissent and its reasons placed in a footnote. Frequently attempts are made by expert witnesses to present a consensus where there is uncertainty rather than stating precisely what is unknown and the potential implications of this lack of knowledge (e.g., long-term effects of environmental pollution). Consensus should not be attempted in uncertain areas and the scientific community should not be vague about what it doesn't know.

The legislator operates best when faced with a list of alternative responses to priority problems -- what can be done. Several actions are usually suggested by the factual description of the problem. These alternatives can be augmented by scientific experts who factually discuss the attendent impacts, costs, side effects, feedback mechanisms, etc. Scientific advice to the political process should stop short of advocacy even though one course of action may be obvious to the scientist. The objective is to reserve decision making to those (elected) officials who are politically responsible and accountable -- not to establish a technocracy nor to lapse into a plebiscite of partially informed citizens on every issue which arises. Even where the issues involve complex technical matters, the ability of the politician to integrate economic, social, raw political, and human intuitional inputs is extremely valuable and should be guarded. As a citizen, the scientist may opt for one or another solution, but in his advisory capacity, to be most effective, he should provide an objective analysis, as complete as possible, of remedial alternatives.

Another aspect of the effective communication of scientific advice to the legislator is recognition of the motivations of human beings which, of necessity, constrict the implementation of decisions. Only the archetypal ivory-tower scientist would wish to pursue his work without consideration of individual human goals and objectives. The interpretation of the facts about consumer and environmental problems should take due regard of the weakness of the flesh despite the willingness of the spirit.

For example, corrective actions will occur much more easily if they can be seen to coincide with immediate self-interest such as direct human health effects, welfare of offspring, damage to property, threat to livelihood, or disruption of the status quo. In contrast, appeals may go unheeded when based on altruism, long-term benefits, good will toward man, voluntary reduction of standard of living to preserve the commons, stewardship of the affluent (noblesse oblige), or subjective esthetic values.

There are possibilities for merging of individual "economic" desires with actions for the long-term common good. For example, ecological principles will be obeyed whether we do it willingly or not. It can be shown that a high-productivity environment is indeed a high-quality environment. Another example of the approach may be found in attitudes toward the less developed countries. We may very well make enormous investments and outright grants in these societies in order to preserve world order. Therefore, it should be practical to underwrite whatever concessions we ask them to make in order to abate environmental degradation. A third example would stress the prudence of knowing more about global systems (research and monitoring), whether or not critical problems exist, simply so we can optimize the economic exploitation of resources and the environment over a very long period of time.

The decision maker can be greatly helped by the purposeful seeking out of those facts and interpretations which strengthen implementation of desired courses of action by enlisting human nature. In fact, it would appear that people will do the right thing even at some personal inconvenience if some reinforcing of their ethical armament is provided by pointing out practicality and prudence. The value of expert advice is apparent when a distinction is made between the implementation of short-term goals and an assurance that a long-term perspective is provided for the evolution of future specific policies. This does not suggest any distortion of the scientific information but only that effort be directed at revealing the connection of good environmental management and personal health and welfare.

## Congressional Consideration of Environmental Hazards

The Pre-1962 Period   Before World War II legislative consideration of environmental and consumer science matters was limited; the following were particularly significant actions:
1862
Land Grant College Act established in each State at least one college in agriculture and the mechanic arts.
1863
National Academy of Sciences chartered.
1890
Weather Bureau established.
1901
National Bureau of Standards established.
1906
Food and Drug Act
1910
Insecticide Act - prevented adulterated or mislabeled pesticides.
1912
Public Health Service created to conduct field investigations and studies in diseases of man and pollution of navigable waters.
1930
Food and Drug Administration established.
1937
National Cancer Institute established.
1938
Food, Drug, and Cosmetic Act. Pesticide residues on food-stuffs were limited. The concept of tolerance was introduced and the administration of the law was to consider the extent to which pesticides were "required or can not be avoided in the production of each such article."

Probably none of the Acts just given involved any debate on the subtle aspects of applied science. The issues were straightforward ones of promoting technology or solving immediately obvious problems and meeting clearly defined needs.

During World War II the Office of Scientific Research and Development demonstrated conclusively that science could be purposely and dependably focused on national goals with enormous return on investment. In 1946, the Atomic Energy Act

created a special agency to develop nuclear technology and also
established the Joint Committee on Atomic Energy in the
Congress. The necessity for government patronage of basic
research was recognized in the establishment of the National
Science Foundation in 1950. During these postwar years,
however, Congressional deliberations still did not include
substantial scientific content. For the most part the funding
was for military or atomic energy programs of a classified
nature. The Committees with the proper jurisdictional
responsibilities brought their recommendations to the floor
of the Senate or House and few questions were asked.

The passage of the Federal Insecticide Fungicide and
Rodenticide Act in 1947 is a case in point. New pesticides,
mainly synthetic organic chemicals, had begun to replace the
older inorganic salts (e.g., arsenicals). The 1910 labeling
act did not contain sufficient authority to regulate quality,
efficacy, and safety in application. A bill was introduced in
early 1946 which was favored by both industry and farm groups.
Final action was not taken that year and the bill was
reintroduced in 1947. Brief hearings were held before the
House Agriculture Committee with testimony presented by the
Production and Marketing Administration of the Department of
Agriculture, the Fish and Wildlife Administration of the
Department of the Interior, the chemical pesticide
manufacturers, farm organizations, and State agricultural
agencies. The possibility for hazards of residues on foodstuffs
and the ecological impact of persistent biocides were hardly
mentioned. The only comment on potential adverse effects
concerned the reluctance of the bee keepers to place their
bees in areas where certain pesticides were being used because
the colonies were killed off.

The bill was favorably reported, passed without debate by
both Houses of Congress and signed into law (P.L. 80-104) on
June 25, 1947. It provided for registration of economic poisons
by the U.S. Department of Agriculture prior to sale, mandatory
labeling including instructions for safe use, reports on
delivery, movement and inventory, and a warning statement to
prevent injury to man, other vertebrate animals, vegetation,
and useful invertebrate animals. Experience has proved that
these policy objectives or restrictions did not adequately
protect all the environmental values at risk (4).

The contaminated cranberry scare in 1959 provides insight
into governmental administrative and regulatory practices for
that period of time. The Delaney Clause (for Rep. James J.
Delaney, D.-N.Y.) of the 1958 Food Additives Amendment to the
Food, Drug and Cosmetic Act states that "no additive shall be

deemed safe if it is found to induce cancer when ingested by man or animal, or if it is found, after tests which are appropriate for the evaluation of the safety of food additives, to induce cancer in man or animal..." The qualifying phrase "appropriate, etc." is usually left out of discussions of this law; but its inclusion shows again the congressional attempt at reason and balance. The effect of the clause was to provide complementary authority to the Food and Drug Administration to establish tolerable residue limits.

Following Department of Agriculture instructions, cranberry bogs were treated after harvest with the herbicide Amitrole. The herbicide manufacturer had applied for a residue tolerance so that Amitrole could be used in preharvest application. Because preliminary animal tests showed the herbicide to cause cancer in rats, no tolerable residue limit was issued by the Food and Drug Administration (FDA). The record is not clear on who gave growers advice to go ahead with preharvest treatment -- the Department of Agriculture, agriculture extension agents, the growers association, or the manufacturers and distributors. Some cranberries were treated, residues were detected, and the FDA (apparently for the first time) ruled that pesticide residues were to be considered as additives under the Delaney clause. The Secretary of Health, Education, and Welfare called a news conference 17 days before Thanksgiving to announce that anybody buying cranberries would be doing so at their own risk -- but the berries were not banned. Scare headlines, bureaucratic ineptness, and consumer bewilderment added up to extensive damage to the cranberry industry.

The political reaction was mixed, with some leaders sympathetic to the FDA caution. Others, including then Senator John F. Kennedy and then Vice-President Richard M. Nixon, were photographed eating cranberry products to show their belief in the wholesomeness of the berries. The Congress authorized and appropriated a $10 million indemnity to the growers on the basis that government bungling had damaged the industry (5).

The political response to regulatory actions which hurt local constituencies was further dramatized recently when New England legislators ate swordfish to counter the impact of the FDA ban because of mercury contamination. The Smithsonian Institution has reported similar amounts of mercury in fish collected in 1890 (6).

The AD-X2 battery additive controversy in 1953 involved the proofs of science vs the acceptance in the marketplace as a test of business regulation by government. A vendor of a chemical purported to extend the life of storage batteries was challenged by the Post Office Department and the Federal Trade

Commission who argued that his product (AD-X2) had no merit according to tests run at the National Bureau of Standards. The vendor produced testimonials from satisfied customers and other tests which showed favorable results. He appealed to members of the Congress and of the Senate Select Committee on Small Business to get the government agencies to treat him fairly.

The agencies involved felt that the law compelled them to use scientific evidence to protect the public by regulating the quality and reliability of commercial products. The vendor (and the Secretary of Commerce and other political leaders) felt that the practical utility of AD-X2 was established by customer satisfaction and that scientific tests could not prove a negative -- i.e., that there was no improvement in battery life. In the political climate of that day, the vendor's position was supported, and the Director of the National Bureau of Standards and the scientific community were severely criticized. The point was made that science should not be concerned with regulatory functions.

The scientific method brings only approximations to the truth; testing for effects may take a very long time and additional tests can always be proposed by protagonists on either side. The "accommodation" which is the usual goal of politics may cause the rejection of cold scientific findings if they are too disruptive to the electorate (6, p. 16).

After "Silent Spring"  Legislative attention to environmental affairs was dramatically intensified by events between 1962 and 1964. Rachel Carson's "Silent Spring" was published in the New Yorker beginning with the issue of July 16, 1962. Her writing skill and the inspired allegory of a bird's song caught the attention of the public, political leaders, and the scientific community. President Kennedy immediately commissioned a study by his scientific advisory committee; and their report, "Use of Pesticides" was published on May 15, 1963. On the next day, Senator Ribicoff's Subcommittee of the Senate Government Operations Committee began 15 months of hearings on "Interagency Coordination in Environmental Hazards (Pesticides)."

On November 18, 1963, the Louisiana Wildlife and Fisheries Commission asked the U.S. Public Health Service for assistance in determining the cause of an extensive fish kill in the Mississippi River. Contaminated discharge from a pesticide manufacturing plant was inferred as the source of toxicity. The press portrayed the fish as analogous to the miner's canary -- with implications for human health all too clear.

The effects of these events was to raise environmental management to a first-priority public-policy issue and thus commanding the close attention of politicians and opinion leaders. Every agency, industry, institution, and profession concerned with environmental manipulation was caused to review its responsibilities. The Senate hearings on pesticides found gaps in the jurisdictions of agencies, lapses in regulation and enforcement, and requirements for new legislation. The most important conclusion was that questions of significance concerning the side effects of pesticides were going unanswered. A major change in attitude that occurred amounted to a loss of confidence in the state of knowledge about cause-and-effect relationships (7).

Public Law 88-305, originated by the Ribicoff investigation, was passed to close the loopholes of "protest registration" whereby a pesticide could be marketed, even if rejected by the government, while the manufacturer appealed the agency decision. Funding was increased for research in improved pest-control methods and pesticide effects on fish and wildlife. The chemical industry undertook improvements in manufacturing methods and plant housekeeping. States strengthened regulations pertaining to aerial spraying and commercial applicators. And yet, no major revision of laws governing chemicals in the environment was forthcoming. The apparently obvious immediate benefits of continued pesticide use overwhelmed the evidence of subtle deleterious effects and the unanswered questions of long-term ecological damage.

Environmental Pollution   Parallel to the concern over pesticides, but surprisingly disconnected from it, was legislative attention to air and water pollution. Pollution-abatement laws are based on the policy objective of preserving the value of common property resources of air and water by denying any right to discharge wastes into them which would decrease their usefulness. The most pressing problems were the gross and obvious pollutants such as particulate matter in air and floating or suspended solids in water. However, the importance of invisible gaseous pollutants such as sulfur oxides, nitrogen oxides, and carbon monoxide in air or dissolved salts and organic material in water was recognized.

The approach in water pollution control is to establish criteria which relate the amount of contaminant to the usability of a particular body of water for a given purpose (e.g., drinking supply, agriculture, industry, sport fishing, etc.). The entire emphasis in implementation has been on short-term localized use, not long-term ecological values.

The emphasis in air pollution control policy is to restrict individual source emissions of contaminants to the point that quality of the ambient air does not endanger public health or welfare.

The air and water pollution control laws also reflect recognition that some substances are so toxic that a zero-discharge regulation may be warranted (e.g., beryllium dusts into air or cyanides into water). However, the long-term ecological or human health implications of inadvertent contamination by trace materials is not anticipated by these laws. For example, hazardous chemicals such as the polychlorinated biphenyls and methyl mercury were not supposed to get into surface waters. Until they were identified by refined analytical techniques, they were not subject to the abatement procedures provided for in statutory policies. As each of these subtle threats is perceived, a study is made of its origin and pathways through the environment and then remedial action is prescribed. Thus we see limits being set for mercury and asbestos in air, and for chlorinated hydrocarbons in water. Pollution laws have limited ability to provide preventive, protective action; the emphasis is reactive abatement of a demonstrated environmental degradation.

Technology Assessment   The environmental impacts of technology were the most important stimulus to deepening Congressional examination of the unanticipated consequences of applied science. At the same time the broader concept of technology assessment in general was being developed in both Houses.

The Subcommittee on Science, Research, and Development (Chaired by Rep. Emilio Daddario, D.-Conn.) of the House Science and Astronautics Committee introduced the concept of technology assessment into many of its ongoing activities without formally so stating. The problems of the adequacy of technology for pollution abatement, the evaluation of fire research and safety, the application of science to urban problems, the International Biological Program, and applied science and the world economy were examined in hearings and staff reports.

Under the auspices of Rep. Daddario's Subcommittee, a seminar was convened in September of 1967 which brought together the leaders of major university and professional society dealing with "science and society" or "technology and culture." These observers, mainly social scientists, affirmed the need for a formal assessment mechanism and discussed the context of social values and national goals within which assessment and decision making must occur (8). A bill was introduced by Rep. Daddario in 1967 (H.R. 6698, 90th Congress) to establish a Technology Assessment Board. The bill was never seriously considered as legislation, but was designed to promote discussion.

In 1969, the Subcommittee received three commissioned reports on technology assessment. In the first report, The National Academy of Sciences (NAS) concluded "that mechanisms for technology assessment beyond those currently operating are clearly needed." Existing mechanisms often were found to have built-in conflicts of interest, such as exist within the Federal Aviation Agency, with responsibility for both regulation of aircraft noise levels and the promotion of the supersonic transport (9).

The NAS panel cautioned against the use of technology assessments in a totally negative sense -- i.e., to prevent change per se. Their report stated, "Ideally, the effort should be to modify goals and criteria of success without dictating the means of achieving them." Similarly, Harvey Brooks has argued that assessment based on too stringent standards of performance could "place a presumption so much against new technology that in fact disincentives to innovation would create penalties to society (10)." This NAS report provided an excellent conceptual framework for thinking about and discussing technology assessment.

In the second report, the National Academy of Engineering (NAE) undertook three preliminary assessments as case studies in order to investigate the methodology of technology assessment. Subsonic aircraft noise, the technology of teaching aids, and multiphasic health screening in hospitals were selected as the case studies (11). A difficult question arose concerning how to secure expert advice when most of the expertise might be associated with interested parties rather than the affected public. While this NAE report demonstrated some aspects of the methodology of technology assessment, its major contribution was to highlight the need for more systematic and fundamental work to bring the "art of TA" up to a more generally useful and reliable level. It was asserted that if a professional atmosphere was constructed by the assessment group, biases from primary employment associations were washed out. Thus in deciding whether to insist on unbiased but perhaps uninformed assessors or to concentrate on expertise, the latter option could be safely taken. All affected parties (insofar as they can be identified) should be assured representation by volunteer or solicited testimony. Technology assessment could be initiated either by the perception of existing problems or by recognition of the potential of a new technology. The NAE group found that all

assessments would be expensive and time consuming and therefore
priorities are necessary. "Criteria for establishing the
priority of topics for assessment include the breadth and
depth of the expected social impact, the visibility of the
problems to legislators and to the people, and the current and
expected rates of development of the technologies."

The NAE study of aircraft noise illustrates the wide range
of considerations that typically enter into a technology
assessment. The investigation considered the impact of five
different assessment strategies upon the following list of
affected parties: airline passengers; airline operators;
airport operators; aircraft and engine manufacturers; airport
neighbors; local taxpayers; local business; local government;
and the Federal Government.

In the third report, the Legislative Reference Service
(now the Congressional Research Service) reviewed a number of
past high-technology issues which had come before the Congress
for resolution or comment, ranging from the AD-X2 battery
additive, to water pollution control, to the nuclear test ban
treaty. This report represents an excellent source book not
only for the individual who would attempt a technology
assessment, but also for the decision maker who will evaluate
existing or future assessments (12). It was concluded that all
technology questions could be subsumed under a larger political
assessment scope. In effect this means that while technical
information is important, it must be integrated with social,
economic, political and institutional factors (as it should be)
into the final decision. Often the Congress does not get
technical input in time to be useful -- and sometimes the
information is ignored or plays little part in final policy
formulation. The primary needs of the Congress were stated in
this report to be (1) an early warning that decision making on
technical issues was impending, and (2) reliable information
sources.

As these reports were received and digested, the Subcommittee
held hearings to further define the sort of new capability
necessary for the Legislative Branch. Legislation providing for
a Congressional Office of Technology Assessment was introduced
by Rep. George P. Miller and others on April 16, 1970 with
bipartisan support. After refinement, the measure was
reintroduced in 1971 in both the House (H.R. 10243) and the
Senate (S. 2302). Finally, the Office of Technology Assessment
was established in October 1972 by Public Law 92-484. A unique
equally bipartisan Technology Assessment Board consisting of
three members each from the majority and minority parties in
the House and in the Senate is the governing body. A Technology

Assessment Advisory Council comprising ten public members, the
Comptroller General, and the Director of the Congressional
Research Service provides liaison beyond the Legislative Branch.

During this period of House activities, some parallel
activities were underway in the Senate which are noteworthy,
although they did not bear the precise name "technology
assessment." The rules of the Senate have never provided a
focal point for science and technology comparable to the House
Subcommittee. In 1965, the Senate Government Operation Committee
established a Subcommittee on Government Research under Sen.
Fred Harris (D.-Okla.). In a series of seminars and hearings
between 1965 and 1967, this group developed the theme "research
in the service of man," concentrating (among several topics) on
the future possibilities and problems of biomedical science.

In 1967, Sen. Edmund Muskie (D.-Me.) and other senators
proposed a Select Committee on Technology and the Human
Environment and outlined a scope for the Select Committee which
would be very close to House initiatives in technology
assessment. Subsequently, Sen. Muskie's Government Operations
Subcommittee on Intergovernmental Relations held two sets of
hearings (March–April, 1967 and March–May, 1969) serving an
educational role on the growing need to assure that society
develop the means to control technology rather than the reverse.
In 1970 a report was inserted in the Congressional Record; but
the resolution (S. Res. 78, 91st Congress) forming the Select
Committee was never reported out by Senate Government
Operations Committee, partially because of the Committee's
preference for the creation of a Joint Committee on
Environmental Quality.

The National Environmental Policy Act  Most recently, both
Houses of the Congress have collaborated on the National
Environmental Policy Act of 1969 (P.L. 91-190). While
responsive to the current surge of interest in the physical
environment, the underlying theme of conducting man's
technological affairs in harmony with nature is once again a
matter of assessing impacts. This Act established an
independent advisory Council on Environmental Quality (CEQ)
in the Executive Office of the President, and requires an
annual report on the status and trends in the quality of the
environment. Environmental impact statements also are called
for on major federal (not private-sector) programs and
activities affecting environmental quality. The Act [Sec.
102(2) (c)] states that every Federal agency shall:

"include in every recommendation or report on proposals for
legislation and other major Federal actions significantly

affecting the quality of the human environment, a detailed
statement by the responsible official on
(i)    the environmental impact of the proposed action,
(ii)   any adverse environmental effects which cannot be
       avoided should the proposal be implemented,
(iii)  alternatives to the proposed action,
(iv)   the relationship between local short-term uses of man's
       environment and the maintenance and enhancement of
       long-term productivity, and
(v)    any irreversible and irretrievable commitments of
       resources which would be involved in the proposed action
       should it be implemented."

A counterpart Congressional unit to the CEQ (as the Joint
Economics Committee is to the Council of Economic Advisors)
appears necessary in the Legislative Branch, since
environmental affairs are scattered over many operating
committees. In a series of maneuvers to accommodate various
personalities and jurisdictional claims, a House Joint
Resolution (No. 1117) was introduced in 1971 to create a Joint
Committee on the Environment and Technology. A large part of
the Congress's technology-assessment task might well be
accomplished by such a Joint Committee. Particularly should it
be given the money for staff and contract studies -- but this
would require perhaps several million dollars per year. As yet
the Congress has failed to complete action on such a Joint
Committee; instead, for the present, it has preferred to
establish an Office of Technology Assessment (OTA), in an
advisor to the Congress capacity.

Politics has been called the art of the possible, and
attaching technology assessment to the coattails of the
environmental-quality movement is an excellent example of the
art in practice. It should be noted that much technology does
not impact directly on the natural environment, but rather has
its primary effect on social and personal interactions. For
example, consider the invasion of privacy by electronic
data-processing techniques, the stresses of crowding, the
cashless society of modern banking, the use of television in
education, the allocation of high-frequency communication
channels, genetic engineering, or the social issues involved
in organ transplants. Nevertheless, formal assessments need to
begin, the environment _is_ important, and much assessment
methodology will be developed in the next few years, regardless
of the topics chosen.

## Elements of Legislation To Regulate Chemicals

The previous discussion has highlighted some of the events and procedural obstacles in Congress's legislative quest for a statutory framework for balance of risks and benefits. The involvement of government began with the first departures from caveat emptor -- the implication (from English common law) that the buyer should beware because he purchases without recourse. Marketplace decisions dominated the laissez-faire period of American economic policy, with government intervention held to a minimum. As business and finance grew and became more complex and sophisticated, the individual was less able to cope with the situation and society called on government to insure fair treatment through regulation. The intervention of science into applications has followed the same course -- government action being necessary to protect public health and a vulnerable common property environment. The citizen is unable to evaluate on his own the consequences of the sophisticated technological products, processes, practices, or changes around him.

The emphasis on freedom which traditionally has characterized our society brings caution to any legislative attempt to restrict choice and innovation. This nation's history demonstrates the value of the freedom of technological innovation. The present development of regulations concerning chemicals seeks not to impose a pattern of behavior, but rather to make certain that our society knows as much as possible about risks and benefits when a decision is made to promote a new technology or consumer product. Experience with exotic chemicals has shown the wisdom of shifting the burden of proof to the entrepreneur or purveyor rather than leaving it in the hands of the individual consumer. It is the purveyor's duty to investigate and report the ramifications of the chemical innovation which he wishes to sell. Some of the elements considered by the Congress in constructing a balanced regulatory system are discussed below.

The Degree of Individual Choice   Three categories of risk are identifiable with respect to the degree of choice the individual user retains. First, there are immediate risks associated with use where no one else is necessarily affected directly, such as the use of automotive seat belts, or participation in some athletic activities, or the use of cosmetics. Of course, it can be argued that society has a stake in every productive human being and that society incurs a cost in any accident on public roads. But where the risk is largely that of the individual decision maker, governmental intervention so far has been limited, for the most part, to information and consumer education. Also in this category are experimental medical treatments as long as they are performed by legitimate physicians and with the informed consent of the patient. It is true, the regulation of the pharmaceutical industry has had a stormy history, but, conceding that preassessment of new drugs should be improved, the patient properly warned of possible side effects can make a personal choice.

On the fringe of this first category are risks from smoking, drinking, taking drugs, and eating exotic foods, herbs, or flavorings. Some of these acts may induce behavior which will harm others. For example, smoking is not regulated except for a governmentally imposed warning, but it has been proposed that smoking be banned in public confined areas such as airplanes, buses, or theaters because of possible deleterious effects on other persons. It gives considerable pause to contemplate resistance to the regulative implementation of the massive accumulated evidence connecting lung cancer with cigarette smoking -- mainly because of the aversion to infringement of personal choice.

The second category of choice is that of personal or collective acceptance of risk for obvious and immediate benefits. For example, chlorination and fluoridation of public water supplies represent the calculated introduction of chemicals into the environment to achieve demonstrated public health benefits. In another instance, industrial hygiene standards and employee safety rules are usually much less stringent than would be set for and expected by the general population as a whole. In general, workers are a selected group -- healthy and not very old or very young. They supposedly accept some higher risks in order to make a living and do it with knowledge. The statistics underlying the cost of workmen's compensation insurance establish the risk/benefit balance for various employment categories. Significantly, studies show that chemists have a shorter life expectancy than do scientists in general, a fact attributed to their occupational contact with a variety of toxic laboratory chemicals.

Government regulation to protect citizens sometimes has unforeseen effects. The Coal Mine Health and Safety Act of 1969 had the purpose of improving conditions for underground miners; there is some evidence that the expense of complying with the regulations promulgated under the law forced some mines to close, adding to Appalachian unemployment. Further, the lessened availability of coal from deep mines could lead to increased strip mining with its associated environmental disruptions. The full social effect of these ricochets from

seemingly straightforward occupational health and safety
legislation is hard to sum up.

Consumer products whose use involves higher risks and less
personal choice are the patent medicines, household chemicals,
and other sophisticated technical products. Individual
ingredients may pose hazards because of misuse or unforeseen
combination with other materials. Detailed labels and
instructions, even if adequate, are not always read. The
question must be raised as to where government's responsibility
for reduction of risk ends, the manufacturer's responsibility
ends, and the consumer's free choice begins, particularly when
it is not mandatory to follow instructions.

The third category of risk is where no choice of avoidance
is possible and everyone is exposed to the risk because of a
generalized introduction of materials into consumer products
or contamination of the environment. Under such circumstances
avoidance is either impossible or so complicated that it is
not feasible for the ordinarily prudent person.

Contaminated water can be purified in the home by boiling;
however, such treatment would not remove heavy metals or
stable organic compounds. Contaminated air could be filtered
through a breathing mask with considerable inconvenience. In
general, however, the hazards associated with this category
are usually less determinable or detectable by the citizen
than for the first two categories. Contact with contamination
in the environment is inadvertent and unnoticed. The greater
impact may be the effects on general human health or on
environmental quality rather than the effect on any one
individual. These general effects may take years or even
generations to become apparent. This is the most important and
critical area for new legislation in regulation of chemicals.
While the entire human environment is at risk, the magnitude
of the hazard is obscure and thus deflated by the propensity
to believe that what you don't know won't hurt you.
Consequently, society must turn to government for prevention
and protection, for the proper evaluation of noneconomic gains
and losses, and for the assessment of the long-term view.
Legislative approaches and public response will be quite
different for this category of choice and risk than for the
regulation of immediate hazards incurred through individual
consumer choice.

Credibility And The Burden Of Proof   While there may be
agreement that the purveyor bears the burden of proof,
arguments remain as to credibility and to the definition of
"proof." Skepticism will often greet tests performed by

manufacturers, or by others funded by them, or by government agencies whose missions promote or involve chemical-manufacturing technology. On the other side of the debate, investigators for consumer and environmental interest groups and regulatory agencies are accused of biased tests and selected data, even in the absence of profit motives. Over a period of time many "independent" laboratories have become identified with a constrained point of view. Thus the public has lost confidence in most such evaluative tests because the charges of inadequacy have so often flown back and forth -- and been shown to be correct.

The detached and disinterested observer (at least, one with any degree of expertise) is difficult to find. In part this is due to the challenge of recent years for scientists to get out of their ivory towers and become "involved." Of those now involved, some are so associated with one or another position that they are no longer credible as neutral investigators. When forming study committees and panels, the National Academy of Sciences (NAS) now asks prospective expert committee members to file a statement "on potential sources of bias" before they can be appointed. It has been suggested that it may be necessary to construct a new institution whose members' duties and responsibilities are only to society and to the truth. That this may be required will no doubt prove a shock to the academic community.

In the meantime, the legislators, accustomed to conflicting expert testimony and recognizing the built-in biases of special interests, must formulate public policy. The compromise inherent in politics cannot be applied to scientific opinions, however, since ultimately only one true explanation is possible.

The difficulty is that proof comes in degrees; science produces knowledge which is probabilistic, so that certainty is never perfect. Replication of tests and independent verification of deduced effects can increase confidence in cause-and-effect relationships and lead to a predictive capability for technology assessment. Nevertheless, regardless of the amount of conclusiveness of scientific evidence on one side of a question or issue a protagonist can always ask additional questions or express the remaining doubt or unanswered questions. The difficulty of balancing practical testing procedures against the need for assurance concerning long-term effects is shown in the following excerpt from the Report to the Surgeon General, USPHS, April 29, 1970 -- Evaluation of Environmental Carcinogens (13). Appendix II -- Comments on 1969 Report of the NAS-NRC Food Protection Committee -- states:

"This Committee has examined a report entitled 'Guidelines for Estimating Toxicologically Insignificant Levels of Chemicals in Food' published in 1969 by the Food Protection Committee, Food and Nutrition Board of the National Academy of Sciences, National Research Council. It records its strong objections to the principles expressed in that report, which states that natural or synthetic substances can be considered safe without experimental support under certain vaguely-stated conditions.

The Food Protection Committee Report assumes that '...a level of insignificance may be determined if: (1) There are available adequate scientific studies that establish safe levels of similar magnitude for at least two analogous substances. (2) The acute or subacute toxicity of the new substance and two analogous substances is of the same nature and degree.' For 'Chemicals in Commercial Production' it recommends that: 'If a chemical has been in commercial production for a substantial period, e.g., 5 years or more, without evidence of toxicological hazard incident to its production or use, if it is not a heavy metal or a compound of a heavy metal, and if it is not intended for use because of its biological activity, it is consistent with sound toxicological judgment to conclude that a level of 0.1 ppm of the chemical in the diet of man is toxicologically insignificant.'

To assume (a) that a 5-year period of use has any meaning for the evaluation of chronic toxicity in man, (b) that any chemical may be considered safe simply because two 'analogous substances' are 'safe,' and (c) that acute or subacute toxicity are reliable guidelines for evaluating long-term toxicity is to display a lack of understanding and appreciation of factors involved in chronic toxicity, particularly of the irreversible and delayed toxic effects which occur in carcinogenesis.

Since the purpose of the report is to recommend guidelines and priorities for selecting chemicals for human use without direct experimental toxicological evaluation, the lack of consideration of irreversible long-term toxic effects (which would not be ruled out by the suggested criteria) makes the suggested approach practically inapplicable and potentially dangerous."

Frequently unappreciated is that proof of a negative is a logical impossibility. There can be no absolute assurance of the absence of hazard or the safety of chemicals in the environment. In testing chemicals, a toxicological experiment which shows no effect at low levels of exposure does not mean there is none. A further experiment with larger numbers of test animals may reveal some impact. Pursuit of proof of no effect can lead to what Alvin Weinberg calls "trans-scientific questions" -- questions incapable of resolution by science. For example, to demonstrate with statistical validity the absence of unwanted effects from exposure to low doses of a single chemical can be calculated to require literally millions of test animals -- an experiment that cannot in practice be carried out.

Lawmakers, mostly lawyers, should note the difference between legal proof and scientific proof. A defendant may be convicted on testimony of a single witness with no chance of replicating the crime situation; however, he may not be convicted on the basis of a very high statistical probability that he conforms to known facts about the criminal.

Responsibility For Testing And Standard Setting  The Congress works through specialized legislative and investigatory committees whose members, over years of exposure to testimony and staff briefings, develop a good working knowledge of those subjects in their jurisdiction. The difficulties of applying scientific knowledge and concepts to regulatory practice are appreciated by these experienced legislators and often unappreciated by the scientific community and others. The intent of the Congress to protect the public against chemical hazards must be converted from statutory authority to a set of working administrative procedures. Toxicologic and epidemiologic tests must be devised which are reproducible and which will predict accurately the effects of chemicals if they are allowed to be used. The results obtained from the use of these protocols lead first to criteria statements or descriptions of what is likely to happen when persons or environmental qualities are exposed to the chemical in question for various times and periods at certain concentrations. As such, criteria are products of scientific research. From the described cause-and-effect relationships, standards or limits can be chosen. Through available regulatory procedures, society can decide to accept a degree of damage or risk in order to gain the benefits of chemical substances. Of necessity standards must be chosen by a politically responsible body (not by scientists) to insure that the concept of social utility is considered.

The Congress usually delegates the design of the testing protocol and standard setting to an administrative agency within the Executive Branch. This follows because there is limited expertise and no scientific research capability within the Congress to allow these technical details to be written into law. During Congressional Committee program overview and annual appropriations hearings, the Congress is provided the

opportunity to determine whether their intentions are being
implemented.

There are occasions, however, when the Legislative Branch
goes further toward specifying the operational features of
regulation. Frustrations with the lack of progress or slowness
in administrative achievements in automobile emission control
led the Congress, in the Clean Air Amendments of 1970 (P.L.
91-604), to set an arbitrary deadline (the 1975 model year) of
a fixed reduction (at least 90 percent) of carbon monoxide and
hydrocarbons from the amounts allowed by standards for the
model year 1970. (The Executive Branch in effect had proposed
this standard for 1980.) It remains to be seen how workable
this legislative fiat will be.

Another example is the Delaney Amendment (P.L. 85-929) to
the Federal Food Drug and Cosmetic Act which proscribes the
use of any food additive which causes cancer in man or animals
when ingested or following appropriate tests. This law has been
interpreted to include inadvertent or "indirect" additives such
as residues from pesticides or packaging materials. The
sensitive techniques of modern analytical chemistry allow the
detection of extremely small quantities of extraneous chemicals
in foodstuffs. Animal testing for carcinogenicity has become
more sophisticated. Some substances, such as DDT, which
routinely contaminate food (and indeed a few naturally
occurring fungal contaminants, such as aflatoxins) have been
shown to cause cancers in test animals. A rigorous enforcement
of the Delaney clause has not yet been pursued, except in
relation to deliberate food additives. While the congressional
intent underlying the Delaney clause is clearcut, difficulty
in defining the long-term effects of very small detectable
amounts of chemicals in foods has prompted industrial challenge
to the Delaney clause; this challenge has been complicated by
the definitional dispute as to whether the clause pertains only
to deliberate addition of synthetic chemicals or whether it
also pertains to "indirect" food additives. (For detailed
discussion of the Delaney clause see page 79.)

Another way that the Congress may insure proper
implementation of its intent is the specification in law of a
role for a scientific body such as the NAS. For example, in
the Clean Air Amendments of 1970 the EPA "...Administrator
shall undertake to enter into appropriate arrangements with
the NAS..." to fund a study as to the technological feasibility
of the automobile industry meeting the 1975 control deadline
included in the Act. The NAS also was named to study the
consequences of defoliant use in Vietnam by the Defense
Procurement Act (P.L. 91-441); and is called upon to judge the

safety of various chemicals under the Food Drug and Cosmetic
Act (U.S. Code, Title 21, Section 201). Over ten additional
assignments were covered in pending legislation as of January
1972. The NAS is called upon to compile rosters for agency
advisory or review committees, or to set up such committees.
The purpose of involving the Academy is to obtain independent
expert scientific consideration by Congressional direction
rather than leaving such supporting work to the discretion of
an Executive Branch Agency administrator.

Research And Information Requirements  The weighing of risk
and benefit requires a balance in available information for
alternative actions. The normal course of events will not
always bring this about. Technologies promoted by established
industries or government agencies may be researched thoroughly.
Alternative technologies which might be superior in their net
worth to society have difficulty receiving enough attention to
bring them to a competitive level. For example, chemical
pesticides have a sales base and practical acceptance which
supports more research on improved chemical pesticides. In
contrast, biological pest-control methods do not constitute a
large market and their application technique requires
different training. Thus the pest problem does not
automatically generate a spectrum of solutions.

Another example is nuclear electric power, which is well
researched as compared with solar-derived energy. The latter
technology is not developed sufficiently to be a candidate in
current national energy policy decisions. (The Congress must
review the allocation of limited R&D resources to guard against
this automatic reinforcement of ongoing technologies.)

A second type of priority problem concerns the technology
of enforcement. Environmental hazards are revealed through
research on impacts and cause-and-effect relationships.
Research for remedial actions is generated by recognition of
the hazard. But the science and engineering knowledge required
for regulatory enforcement is also critically important to a
successful balance of risks and benefits. In the case of
chemicals, the legislator must be aware that several areas of
science need to be strengthened. Hazard is often equated with
certain biological end points -- e.g., with cancer, birth
defects, or genetic changes. Ascertaining whether the use of
any particular chemical leads to such disasters is expensive,
requires technical personnel who are at present in short
supply, and takes a long time. In the absence of improved test
methods and procedures, legislations designed to establish
the magnitude of the acceptable risk to human health or the

environment might simply result in retarding the development
of all new chemical products. Conceivably, society could be
denied the benefits of highly efficacious products because it
could not afford to evaluate potential hazards.

Similarly, much hazard evaluation or assessment can be
accomplished through environmental epidemiology; but the state
of the art is relatively weak. With current techniques it is
very difficult if not impossible to separate chemical effects
from socioeconomic factors and personal habits.

The science and profession of ecology has been thrust to
the forefront as the integrating discipline that can make
sense out of complex environmental problems. Because there are
only a limited number of trained ecologists in the world, it
may take decades to strengthen and expand this work force.
Apart from this, ecology is still more capable of retrospective
analysis of adverse effects than it is of prediction. The very-
long-term, tedious research in the study of environmental
effects is not attractive to scientists when compared with the
glamor and immediate results to be expected of other
life-science projects.

In the context of world health problems, research on subtle
hazards from chemicals should be contrasted with other demands
for the same funds, animal colonies, scarce toxicologists and
pharmacologists, and laboratory facilities. The rich nations
may well be able to afford a high degree of risk avoidance.
However, there is a further obligation to use our scientific
and other resources so as to promote all human welfare. An
immediate instance is the foreign-relations aspect of the
regulation of chemicals. Recently, the charge was made that
U.S. suppliers were selling remaining stocks of cyclamate-
sweetened soft drinks in other countries after this additive
was banned here.

Priorities must be set for research on chemical hazards
after the appropriate resources have been allocated to this
field in competition with grants for other public-health and
environmental-risk studies. There are thousands of synthetic
and natural substances to consider. As stated by the NAS Food
Protection Committee: "All environmental exposures must be
subjected to scientific evaluation, but not all exposures
require experimental toxicological study." The application of
experience and sound judgment is necessary. However, the
critical limitation of such judgment is indicated by the
recent decision of the FDA to review the status of hundreds of
food additives which had been on the Generally Regarded As Safe
(GRAS) list. The Congress must review administrative agency
research plans to see that fads, topical events, or scientific

orthodoxy have not distorted the research support of regulatory
decision making.

Non-Regulatory Protective Mechanisms  The balancing of risk
and benefit does not rely entirely on government investigation
of chemical hazards. Several other existing checks and
evaluations provide safeguards that should be augmented rather
than disregarded in erecting an improved assessment system.

The research chemist himself is the first person to be
threatened by a new chemical substance. His training may warn
him of potential harm by analogies between new materials and
the structure or composition of known toxicants. Laboratory
safety and self-interest should assure an early evaluation of
possible hazards. With varying degrees of rigor, industrial
hygiene policies require research into both acute and chronic
effects as development toward commercial use proceeds.

Product-liability law is being continually redefined and
expanded by the courts. Labels and instructions are no longer
sufficient to avoid claims when an unexpected effect shows up.
If use or disposal will require special measures, these must
be developed concurrently with the marketing aspects of new
chemicals.

Workmen's compensation laws, insurance requirements, and
transportation restrictions add to the motivation of industrial
chemists to be informed on the products they sell. Materials
balances and waste control in manufacturing operations are good
housekeeping techniques which minimize inadvertent environmental
contamination and make economic sense.

Summary Of Legislative Approaches  To recapitulate, the
following are some of the approaches and elements in
constructing workable and enforceable regulations which can
increase the prospect of an optimum risk-benefit balance in
using chemicals:

Labeling requirements for application directions, warning of
hazards, and disposal instructions.

Transportation, packaging, and handling procedures to minimize
accidental release to the environment or contamination of
other commodities.

Wastes management and control. Standards for specific
contaminants of air and water.

Registration of chemical products or disclosure of production
and uses can alert government authorities that new compounds
are entering the environment in certain ways. Assessment

investigations may then be initiated. Costs of testing may be charged to the purveyor.

Reporting of materials flows in manufacturing and processing may be required for compounds of known potential hazard so that government monitoring can keep track of them. The right of entry may be necessary.

Licensing of application personnel can prevent untrained workers or the public from using certain hazardous materials whose benefits can be safely obtained if proper precautions are taken.

Allowable residues, exposure limits, or ambient environmental concentrations can be specified as is done for certain air and water contaminants and pesticides. This forces the manufacturing sources and users to conform their activities to a safe pattern.

Restriction of use or an outright ban on some chemicals may be found to be necessary.

Surveillance programs may be maintained on human health (epidemiology of environmental hazards) and ecological status (including indicators of environmental quality). This continuous search for unanticipated impacts could provide the first clue in many instances of subtle effects of chemicals.

Liability for accidents and authority for immediate governmental agency cleanup action (with the cost borne by the responsible party) are in effect for oil transportation and storage and will be extended to hazardous materials soon under provisions of the Water Quality Improvement Act of 1970. Further extension to chemical products could be envisioned.

Compensation may be necessary for the loss of proprietary information or the seizure of contaminated commodities in the course of enforcement action.

All of these procedures have been suggested from time to time and many of them are already incorporated into law. We are now concerned with the less obvious, subtle, long-term effects of chemicals. New techniques may have to be devised to give adequate protection.

## The Trend Toward Full Disclosure
Legislation often develops by analogy to previous successful means in satisfying the wishes of the electorate. In the period following the stock market crash of 1929 the financial community was challenged to restore public confidence in the basic processes of the free enterprise system. Society, through

its representatives in the Congress, constructed the Securities
Act of 1933 with its concept of a prospectus for stocks and
bonds which would enable the investor to make an informed
decision when securities were offered for sale. The language
of that Act expresses the need for full disclosure of
information that is "...necessary or appropriate in the public
interest or for the protection of investors." No offering is
allowed by the Securities and Exchange Commission if the
registration statement "...includes any untrue statement of a
material fact or omits to state any material fact required to
be stated therein or necessary to make the statements therein
not misleading."

The preintroductory certification that chemicals will be
nonhazardous in use is not a simple matter. It has been
proposed on a number of occasions (14, 15). Such a policy
would prohibit the general use of any synthetic material,
trace metal or chemical until approved by a government agency.
Manufacturers would provide all necessary data to establish
levels of safe usage, standards and regulations to assure a
proper risk/benefit balance. Disclosure would include
information now normally withheld for proprietary reasons or
because it would detract from marketability of the product.
Much of the distrust of the present system is based on the
belief that proponents of a technology or innovation hide
information on adverse effects besides exaggerating claims on
utility and efficacy. This breeds a disruptive and delaying
sequence of challenges which obscure the difference between
what is known and not revealed and what is not known. The
restoration of credibility will require full disclosure by
proponents plus a capability to generate the missing
information.

The National Environmental Policy Act (NEPA) of 1969 directs
all agencies of government to prepare a detailed impact
statement for proposed actions affecting the quality of the
human environment. Adjudication of this law in recent court
cases shows that full disclosure was intended by the Congress.
The impact statement must examine broadly any adverse
environmental effects, alternatives to the proposed action,
and any irreversible and irretrievable commitments of resources.
This information is available to the public and must be
considered along with economic and technical factors in
decision making. The NEPA, however, does not mandate a
negative decision even if environmental effects appear to be
extremely adverse. Nevertheless, it does assure that more is
known about the secondary consequences of applied science.

The concept of full disclosure must also include the integration of impacts from a number of sources. For example, genetic-mutation effects can result from radiation, physical changes, or chemical reactions. If some level of genetic change (above that of natural background) is accepted by society, then there remains the problem of allocating this damage among these contributing agents. To this complexity must be added the chance synergistic effects, where combinations of agents in the environment interact to create greater hazards than their additive effects alone.

Control of the exposure of citizens can hardly be regarded as limited to one nation, since many environmental threats are mobile and persistent and diffuse throughout the world. Thus, a regulatory system for chemicals must ultimately be coordinated with the regulation of other insults to human health and environmental quality in an international agreement as to risks and benefits.

In the face of these challenges and difficulties it may seem fatuous to pursue a legislative construction of an equitable regulatory system. But what are the alternatives? (1) To muddle through, experiencing continuing episodes such as mercury in fresh waters, polychlorinated biphenyl (PCB) effects on fish-eating birds, and cyclamates in foodstuffs. (2) To absorb the long-term subtle degradation of the human species and the productivity of the living environment. (3) To retreat to a pre-synthetic-chemical standard of living by arbitrarily banning the use of such products.

An optimist can offer a better scenario. The same high level of science which generates new chemicals can give us sophisticated but practical means of evaluating their potential for good or harm. A full disclosure of this information can allow present decision-making institutions to choose an optimum balance for society.

While working for a substantial improvement we should remember what Dr. Rene Dubos told the Congress a few years ago,

"Unfortunately it will always remain impossible to predict from laboratory experiments all the threats to health that can arise from technological innovation... We must abandon, in fact, the utopian hope that regulations can protect us completely from all health dangers in the modern world." (16)

## References

1.  National Research Council, Committee of Food Protection, Food and Nutrition Board, Division of Biology and Agriculture, "Food Colors" (1971), pp. 2-50.

2.  _____, "Science," 173:4000, 902 (September 3, 1971).

3.  USPHS, Report to the Surgeon General, The Ad Hoc Committee on the Evaluation of the Low Levels of Environmental Chemical Carcinogens (National Cancer Institute), April 22, 1970.

4.  U.S. Congress. House of Representatives. Science and Astronautics Committee Subcommittee on Science Research and Development. "Technical Information for Congress" (April 25, 1969).

5.  Midwest Research Institute, "An Analysis of Unstructured Technology Assessments," September 17, 1971.

6.  Jenkins, Dale W., "The Toxic Metals in Your Future -- and Your Past," April, 1972, p. 66.

7.  U.S. Congress. Senate. Committee on Government Operations, Interagency Environmental Hazards Coordination: "Pesticides and Public Policy" (July 21, 1966). Senate Rept. No. 89-1379.

8.  U.S. Congress. House of Representatives. Committee on Science and Astronautics. "Technology Assessment Seminar." Proceedings before the Subcommittee on Science, Research, and Development of the ... September 21 and 22, 1967, 90th Congress, first session. Washington, D.C., U.S. Government Printing Office, 1967, 184 pages.
    Initial seminar of technology assessment help by the Subcommittee on Science, Research and Development to provide the Committee with assistance in developing issues for later Congressional hearings and consideration of technology assessment.

9.  U.S. Congress. House of Representatives. Committee on Science and Astronautics. "Technology: Processes of Assessment and Choice." Report of the National Academy of Sciences, July 1969. 89th Congress. Washington, D.C., U.S. Government Printing Office, 1969, 163 pages.

10. U.S. Congress. Senate. Committee on Interior and Insular Affairs. Joint House-Senate Colloquium to Discuss a National Policy for the Environment, 90th Congress, July 17, 1968, p. 71.

11. U.S. Congress. House of Representatives. Committee on Science and Astronautics. "A Study of Technology Assessment." Report of the Committee on Public Engineering Policy, National Academy of Engineering, July 1969. Washington, D.C., Government Printing Office, 1969, 208 pages.

12. U.S. Congress. House of Representatives. Committee on Science and Astronautics. "Technical Information for Congress." Report to the Subcommittee on Science, Research, and Development of the ... Prepared by the Science Policy Research Division, Congressional Research Service, Library of Congress. 92nd Congress, 1st session. Revised April 25, 1971, Washington, D.C., U.S. Government Printing Office, 1971, 845 pages (Committee Print).

13. U.S. Congress. Senate. Subcommittee on Agricultural Research and General Legislation of the Committee on Agriculture and Forestry, Hearings on the Federal Environmental Pesticide Control Act, March 23-26, 1971, pp. 676-699.

14. DHEW, "A Strategy for a Livable Environment," a report to the Secretary of HEW by the Task Force on Environmental Health and Related Problems, June 1967, p. 20.

15. Council on Environmental Quality, The First Annual Report, August 1970, p. 59.

16. U.S. Congress. House of Representatives. Hearings on the Adequacy of Technology for Pollution Abatement before the Subcommittee on Science, Research and Development of the Committee on Science and Astronautics, 89th Congress, second Session, Vol. II., p. 846.

# 2

## PUBLIC HEALTH HAZARDS FROM CHEMICALS IN CONSUMER PRODUCTS

Samuel S. Epstein

CONTENTS

## Introduction

Pressures to raise the standard of living in America and other
industrialized societies have resulted in an unprecedented
escalation in the rate of technological innovation. The
consumer and economic benefits of particular innovations are
usually apparent early in their development and lead to their
rapid introduction into commerce. The attendant social costs
and untoward side effects are in the short run often less
apparent than the benefits, and thus tend to be "externalized"
or discounted.

Concurrently, new methods for the identification of
potential consumer product hazards have evolved. In the past,
concern was largely for acute toxic hazards. However, with
increasing public knowledge of the chronic, long-term hazards
of consumer products, pressure has mounted to the point where
some form of "preassessment" is now seen as an integral element
of public policy.

It is clearly unrealistic to expect industry to voluntarily
and universally devote the appropriate time and resources to
the evaluation of long-term hazards. Thus, legislation and
regulatory mechanisms have gradually evolved into a public
policy that provides minimum requirements for preassessment of
product safety, both short- and long-term, and both to
the individual and to the environment. Another reason for the
establishment of regulatory requirements prescribing minimum
standards for preassessment of such hazards is to eliminate the
economic advantage obtained by the manufacturer who does not
respond to voluntary standards or guidelines, while a more
conscientious competitor conforms to, or often exceeds, what
are considered reasonable standards of responsible practice.
However, increasingly stringent regulatory requirements for
preassessment of product safety are now generally regarded by
some segments of industry as excessive and as impediments to
innovation. More stringent regulatory requirements are also
being directed to products with already-established market
positions. Such "postassessment" is an effort to investigate
newly appreciated potential hazards and in some cases to
substantiate suspected absence of efficacy.

Concerns for consumer product safety -- and also for
environmental quality and occupational safety -- are now
burgeoning and some classic assumptions regarding the so-called
free market economy are now under challenge. As a result,
apparent conflicts have developed between social policies that
foster continued economic and material growth vs concerns for
consumer product safety in particular and for environmental
safety and management in general. Such conflicts are usually

exacerbated when consumer hazards arise from involuntary or
inadvertent exposure, in which the consumer has little or no
intent or choice, as opposed to readily identifiable hazards
to which the consumer exposes himself with direct choice and
intent. The scope and breadth of the various factions and
viewpoints represented in these issues is reflected in
divergent, and sometimes polarized, current attitudes to
recent restrictions on consumer products such as DDT and the
cyclamates.

## Modes Of Human Exposure To Chemicals In Consumer Products
Chemical consumer products may be simply classified by general
class and subclass. Examples of such classes include cosmetics,
therapeutic drugs, household chemicals (such as detergents),
pesticides, food additives, feed additives, and fuel additives.
While such classification has a descriptive and functional
basis, it is of limited value as an index of modes of human
exposure to products with regard to intent and free choice.
Three major modes of exposure may be conveniently identified,
as follows:

## Readily Identifiable Chemicals Used With Consumer Intent  This
category of products, including detergents, cosmetics, and
drugs, are purchased as such and in a form readily identifiable
by the consumer. Exposure of the consumer to any effects of
such products, whether beneficial or hazardous, results from a
deliberate and voluntary action on the consumer's part. The
consumer's real freedom of choice is, however, limited; for,
in general, he is not informed of the ingredients of the
product, nor of its benefits, real or alleged, nor of its
hazards.

## Poorly Identifiable Chemicals Used With Limited Consumer Intent And Choice  A second and less obvious category are products,
such as food and feed additives, which are not easily and
readily identifiable as such. Consumer exposure to such
products is generally both unwitting and involuntary. For
instance, consumers are not informed, by labeling or other
measures, that the meat they buy comes from cattle or poultry
treated with a wide range of feed additives, antibiotics, and
other growth-promoting agents. Even if they were so informed,
present marketing conditions would allow them little choice
but to buy additive-treated meat, as no practical alternatives
are available. While such consumer exposure is generally both
involuntary and unwitting, these products are of course used
by industry with specific intent.

Non-Identifiable Chemicals Used Without Consumer Intent or
Choice  A third category of consumer products are accidental
environmental pollutants, such as pesticides, which may
indirectly contaminate food or meat. Consumer exposure to these
is again unwitting and involuntary but, in this case, it occurs
in the absence of specific intent by industry.

There is considerable overlap between these three major
modes of exposure to chemicals in consumer products. For
instance, the consumer may be exposed to the effects of DDT,
present as an accidental contaminant in meat, bread, or milk.
Alternatively, he may be exposed to DDT as a result of a
deliberate and voluntary action, following domestic use of a
DDT-containing formulation.

Routes Of Human Exposure To Chemicals In Consumer Products
There are three major routes of human exposure to any category
of chemical consumer product -- skin or mucous membrane contact,
ingestion, and inhalation. For therapeutic drugs, there is a
fourth and common route -- the parenteral, such as by
intravenous, subcutaneous, or intramuscular injection. The
effects of any product may be restricted to the initial route
of contact and exposure, such as the skin, mucous membrane,
and lung, or may become generalized by subsequent absorption
from these sites.

For any particular product, it is possible that exposure
will occur through more than one route. For example, with
domestic formulations of insecticide aerosols, it is likely
that exposure will occur by direct skin contact, by eating
food contaminated with the aerosol, and most importantly, by
inhalation. Similar multiple routes of exposure also obtain
for cosmetics, such as hair sprays, dispensed in aerosol form.
Certain ingredients of lipstick may be directly absorbed
through the skin and also may be swallowed in saliva. Exposure
to detergents may occur directly through the housewife's skin,
by accidental splashing into eyes, by accidental ingestion --
particularly by young children -- and possibly by inhalation
of powdered detergent dust. Enzyme ingredients of certain
detergent formulations have been shown to produce allergic
bronchiolitis following occupational exposure (1), although
there is, as yet, no such evidence in housewives using these
formulations. Additionally, certain detergent ingredients may
partially resist degradation in sewage treatment plants or may
otherwise contaminate drinking waters.

## Categories Of Toxic Effects Due To Chemicals In Consumer Products

Chemicals in consumer products, like any other category of synthetic or naturally occurring chemical, may induce a wide range of adverse biological effects in humans. When these effects are adverse, they are generically and collectively termed toxicity. Short term (acute and subacute) or long term (chronic) toxicity per se may be expressed in fetal, neonatal, perinatal, childhood, or adult life, in a wide range of effects extending from impairment of health and fitness to mortality. More specific and unique manifestations of chronic toxicity include induction of cancer (carcinogenicity), induction of birth defects (teratogenicity) and induction of heritable genetic damage (mutagenicity). The possibility that chronic toxicity may also manifest in immunological impairment or in psychobehavioral disorders has yet to be explored in depth.

Acute and subacute toxic effects are obvious, and the causal relationships between them and consumer exposure to particular chemicals are in general readily established. As a result, industry has traditionally undertaken routine testing to avoid or minimize short-term toxicity. Concern has more recently been extended to chronic toxicity, particularly carcinogenicity, teratogenicity, and mutagenicity, for which legislative authority and regulatory requirements have often been belatedly and imperfectly developed and for which routine industrial testing is still often inadequate.

Certain chemicals may induce any one or more of these types of toxic effects. In addition, different classes of chemicals may interact outside the body and in the products themselves (in vitro) and in the body (in vivo) to produce otherwise unanticipated synergistic toxicity. Synergistic effects can also result from interactions between specific synthetic chemicals, such as pesticides, food additives, and drugs, and otherwise harmless and common naturally-occuring chemicals.

## Efficacy And Social Utility

There are two questions relevant to efficacy and social utility. Firstly, does the innovation or chemical product comply with minimal requirements for efficacy and achieve its narrowly stated objective, as dictated by Federal Trade Commission (FTC) policies? Secondly (and this is the more recent concept), does the innovation satisfy the requirement for utility in a broader social context? While it is not entirely possible to divorce this broader concept from possible bias and from the value

judgments of special interest groups, attempts have been made
to introduce such distinctions into legislation. Senator
Nelson has recently advocated the position that food additives
should be both "effective," in that their use will achieve a
stated objective, and also "necessary," in that this objective
will have broad societal and economic utility (2). (See also
Criteria and Standards..., later in this chapter.)

## Chemicals Not Complying With Even Minimal Requirements For Efficacy

Therapeutic Drugs  A recent National Academy of Sciences (NAS)
report (3) has revealed that approximately 60 percent of
prescription drugs and combination antibiotics in common use
are not efficacious. Additionally, 80 percent of claims for
common prescription drugs have not been substantiated (3).
This is in contravention of the 1962 Kefauver-Harris Amendment
to the Food, Drug, and Cosmetic Act (P.L. 87-781), which
imposes a requirement for efficacy on all prescription drugs.
DDT A major use of DDT in the United States has been for
cotton insect pests, which are, however, largely DDT-resistant
(4, 5).
Monosodium Glutamate This has been used to flavor infant foods,
although there are no available data that infants have
preferential discrimination for flavored foods.

## Chemicals Complying With Minimal Requirements For Efficacy, But Without Broad Societal Utility

Food Dyes  These include dyes, such as Citrus Red 2, used to
redden Florida oranges, and nitrate-nitrite additives, used to
redden and improve the appearance of meat. These dyes improve
marketability by catering to consumer desires, which are,
however, often artificially engendered by promotional practices.
Sweetening Agents  These include agents, such as cyclamates,
which until recently were extensively used in food and drinks
consumed by children as well as adults.
Flavoring Agents  These include agents, such as monosodium
glutamate, that are used to enhance the flavor of foods.
DDT  This efficiently kills susceptible insects, such as
malaria-transmitting anophelines, in areas outside the United
States.
Mirex  This efficiently kills various susceptible insects,
including the "imported fire ant." However, there is little
evidence that this ant poses any threat to man, animals, or
agriculture greater than bees or wasps! At worst, the ant is
a minor pest (6). Yet, large-scale programs have been vigorously
advocated for the extensive use of Mirex, a carcinogenic (7)

and highly persistent chlorinated hydrocarbon insecticide, for
the eradication of the "fire ant." (8)
NTA  Nitrilotriacetic Acid (NTA) was introduced as a partial
substitute for phosphates in heavy duty detergents (9). While
NTA is a highly effective detergent builder, the major impetus
for the development of NTA-based detergent formulations
stemmed from concern about the deterioration of water quality
due to cultural eutrophication induced by phosphates. The
available evidence indicates that the use of NTA alone,
especially without concomitant removal of phosphates at sewage
treatment stages, is unlikely to achieve the intended objective
of preventing or reducing eutrophication (9).

## Matching Benefits Or Efficacy Against Hazards

The evident need of industrialized societies to use a wide
range of synthetic chemicals makes it essential also to
recognize and estimate their human and environmental hazards
or costs and the acceptability of these costs with regard to
efficacy or matching benefits (10). Such societal costing
must be in each case weighted by various factors, including
the persistence and environmental mobility of the chemical,
its degradation and pyrolytic products and contaminants, the
size of the exposed population, and the reversibility of the
adverse effect. The scope and magnitude of the human costs is
not generally appreciated, especially as in any specific
instance it may not be feasible to demonstrate direct causal
relationships between a particular pollutant and the induced
adverse effect.

The costs to society of one child with severe brain damage
following lead poisoning, based on remedial and custodial care
alone and excluding deprivation of earnings, have been recently
estimated to be about $250,000 (11). Similar or greater cost
can be stated for cancer induced by environmental pollutants,
carcinogenic drugs, or occupational exposure. Such costing is
clearly not presently feasible for inherited genetic damage or
mutations, the scope and nature of whose future effect --
extending perhaps up to forty generations hence -- cannot be
predicted. Environmental costs, such as cultural eutrophication
in lakes induced by phosphate detergents, or property damage
from air pollutants, have until recently been ignored or
discounted as beyond the scope of a manufacturer's concerns.
There is growing recognition of the fact that many human and
environmental costs which hitherto have been "externalized"
must now be "internalized."

Hazards from a particular chemical product need not
necessarily be accepted even when matching benefits appear
high. Frequently equally effective or efficacious but either
nonhazardous or less-hazardous alternatives are available.
The mandatory criterion of efficacy, once extended from
therapeutic drugs to other consumer products, such as food
and fuel additives and pesticides, may well simplify these
equations, especially for hazards from chemical products with
no demonstrable benefits for the general population.

The imposition of a requirement for broad social utility
may even further simplify the benefit-hazard equation. To
illustrate: methoxychlor can replace the highly persistent
and carcinogenic DDT, whose efficacy for cotton insect control
is now questionable due to the emergence of DDT resistance
(4, 5). Such concepts of social utility have been recently
emphasized by a leading representative of the food industry,
who recommended that food additives be excluded from products
unless they either significantly improve the quality or
nutritive value of the food or lower its cost, as well as
being safe (12).

## Methods Of Testing For Toxicity Of Chemicals In Consumer Products

Historical Perspectives   In the past, the techniques for
determining different classes of toxic effects have been
studied and applied independently and by nonconverging
disciplines. Chemicals to which humans are exposed should be
tested for acute and chronic toxicity per se and also for the
more specific effects of carcinogenicity, teratogenicity and
mutagenicity. Toxicity per se has largely been the province of
classical pharmacologists and toxicologists, generally with
little interest in carcinogenesis or mutagenesis. This
parochialism was exemplified in the commonly held mid-fifties
view that the chronic toxicity test is inappropriate for
determining carcinogenicity (13). The regulatory requirement
for the evaluation of the teratogenicity of drugs -- imposed
somewhat indirectly, however, as a three-generation
reproductive test -- in response to the thalidomide disaster,
is another illustration of the effect of this separation of
disciplines. Mutagenesis has been even more isolated than other
aspects of toxicology. Indeed, articles on mutagenic hazards
are even today relative rarities in toxicological and public
health journals and, in general, appear only in
small-circulation genetic journals. Such fragmentation of
toxicological research appears to be artificial as well as

restrictive. New organizational patterns and training programs
are needed to coordinate toxicological approaches, and to make
toxicology more responsive to current needs.

New and more sophisticated methods for toxicity testing,
which are more sensitive and responsive to low, and even
ambient, levels of individual chemical agents, such as
accidental pesticide contaminants, and various mixtures of
these agents, reflecting more realistic patterns of
environmental exposure, are being gradually developed.
Illustrative is the recent demonstration (14) that a wide
range of nonspecific stresses, including temporary deprivation
of food, cage crowding, parturition, and lactation, markedly
increases the toxicity to rodents of ambient levels of DDT.

Test Chemicals   Toxicity testing clearly should not be
arbitrarily confined to the parent chemical per se;
consideration also must be given to extensive testing of its
chemical and metabolic derivatives, its pyrolytic and
degradation products, and its contaminants and reaction
products. These considerations are further accentuated when
the various derivatives or degradation products are
demonstrated to be of potential toxicological or environmental
significance. Illustrative are the occurrence of
polychlorophenol and dioxin contaminants and their dioxin
pyrolytic products in phenoxy herbicides (15, 16),
cyclohexylamine as a contaminant and human metabolic product
of the sweetening agent cyclamate (17), and the
uncharacterized biodegradation products of the detergent-builder
NTA (18). It is thus apparent that comprehensive safety testing
demands the availability of detailed chemical and comparative
metabolic data concerning the agent under test. The requirements
for such data may necessitate carefully controlled metabolic
studies in human volunteers, once safety has been established
in comprehensive animal tests.

In any form of toxicity testing, agents should be
administered acutely, subacutely, and chronically, to reflect
the function of liver microsomal enzyme systems in activation
and detoxification. It also may be necessary in particular
circumstances to test for effects of concomitantly administered
and otherwise nontoxic chemicals that may induce or inhibit
microsomal enzyme function.

Experiments also can be designed to reflect the role of
possible interactions between test chemicals -- administered by
any route -- and dietary factors and other chemicals, such as
accidental and intentional food additives and drugs.

Routes Of Testing   Routes of test administration should, <u>inter alia</u>, reflect modes of human exposure. While inhalation is the obvious route for testing of air pollutants, the importance of this route for other classes of chemical agents has been generally underestimated. For example: respiratory exposure is of particular human significance for pesticide and other aerosols, as this represents the major route of human exposure. (See the discussion of Chronic Toxicity Tests, later in this chapter.)

While useful information is often derived from tests involving inappropriate routes of administration, extrapolation from these data to human experience should clearly be cautious. However, to demonstrate the presence of weak agents and carcinogens in the environment, the most sensitive available test systems should be used, and the factor of comparability of route of administration may be initially subordinated to the requirement of sensitivity. Once an adverse effect has been clearly established, the quantitative relevance of the experimental data to the human situation should be considered before regulatory approaches can be reasonably developed. At this stage, it becomes appropriate to weight factors such as the route of administration. To use such factors in a limiting sense, and to insist on precise initial comparability between test systems and human exposure before the problem of hazard is established, may effectively limit the possibility of detecting weak environmental carcinogens. Such limitations would indeed challenge the human implications of all but the most recent data on experimental tobacco carcinogenesis.

Test Species   In standard toxicological practice, two mammalian species are tested for toxicity per se, carcinogenicity, mutagenicity, and teratogenicity. In certain circumstances, when there is specific information that the rodent metabolism of the chemical in question is qualitatively different from that in humans, other more appropriate species, such as pigs and subhuman primates, may also be tested.

Test Methods
Acute And Subacute Toxicity Tests   In acute tests, the agent is administered on a single occasion. In subacute tests, the agent is administered on repeated occasions, extending from one week to three months. Routes of administration include the oral, respiratory, and parenteral; exposure of the skin and eye are specialized types of toxicity tests to be discussed separately.

Acute oral toxicity is an index of the lethality of an agent following single oral administration (Table 1). As in all other toxicity tests, effects are dependent on a wide range of variable factors, including age, sex, weight, nutritional status, and method of housing of test animals. These must be rigorously standardized if results are to be reproducible. It is usual to measure acute toxicity on the basis of the number of animals killed at different dose levels of the test agent; toxic effects can also be measured in a variety of other ways, including weight loss. The $LD_{50}$ is that dose which is lethal to 50 percent of the animals tested. As indicated in Table 1, the greater the $LD_{50}$ the lower is the toxicity of the agent. Doses are usually expressed on a body weight basis; for example, mg/kg is the dose in milligrams per kilogram of body weight.

In oral toxicity tests, the agent may be administered in water, food, capsules, or by stomach tube (gavage). Ingestion tests are acute oral toxicity tests in which particular attention is paid to possible damage to the mouth, pharynx, esophagus, and stomach, in attempts to predict the effects of accidental swallowing of caustic materials, particularly by young children.

Eye Irritation   Short-term eye irritation tests in animals are standard for agents, such as detergents, which are likely to be splashed into the eye. In the standard "Federal Hazardous Substances Act" (FHSA) Tests, a small volume (0.1 ml) of the detergent is instilled into the conjunctival sac of six rabbits whose eyelids are held closed for one second. Eye damage is scored for up to three days subsequently. More prolonged observation, for up to two weeks, is however necessary to differentiate between the effects of caustic and noncaustic detergents. Other variations of the eye irritation test include washing out the test agent from the eyes one second after its

Table 1   Quantities Required To Produce Lethal Effects (19)

| Acute Oral Toxicity $LD_{50}$ (mg/kg) | Quantity |
| --- | --- |
| Less than 5 | A few drops |
| 5-50 | A pinch to one teaspoonful |
| 50-500 | 1 teaspoonful to 2 teaspoonfuls |
| 500-5,000 | 1 ounce to 1 pint (1 pound) |
| 5,000-15,000 | 1 pint to 1 quart (2 pounds) |

instillation, as rabbits do not have a protective tear
response, as do primates.

Primary Skin Irritation, Allergic Sensitization, And
Percutaneous Toxicity    FHSA procedures for primary skin
irritation tests are based on application of pastes of the
test agents, such as detergents, to the shaved skin of rabbits
for periods of up to one hour, followed by rinsing and
observation for up to three days.

More modern procedures are based on closed-patch tests in
albino rabbits and human volunteers. Small volumes of
solutions, e.g., of detergents or their ingredients, are
applied to discrete areas on the intact and abraded shaved
skin on the backs of albino rabbits. The solutions are allowed
to dry and then covered with small patch bandages for 24 hours
and the skin is then inspected for primary irritation. The
reactions are graded from slight redness to swelling and
blistering. Human volunteers can be similarly studied,
sometimes with the repeated-insult method, in which serial
applications of test solutions are made at the same site.

Besides these patch tests, allergic sensitization can also
be investigated by pricking, scratching, or injecting dilute
solutions into the skin. Additional tests include immersion of
limbs of rabbits or volunteers in test solutions and also the
use of household tests, in which volunteer families use the
product under evaluation. Periodic inspection is made to
determine whether skin irritation or sensitization has occurred.

Occupational experience in handling detergent formulations
is also likely to give indications of potential consumer
hazards from cutaneous allergic sensitization, as indeed was
the case with enzyme detergents, quite apart from pulmonary
sensitization.

The object of the percutaneous test is to determine whether
general or systemic toxicity can result from absorption of
toxic components of products, such as cosmetics or detergents,
through intact, inflamed, or abraded skin. Concentrated
solutions of detergent pastes are applied daily for five days
a week over a three-month period to the intact or abraded skin
of albino rabbits, which is observed for evidence of local
skin and other toxicity; furthermore, the rabbits are autopsied
for gross and histological examination at the end of the test
period.

Chronic Toxicity Tests    The object of chronic toxicity tests is
to determine the effects on experimental animals of life-long
or long-term exposure to the effects of a particular product or
ingredient. It is standard practice to use at least two species,
generally mice and rats, and four groups of animals; and to use

an untreated or solvent-treated control group and high-, intermediate-, and low-dose test groups. Effects are measured by deaths and by weight loss and also by more subtle changes, such as alterations in liver enzyme function. At the termination of experiments, animals are carefully autopsied and various organs are histologically examined. While traditionally the chronic toxicity test was regarded as inappropriate for determining carcinogenicity (13), such distinctions are no longer considered tenable (20).

The standard route for chronic toxicity tests is the oral. A much-neglected route, largely for technical reasons, is the respiratory. For example, there is no evidence in the "open" literature that those pesticides to which humans are exposed by inhalation over prolonged periods -- e.g., Shell No-Pest Strip (Vapona or Dichlorvos) -- have been subjected to chronic inhalation toxicity tests.

Carcinogenicity Tests  Although the chronic oral toxicity test is standard for determination of carcinogenicity for most classes of products and chemicals (21-23), other routes and techniques are available in particular circumstances. These include repeated skin painting in mice, single or repeated subcutaneous injections in mice, repeated subcutaneous injections in rats, bladder implantation, and intratracheal installation.

In attempts to reduce the gross insensitivity (due to the small number of animals tested) of carcinogenicity tests, there has been growing a tendency to commence carcinogenicity testing in infant rodents, as these are generally more sensitive to chemical carcinogens than adults (24, 25). This approach was used in the Bionetics study (26), supported by a contract from the National Cancer Institute (NCI), in which over 140 pesticides and industrial chemicals were tested for carcinogenicity. Two strains of mice were tested with maximally tolerated doses of chemicals by repeated oral administration from the 7th day of life until sacrifice at the age of 18 months. (See also Insensitivity of Test Methods, below.)

It has been known for nearly the last decade that administration of carcinogens, particularly N-nitroso compounds, to animals in the latter part of pregnancy can produce a high incidence of malignant tumors in their progeny (27). Interest in the practical implications of transplacental carcinogenicity testing has been greatly stimulated by recent reports on the occurrence of vaginal cancer in postpubertal girls (28) whose mothers were treated with high doses of diethylstilbestrol during pregnancy. Yet diethylstibestrol is still used as a contraceptive ("morning-after") pill.

Teratogenicity Tests  The ability of chemicals or other agents
to produce birth defects is determined by their administration
to pregnant animals, generally rodents, during the phase of
active organ development of the growing embryo (organogenesis)
(29, 30). Agents are administered to animals by oral, or less
commonly by other routes, on a single occasion and also
repeatedly during organogenesis. Shortly before anticipated
birth, embryos are harvested by Caesarean section and examined.
Parameters considered in test and concurrent control animals
include the incidence of abnormal fetuses per litter, the
incidence of specific congenital abnormalities, the incidence
of fetal mortality, maternal weight gains in pregnancy, and
maternal and fetal organ/body weight ratios. Additionally,
some pregnant animals are allowed to give birth in order to
identify abnormalities that may be manifest only in the
perinatal period or in the subsequent adult life of the $F_1$
progeny.

Mutagenicity Tests  Various methods are now available for
mutagenicity testing. Systems of bacteria or yeasts have been
categorized as ancillary submammalian systems, with the
presumption of human relevance. More definitive test systems,
however, are based on the use of intact whole mammals. The
human relevance of data obtained from ancillary tests systems
is uncertain, in view of factors such as cell uptake and
metabolism, which markedly differ in mammalian and microbial
systems (31, 32).

Since no single method can detect all possible types of
mutations, a combination of methods must be used. A positive
result in any mammalian system represents evidence of a
potential mutagenic hazard (31). The mammalian tests are
practical and sensitive and their results can be extrapolated
to man with some confidence (31, 32)

Standard mammalian test systems include the dominant lethal
assay, in which male mice or rats are treated with the chemical
under test and then mated to untreated females. Certain forms
of genetic damage induced in male germ cells will manifest
themselves by inducing death of the fertilized embryo shortly
after implantation. This can be recognized by sacrificing the
pregnant rodents in midpregnancy. A second test system is the
cytogenetic assay, in which adult male or female rodents or
other test species are treated with the agent under test.
Bone marrow cells, peripheral lymphocytes, and testicular cells
are then examined microscopically for the induction of
chromosome damage, as manifested by structural or numerical
aberrations. The third in vivo test for mutagenicity is the
host-mediated assay. This is a test for the induction of gene

mutations, which cannot be recognized microscopically, but
which can be detected in microbial systems by standard
nutritional-dependency tests. Nonvirulent microbial suspensions
are injected intraperitoneally into rodents which are then
dosed with the test agent. A few hours later the bacteria are
recovered from the animal and examined to determine whether
mutations have occurred.

## Insensitivity Of Test Methods

For carcinogenicity, teratogenicity, and mutagenicity, chemicals
are tested at higher levels than those of general human
exposure (33). Irrespective of the route of administration,
maximally tolerated doses (MTD) are recommended for this
purpose as the highest dose in dose-response studies (33).
Testing at high doses is now generally regarded as essential
to the attempt to reduce the gross insensitivity imposed on
animal tests by the small size of samples routinely tested,
such as 50 or so rats or mice per dose level per chemical,
compared with the millions of humans at presumptive risk (33).

To illustrate, assume that man is as sensitive to a
particular carcinogen or teratogen as the rat or mouse. Assume
further that this particular agent will produce cancer or a
birth defect in one out of 10,000 humans exposed. Then the
chances of detecting this in groups of 50 rats or mice, tested
at ambient human exposure levels, are very low. Indeed, samples
of 10,000 rats or mice would be required to yield one cancer
or teratogenic event, over and above any spontaneous
occurrences; for statistical significance, perhaps 30,000
rodents would be needed (34). Of course, in any particular
instance, humans may be less or more sensitive than rodents to
the chemical in question. There is consequently no valid basis
for the prediction of the relative sensitivities of test
animals and man. Thus, meclizine, an antihistamine drug used
in treatment of morning sickness, is teratogenic in the rat,
but not apparently so in the few studies on women (35, 36).
In contrast, for thalidomide the lowest effective human
teratogenic dose is 0.5 mg/kg/day; the corresponding values
for the mouse, rat, dog, and hamster are 30, 50, 100, and
350 mg/kg/day, respectively (37). Thus, humans are 60 times
more sensitive than mice, 100 times more sensitive than rats,
200 times more sensitive than dogs, and 700 times more
sensitive than hamsters.

Similar considerations obtain for certain aromatic amines,
such as 2-naphthylamine, which are potent bladder carcinogens
for man and dogs, but not for rats, mice, guinea pigs, and
rabbits (38). Hence, to attempt to predict a safe level for

thalidomide or for 2-naphthylamine from rodent data or from
derived mathematical models would expose humans to obvious
hazards.

Apart from the gross insensitivity of animal test systems,
and the impossibility of gauging human sensitivity from animal
tests, ample data on interactions between carcinogens further
confirm that it is not possible to predict safe levels of
carcinogens based on an arbitrary fraction of the lowest
effective animal dose in a particular experimental situation.
As Health, Education, and Welfare Secretary Arthur Fleming
stated over ten years ago before the House Committee on
Interstate and Foreign Commerce, "...scientifically, there is
no way to determine a safe level for a substance known to
produce cancer in animals." (39)

Thus, the production of hepatomas in trout by feeding as
little as 0.4 parts per billion of aflatoxin $B_1$ is sharply
enhanced by addition of various noncarcinogenic oils to the
diet (40). Similarly, carcinogenesis for mouse skin at low
concentration of benzo(a)pyrene and benz(a)anthracene is
increased 1,000-fold by the use of the noncarcinogenic
n-dodecane as a solvent (41). Intratracheal instillation of
benzo(a)pyrene and ferric oxide in adult hamsters elicited a
high incidence of lower respiratory tract tumors only in
animals pretreated at birth with a single low dose of
diethylnitrosamine (42). Such considerations underlie the
1958 Delaney Amendment, which imposes a zero tolerance for
carcinogenic food additives.

It also must be emphasized that testing at high dosages
does not produce false positive carcinogenic, teratogenic, or
mutagenic results. There is no basis for the contention that
all chemicals are carcinogenic, teratogenic, or mutagenic at
high doses. To illustrate, in the aforementioned Bionetics
study, about 140 pesticides were tested orally in mice of both
sexes and strains at maximally tolerated doses from the first
week of life until sacrifice at 18 months; less than 10 percent
of these were found to be carcinogenic (26). A similar low
incidence of teratogenicity was detected in the Bionetics
survey on pesticides and industrial compounds (29).

It is now clearly recognized that current toxicological
techniques are insensitive and relatively limited in their
ability to detect weak carcinogens, teratogens, and mutagens,
both individually and in various combinations or mixtures
realistically reflecting low or ambient levels and patterns of
environmental exposure. While this is largely due to the
relatively small numbers of animals tested compared with the
massive human populations at presumptive risk, it also reflects

the simplistic nature of toxicological approaches, which are
generally based on the testing of single chemical agents in
isolation from the multitude of other chemicals to which human
populations are concurrently exposed. Thus, the potential for
a wide range of interactions, that may markedly enhance or
synergize toxicity, is not reflected in standard toxicological
practice.

## Methods Of Recognizing Adverse Effects Of Chemicals In Human Populations

Monitoring Of Known Toxic Chemicals  Persistent chemicals,
chemical and metabolic derivatives of less persistent chemicals,
and their reaction and pyrolytic products, should be detected
and monitored in the environment -- air, water, soil, and
food -- and in body fluids or tissues of plants, animals, and
man. Only those chemicals or degradation products with known
or presumed toxicological effect or relevance require
monitoring.

Epidemiology  Even with well-planned and well-executed
toxicologic testing, it is likely that unexpected adverse
effects from toxic chemicals will be seen in humans, reflecting
the insensitivity or inappropriateness of the test systems.
Epidemiological surveys of human and animal populations may
provide post hoc information on geographical or temporal
clusters of unusual types or frequencies of adverse effects --
including cancer, birth defects, and mutations -- after
exposure to undetected or untested chemical agents in the
environment.
    Epidemiologic techniques serve to detect trends or
fluctuations in mortality, morbidity, or disease patterns.
Provided that clear differentials in exposure levels to specific
chemicals or products exist in the general population,
epidemiology may then correlate particular toxic effects with
a particular chemical; the relationship between heavy cigarette
smoking and lung cancer is a classic example of such a
relationship. However, these relationships are more difficult
to establish when exposure differentials are minimal, as with
a food additive or a feed additive residue consumed by the
general population at not widely dissimilar levels.
Additionally, logistic considerations, quite apart from
inadequate current surveillance systems, may limit the utility
of epidemiological approaches even when temporal or
geographical clusters of adverse effects have developed. It is
disquieting to realize that no major known human teratogen --

X-rays, German measles, mercury, or thalidomide -- has been
identified by prospective epidemiological approaches, even in
industrialized countries with good medical facilities (29).
Thalidomide teratogenicity was recognized only by the bizarre
deformities it produced. In all likelihood, thalidomide would
still be in wide use as a "safe" drug had it produced
relatively common anomalies, such as cleft palate or atrial
septal defects.

One of the most critical needs is the development of a
comprehensive national surveillance and registration system
for birth defects and for mutations. This could operate simply
by referral of any obvious birth defects to a specialized
regional center. As the incidence of obvious birth defects in
the United States is approximately 2 percent of all live
births, this sample would be likely to uncover the effects
induced by environmental teratogens or mutagens. Recognition
of temporal or geographical clustering of such effects might
permit the isolation of causal environmental influences.

To be of value in monitoring mutation rates, special
indicator traits must also be selected. These would have to be
dominant, unique, present obviously and conspicuously at
birth, and be associated with sterility, to obviate the
possibility of parental transmission. In addition to relatively
gross approaches such as this, more refined cytogenic and
biochemical monitoring procedures could be developed for both
intrauterine and neonatal tests.

The counting of spontaneous abortions has been recently
recommended as a simple and practical method for monitoring
mutation rates (43). The required parameters would include the
proportion of pregnancies spontaneously aborting; the
proportion of analyzable abortuses with chromosome aberrations;
and the incidence of chromosome aberrations (such as trisomy,
XO and polyploidy).* Teratogens may also produce chromosome
aberrations, but as their effects appear after fertilization,
the aberrations will be sporadic against a normal background.
The action of teratogens would, therefore, be recognized by an
increase in abortions with a basically normal karyotype.

---

*The most informative single statistic for monitoring the
mutation rate would be the proportion of all pregnancies with
an XO abortus; the spontaneous incidence of these is
approximately one percent. The same data could be used to
monitor for polyploidy, nondisjunction -- parallel increase of
both trisomy and XO -- and for teratogenic effects, all of
which would also be detected amongst full-term pregnancies.

Apart from testing of first generation progeny, the feasibility of monitoring peripheral blood cells for cytogenic aberrations and for protein changes -- resulting from altered gene function -- may give more immediate measures of enhanced mutation rates.

High-risk occupational groups have in the past provided the general public with important epidemiologic data relating to hazardous chemicals, such as carbon monoxide, aromatic amines, dioxins, nitrosamines, asbestos, enzyme detergents, and heavy metals. In this connection, it should be pointed out that existing proprietary standards relate to only a small fraction of those toxic chemicals to which workmen are exposed; furthermore, these standards are generally obsolete and ignore or minimize delayed toxic effects, particularly cancer and chronic respiratory disease.

Epidemiologic studies may provide retrospective data on the carcinogenicity of chemicals in current use. However, human experience generally affords only limited indications as to safety or hazard in this area. A prime reason for this is the long latent period elapsing between exposure to carcinogenic chemicals and the subsequent development of cancer. To illustrate, the latent period for the induction of bladder cancer and of lung mesotheliomas following occupational exposure to aromatic amines and asbestos may average 18 and 30 years, respectively. Adverse genetic effects induced by chemical mutagens also have latent periods frequently extending over many generations. Additional difficulties include isolating the effects of any single chemical from the multitude of others to which populations are concurrently exposed, and the lack of baseline data on regional and national incidences of birth defects, besides other adverse human effects. These epidemiological limitations are compounded when the population at large is exposed to weak carcinogens, mutagens, or teratogens and when there are no sharp differentials in levels of human exposure. Even with tobacco, where such exposure differentials clearly obtain, the epidemiological demonstration of causal relationships between smoking and lung cancer has been long delayed for these other reasons.

## Poisoning From Chemicals In Consumer Products As A Public Health Hazard

Annual estimates by the National Safety Council and the National Center for Health Statistics of the Department of Health, Education and Welfare (HEW), for injury and poisoning in and around the home indicate that, yearly, 30,000 people are killed, 110,000 permanently disabled, 585,000 hospitalized and

more than 20 million injured seriously enough to require
medical treatment or to be disabled for one day or more (44,
44). Most of these casualties are associated with consumer
products. The cost to the economy, individual consumers, and
manufacturers runs to billions of dollars annually.

Based on tabulations of the National Clearing House for
Poison Control Centers, the FDA Bureau of Product Safety
estimates that there are approximately 500,000 to 1,000,000
annual ingestions of potentially poisonous household products
by both sexes and all ages (46). There are also grounds for
believing that the number of deaths resulting from these
poisonings are grossly underestimated in officially reported
figures.

Poisonings from pesticide products are approximately 75,000
per year (46, and Table 2). Injuries from laundry cleaning and
polishing products are estimated to be about 250,000 annually.
Approximately 62 percent of the poisonings occur in children
under the age of five years. The ability of the Bureau of
Product Safety of the FDA to obtain more accurate, rapid, and
comprehensive statistics on accidents and injuries has been
augmented by the recent creation of a National Electronic
Injury Surveillance System (47).

Table 2  HEW Estimates On Annual Injuries From Chemical
Consumer Products (46)

### Laundering, Cleaning, and Polishing Products

| | |
|---|---|
| Poisonings from soaps, detergents, cleaners | 40,000 |
| Poisonings from bleaches | 35,000 |
| Poisonings from disinfectants and deodorizers | 20,000 |
| Poisonings from furniture polish | 20,000 |
| Poisonings from lye corrosives | 15,000 |
| Other poisonings from laundering, cleaning and polishing products | 20,000 |
| Other injuries from laundering, cleaning and polishing products | 100,000 |
| Total | 250,000 |

### Pesticides

| | |
|---|---|
| Poisonings from insecticides | 35,000 |
| Poisonings from rodenticides | 20,000 |
| Other poisonings from pesticides | 20,000 |
| Total | 75,000 |

   Poisoning from cleaning products can cause a wide range of
injuries ranging from surface burns to the lips, mouth, skin,
and eyes, to corrosion of the esophagus and stomach which may
be fatal. Even small quantities of petroleum distillate-based
furniture polish reaching the lungs can cause chemical
pneumonia.

   Prevention of accidental poisoning requires the repackaging
of products with child-resistant spouts or other forms of
protective packaging, and the use of less toxic and caustic
ingredients in household cleaning products. Certain standard
current products, such as strongly alkaline dishwasher
detergents and furniture polishes, can be reformulated with
similarly effective, but less hazardous, ingredients. Warning
labeling, as required by the FHSA, clearly will not alone
prevent accidental childhood poisoning.

## Carcinogenicity As A Public Health Hazard

More than 25 percent (51 million) of the 200 million people
now living in the United States will develop some form of
cancer (48, 49). Even with available methods of treatment,
34 million of these will die of cancer. In 1969, 323,000 people
died of cancer in the United States. Cancer is thus a leading
cause of early death (Table 3).

   The rate of increase of cancer deaths is more rapid than the
rate of increase in population and is even more rapid than the
increase in the rate of death (49). This increase in new cancer
cases is real and is over and above that due to the increase
in median age of the population.

   The economic impact of cancer is massive. The direct costs
of hospitalization and all medical care for cancer in 1969
exceeded $500 million (50). The indirect costs of cancer,
including loss of earnings during illness and over the balance
of normal life expectancy, brought the total costs of cancer
to over $13 billion for 1969.

Table 3  U.S. Deaths From Various Causes (49)

| | |
|---|---:|
| Cancer (1969) | 323,000 |
| World War II | 292,000 |
| Auto accidents (1969) | 59,600 |
| Vietnam War (6 years) | 41,000 |
| Korean War (3 years) | 34,000 |
| Polio (1952 - worst year) | 3,300 |

There is now growing recognition that the majority of human
cancers are due to chemical carcinogens in the environment and
that they are hence ultimately preventable (51, 52, 53, 54).
The World Health Organization has estimated that over 75
percent of human cancers are influenced by environmental
factors (52). It has also been estimated that approximately
90 percent of human cancers are chemical in origin (54). Other
estimates indicate that between 60 to 80 percent of human
cancers are environmental in origin. The basis for these
estimates largely derives from epidemiological studies, which
have revealed wide geographic variations in the incidence of
cancer of various organs in the general population (53, 55).
In some of these studies, the role of specific environmental
carcinogens has been implicated or identified.

The best-documented and most-significant data on
carcinogenesis due to environmental chemicals are those on
tobacco. It has been suspected for several decades that heavy
tobacco smoking is directly and causally related to chronic
lung disease, especially cancer. Over 29 retrospective
epidemiologic studies on lung cancer, generally substantiating
the causative role of smoking, have been published from 1939
to 1964 (56). One of the most important of these studies
demonstrated unambiguously that the incidence of lung cancer
could be positively correlated with cigarette smoking (57).
Mortality rates from lung cancer have increased exponentially
over the last few decades, in both men and women, particularly
in the United States, and have now reached epidemic
proportions (58). There are also many studies which demonstrate
the contributory role of urban air pollution to lung cancer,
in addition to the identification of numerous classes of
chemical carcinogens in polluted urban air. These studies have
shown that there is an excess of lung cancer deaths in smokers
living in polluted urban areas, when contrasted with those
living in nonpolluted rural areas (59). Similar strong regional
variations in the occurrence of a wide range of other organ
cancers are now well recognized (60-67). The high incidence of
cancer of the oral cavity in Asia, representing some 35 percent
of all Asiatic cancers, in contrast to one percent of all
European cancers, is clearly related to the chewing of betel
nuts and tobacco leaves. The high incidence of liver cancer in
the Bantu and in Guam may well be due to dietary contamination
with aflatoxin (68), a potent fungal carcinogen, and to eating
Cycad plants, containing azoxyglucoside carcinogens (61, 62,
69-71). The high incidence of gastric cancer in Japan, Iceland,
and Chile has been associated with high dietary intake of
fish; suggestions have been made implicating nitrosamines,

formed by reactions between secondary amines in fish and
nitrite preservatives. The high incidence of cancer of the
esophagus, in Zambians drinking Kachasu spirits and in the
Calvados area of France and in other clearly defined geographic
areas, may be related to contamination of alcoholic drinks or
food with nitrosamines, some of which produce esophageal cancer
in experimental animals (66, 67, 72, 73).

More restricted data on chemical carcinogenesis in humans
derive from follow-up studies on patients treated with
carcinogenic drugs (74-78). These include immunosuppressive
agents, used in transplant therapy; alkylating agents, used in
treatment of cancer and to a lesser extent autoimmune disease;
radioactive phosphorus, used in treatment of polycythemia vera;
estrogens, used for treatment of prostatic cancer and for
hormone replacement therapy in women; and diethylstilbestrol
(see Carcinogenicity Tests, above).

Data on occupational carcinogenesis extend back to the
eighteenth century, with the discovery by Sir Percival Pott of
a high incidence of scrotal cancers in young British chimney
sweeps exposed to soot. A very wide range of occupational
cancers has since been identified and studied in detail (79-82).
These include bladder cancer in the aniline dye and rubber
industry, caused by chemicals including 2-naphthylamine,
benzidine, 2-aminodiphenyl, and 2-nitrodiphenyl (83, 84); lung
cancer in uranium miners of Colorado, in coke oven workers, in
nitrogen mustard factories in Japan and in U.S. workers even
briefly exposed to bis- (chloromethyl) ether (85-87); skin
cancer in cutting and shale oil workers; nasal-sinus cancer
in wood workers; lung cancer and pleural mesotheliomas in
insulation workers and in others, such as construction workers,
exposed to asbestos (88, 89); cancer of the pancreas and
lymphomas in organic chemists (90); and cancer of the cervix
in prostitutes.

From both toxicological and epidemiological standpoints, it
is useful to differentiate potent from weak carcinogens.
Potent carcinogens such as aflatoxins (68) and nitrosamines
(67) can produce cancer in experimental animals, even at the
very low levels in which they have been found in certain foods.
Identification of these carcinogens in food has encouraged
attempts to link their distribution with local patterns of
cancer incidence.

However, the effects of weak carcinogens, such as
atmospheric pollutants and certain pesticides and food
additives, may easily escape detection by conventional
biological tests. Additionally, as such weak carcinogens are

unlikely to be clearly implicated epidemiologically, they may pose greater hazards than more obvious potent carcinogens.

## Mutagenicity As A Public Health Hazard

The first indication that environmental pollutants may influence the genetic constitution of future populations appeared some four decades ago upon the discovery that ionizing radiation induces mutations. The subsequent development of atomic energy has added a new dimension and enhanced awareness to the problem of genetic hazards. Partial safeguards have been accordingly developed to minimize radiation exposure. Once radiation-induced mutagenesis was discovered, there were reasons to suspect that some chemicals would act similarly, but proof of this was delayed until World War II, when mustard gas was shown to induce mutations in fruit flies. Many and varied types of chemicals have subsequently been shown to be mutagenic. The likelihood that some highly mutagenic chemicals may come into wide use, or indeed may already be in wide use, is now a serious concern.

A mutation is defined as any inheritable change in the genetic material. This may be a chemical transformation of an individual gene, which is designated a gene or point mutation, that causes it to have an altered function. Alternatively, the change may involve a rearrangement, or a gain or loss, of parts of a chromosome which may be microscopically visible, and which is designated a chromosome aberration. In many systems these are easily distinguished, but classification of an individual defect in human studies -- the decision as to whether some defect is due to a point mutation or a chromosome aberration -- is not always possible.

Mutations may occur in any somatic (body) or germ (ovum or sperm) cell. The result is frequently the death of the particular cell involved, and generally this causes only local and transient damage. However, if the genetic functioning of the cell is altered, while the capacity for cell division is unimpaired, the mutation may be transmitted to descendant cells. These effects may result in cancer in somatic cells of the adult or embryo or in birth defects in somatic cells of the embryo.

Mutations in germ cells are most serious as these may be transmitted to future generations. It should be emphasized that there is no single type of inherited mutagenic effect. Since every part of the body and every metabolic process is under at least some genetic control, the range of effects produced by gene alterations includes all conceivable types of structure and process. At one extreme are consequences so

severe (so-called lethal effects) that the individual may be
aborted, stillborn, or incapable of survival after birth. If
cell death occurs very early in embryonic development, it may
never be detected; extensive cell death at a later stage may
lead to abortions. Approximately one-fourth of spontaneous
abortions show detectable chromosome aberrations. There is no
way at present to know how many of the remainder are caused by
gene mutations or by visually undetectable chromosome
aberrations. If the embryo survives until birth, a variety of
physical abnormalities may manifest themselves. There are
numerous known inherited diseases, and probably many more that
are unknown, all of which owe their ultimate cause to mutations.
While these are individually rare, collectively they are at the
root of many problems in the area of public health. At the
other extreme are gene mutations with mild effects. Finally,
those with still smaller effects may be imperceptible.

Mutations can produce a wide diversity of deleterious
effects. Many mutations produce effects similar to those
arising from nongenetic causes. The impact of environmental
mutagens is thus statistical rather than unique. This problem
is further complicated by the time distribution of mutational
effects.

Some mutant genes are dominant, in which case the
abnormality or disease will appear in the immediate generation
following occurrence of the mutation. Dominant mutations
express themselves as early fetal deaths, or in abnormalities
such as achondroplasia, polydactyly, retinoblastoma, and
sterility.

On the other hand, the mutation may be recessive, requiring
the presence of abnormal genes in both homologous chromosomes --
one derived from each parent -- to produce the defect.
Recessive mutations, such as albinism, Fanconi's anemia,
amaurotic idiocy, and phenylketonuria, may therefore be
unexpressed for many generations. The major effects of
increased mutation rates would thus be less obvious and spread
over many generations, and would include ill-defined
abnormalities, such as premature aging, enhanced susceptibility
to various diseases (notably leukemia and cancer), and
alterations in sex ratios (91, 92).

The great majority of mutations are harmful or at best
neutral. This has been established experimentally and follows
from the principle of natural selection (91). Natural selection
has previously eliminated those individuals whose mutant genes
caused them to be abnormal. As a result, an approximate
equilibrium has been established between the introduction of
new mutant genes into the population and elimination of old

mutant genes by natural selection. With present high standards
of living and health care in the United States, many individuals
carrying mutations that in the past would have caused death or
reduced fertility now persist. The equilibrium is thus out of
balance, and new mutants are being added to the population
faster than they can be eliminated by natural processes. This,
coupled with the near-eradication of many infectious diseases,
makes it likely that future medical problems will be of
increasingly genetic origin. As Lederberg recently stated,

"If we give proper weight to the genetic component of many
common diseases which have a more complex etiology than the
textbook examples of Mendelian defects, we can calculate that
at least 25 percent of our health burden is of genetic origin.
This figure is a very conservative estimate in view of the
genetic component of such griefs as schizophrenia, diabetes,
atherosclerosis, mental retardation, early senility, and many
congenital malformations. In fact, the genetic factor in
disease is bound to increase to an even larger proportion, for
as we deal with infectious disease and other environmental
insults, the genetic legacy of the species will compete only
with traumatic accidents as the major factor in health." (93)

A mutation, once it has occurred, may be transmitted to
succeeding generations. If the gene causes a lethal or
sterilizing effect, it will persist only one generation and
affect only one person. On the other hand, if it causes only
slight impairment of health, it may be transmitted from
generation to generation. There is, therefore, generally an
inverse relation between the severity of the gene effect and
the number of persons that will be exposed to this effect. The
effects of mild mutations could otherwise be dismissed as
relatively unimportant, but in any overall consideration, the
consequences to many persons mildly affected may be comparable
to the effect upon one individual severely affected.
Experiments on Drosophila show that mildly deleterious
mutations occur with much greater frequency than more severe
mutants. Thus, although an increased mutation rate would cause
a corresponding increase in severe abnormalities and genetic
diseases, the major statistical impact of a mutational increase
would be to add to the burden of mild mutation effects, which
would have major public-health consequences while being most
difficult to detect.
Chemical mutagens in the environment pose hazards which have
not yet been quantified, although sensitive and practical
mammalian test systems are available. A report of the genetic

study section of the National Institutes of Health states
that,

"There is reason to fear that some chemicals may constitute
as important a risk as radiation, possibly a more serious one.
Although knowledge of chemical mutagenesis in man is much less
certain than that of radiation, a number of chemicals -- some
with widespread use -- are known to induce genetic damage in
some organisms. To consider only radiation hazards is to
ignore what may be the submerged part of the iceberg....
Recent investigations have revealed chemical compounds that
are highly mutagenic in experimental organisms, in
concentrations that are not toxic and that have no overt
effect on fertility...." (92)

Fortunately, recent recognition of genetic hazards due to
chemicals has been paralleled by the development of various
tests for mutagenicity (91). A variety of submammalian test
organisms -- bacteria, Neurospora, yeasts, and Drosophila --
are available to help elucidate basic mechanisms. But in view
of the wide metabolic and biochemical discrepancies between
these systems and man, submammalian tests should be used to
provide data ancillary to more relevant test systems. Of these,
three in vivo mammalian tests are practical and sensitive --
in vivo cytogenetics, the host-mediated assay, and the dominant
lethal assay; results from these three tests can be
extrapolated to man with some confidence (91).
Ethyleneimines are good examples of highly mutagenic
chemicals which are used for many purposes, including therapy
of neoplastic and nonneoplastic diseases, chemosterilant
insecticides, pigment dyeing and printing, fireproofing and
creaseproofing of fabrics and textiles, as ingredients in solid
rocket fuels, intermediates in many industrial synthesis, and
as cross-linking agents in starches and shampoos. Ethyleneimines
have also been proposed for rodent and plant control.
Another example of a mutagen in common use until recently is
trimethylphosphate (TMP), which until recently was added to
gasoline, on a regional basis, at concentrations of 0.25 gram
per gallon for controlling surface ignition and spark plug
fouling due to the use of alkyl lead additives (94, 95). It
also is used as a methylating agent, chemical intermediate in
production of polymethyl polyphosphates, flame-retardant solvent
for paints and polymers, and catalyst in preparation of polymers
and resins. TMP is mutagenic in the dominant lethal assay in
mice, and produces chromosomal damage in bone marrow cells of

rats following oral or parenteral administration at subtoxic
doses (96, 97).

It, however, is difficult to estimate mutagenic hazards to
which the general population has been exposed in the absence
of information on the concentration of unreacted TMP and of
biologically active pyrolytic products in automobile exhaust.
Such problems hitherto have not received adequate consideration.
According to a recent statement by a major manufacturer (98),

"We have not attempted to detect trimethylphosphate in
exhaust, but it is reasonable to assume that a portion -- maybe
one percent -- may appear unreacted in the exhaust."

Similar considerations apply to fuel additive formulations
based on triaryl phosphates, some of which have been used to
replace TMP (99, 100). In a recent unpublished study, it was
found that approximately one quarter of one percent of the
triaryl phosphate added to gasoline appeared in unreacted form
in exhaust, representing a concentration in exhaust of 70
micrograms per cubic meter (101).

An additional source of prolonged exposure of large
population groups to TMP results from the extensive use of the
previously mentioned insecticide Vapona or Dichlorvos (Shell
No-Pest Strip). (See Chronic Toxicity Tests, above.) TMP is
one of the usual ingredients of Vapona (102, 103), being
present as an impurity together with other unlabeled "related
compounds" in commercial formulations. Additionally, Vapona
itself is mutagenic in microbial systems (104). Most serious
is the fact that Vapona itself induces alkylating effects
(cross-linkage between macromolecules such as DNA) both in
vitro (105) and in vivo (106). Most carcinogens and mutagens,
or their proximate activated forms, are alkylating agents (107);
hence the property of alkylation indicates strong presumption
of carcinogenic and mutagenic hazards in the absence of
specific evidence to the contrary.

Teratogenicity As A Public Health Hazard
Teratology is the study of congenital malformations. These are
generally defined as structural abnormalities which can be
recognized at or shortly after birth, and which can cause
disability or death. In its less restricted definition,
teratology also includes microscopic, biochemical, and
functional abnormalities of prenatal origin.*

---

*Teratological effects are quite distinct from mutagenic.
However, some teratological effects may be due to the induction
of somatic mutations in embryonic cells.

The standard definition of teratology has, however, recently been challenged by scientists from Dow Chemical Co. (108). Following the experimental induction of a wide range of skeletal abnormalities in rats by phenoxy herbicides, the following alternative definition has been proffered: "That degree of embryotoxicity which seriously interferes with normal development or survival of the offspring."

This suggested redefinition, however, would exclude common birth defects such as cleft palate (30, 109). In turn, it could seriously hinder the adoption of effective regulatory approaches concerned with prevention of exposure of pregnant women to teratogenic agents in the environment.

The incidence of human congenital malformation is unknown in the absence of a comprehensive national surveillance system and registry; it has been variously estimated as ranging from 3 to 7 percent of total live births. Congenital malformations pose incalculable personal, familial, and social stresses. As previously mentioned, the financial cost to society of one seriously retarded child approximates to $250,000 computed on the basis of remedial and custodial care alone, excluding deprivation of earnings (11).

Three major categories of human teratogens have so far been identified: viral infections, X-irradiation, and chemicals, such as mercurials, thalidomide and diethylstilbestrol. Although the teratogenicity of various chemicals has been experimentally recognized for several decades, only after the thalidomide disaster of 1962 were legislative requirements for three-generation reproductive tests established for pesticides and drugs. This requirement was informally extended to teratogenicity tests in 1966. The appropriateness of three-generation tests for determination of teratogenicity has, however, recently been questioned (29).

The possible carcinogenic effects of teratogens is largely unknown, as pregnant animals are generally sacrificed by Caesarean section in teratogenicity experiments. However, recent studies indicate that N-nitroso compounds may induce carcinogenic effects, particularly of the central nervous system (CNS), when administered to rodents after the completion of organogenesis (27). The exact situation is unclear, because administration of such agents during organogenesis may also produce fetotoxicity or growth disturbances, particularly of the CNS.

These findings are of particular practical importance in view of the ease of synthesis of N-nitroso compounds from simple precursors -- nitrites and amides or amines -- which are widely distributed in the environment, and also in view of strong epidemiological data implicating the influence of

prenatal events in childhood tumors of the CNS and elsewhere
(110). Such evidence includes peaks in mortality of major
childhood tumors under the age of 5 years, the occasional
association between such tumors and growth disturbances, such
as hamartomas and congenital hemihypertrophy, and the increased
tumor risk in the siblings of children with brain and other
tumors.

A more compelling current issue related to transplacental
carcinogenesis in humans concerns diethylstilbestrol (DES), a
synthetic stilbene with estrogenic activity. There have been
recent reports on the induction of adenocarcinoma of the
vagina, an otherwise excessively rare tumor, in postpubertal
girls whose mothers were treated with DES for threatened
abortion (28). Over 80 such cases of transplacental
carcinogenesis due to DES have to date been identified (111).
DES has long been known to be carcinogenic to many species of
test animals (112), and to produce a high incidence of mammary
carcinomas when fed to mice at levels as low as 0.2 micrograms
per gram (113).

The use of DES as a feed additive to fatten cattle in
feedlots was considered of sufficient danger to public health
that it was banned by the FDA as of January 1973, following
repeated findings of illegal residues in meal. Its use for
implants was subsequently banned also. Yet at this writing it
is still widely used as a contraceptive "morning-after" pill,
as previously discussed.

Regulatory Controls Over Chemicals In Consumer Products
There are a wide range of controls which -- with varying
degrees of effectiveness -- regulate the manufacture,
distribution and sale of chemical consumer products.
Historically, the Food and Drug Administration (FDA) has had
the principal administrative and responsibility for federal
law, discharging functions through five principle Bureaus --
Food; Drugs; Veterinary Medicine; Product Safety; and
Radiological Health. Responsibility for product safety was
transferred in October 1972 to the then-established Consumer
Product Safety Commission. Responsibility for biological
standards in July 1972 was transferred from the National
Institutes of Health to the FDA. In addition, there is a
Regional Operations Office which administers all FDA activities
through 17 district offices in 10 regions.

FDA's Legislative Domain (47)  The Food and Drug Administration
is the governmental agency with prime responsibility for
protecting the health and safety of Americans, a responsibility

which has grown beyond food and drugs with the passage of new legislation over the years. Here is a chronological listing of the major laws the agency enforces.

The Tea Importation Act (29 Stat 604), enacted in 1897, requires that all tea imported into the U.S. meets certain quality standards.

The Federal Food, Drug and Cosmetic Act (34 Stat 768), enacted in 1906 as the nation's first major food and drug law, was replaced in 1938 by another act of the same name (21 USC 301-392) that requires pure and wholesome foods, safe and effective drugs, safe cosmetics, truthful labeling, inspection of drug manufacturing plants every two years, and testing of drugs, coloring additives and food chemicals by the FDA.

The Filled Milk Act (42 Stat 1486), enacted in 1923, prohibits interstate distribution of milk products in which butterfat is replaced with vegetable oils.

The Import Milk Act (44 Stat 1101), enacted in 1927, prohibits the importation of milk and cream unless importers certify it was produced under sanitary conditions.

The Food Additives Amendment (72 Stat 1784), enacted in 1958, prohibits the use of new food additives until safety is established and regulations are issued on usage.

The Color Additives Amendment (74 Stat 397), enacted in 1960, permits the FDA to establish by regulation the conditions for safe usage of color additives in foods, drugs and cosmetics, and to require manufacturers to prove their safety.

The Federal Hazardous Substances Labeling Act (74 Stat 372), enacted in 1960, requires all household containers of potentially dangerous substances to be conspicuously labeled to warn the user of danger.

The Drug Amendments of 1962 (76 Stat 780), the so-called Kefauver-Harris amendments, strengthen new-drug clearance procedures and require proof of effectiveness before marketing.

The Child Protection Act of 1966 (80 Stat 1303), banned from interstate commerce toys and articles so hazardous that adequate warnings could not be written.

The Fair Packaging and Labeling Act (80 Stat 1296), enacted in 1966, requires complete and prominent labeling information on packages and containers to aid shoppers in comparing values and to prevent deceptive packaging practices. FDA jurisdiction

extends to the packaging of foods, drugs, medical devices and
cosmetics.

The Flammable Fabrics Act (67 Stat 111), enacted in 1953 with
amendments in 1967 (81 Stat 568), directs the FDA to study and
investigate deaths, injuries and losses resulting from
accidental burns caused by products, plastics and other
related materials. The FDA does not establish standards or
enforce them.

The Radiation Control for Health and Safety Act (82 Stat 1173),
was enacted in 1968 as an amendment to the Public Health
Service Act. It protects the public from unnecessary exposure
to radiation from electronic products.

The Child Protection and Toy Safety Act of 1969 (83 Stat 187),
bans toys and other children's articles that have electrical,
mechanical or thermal hazards.

The Public Health Service Act (58 Stat 682), enacted in 1944,
contains four sections that were transferred to FDA jurisdiction
in 1969. They cover milk supplies; food, water and sanitary
facilities for travelers; sanitary practices in restaurants
and food-service establishments; the harvesting and handling
of shellfish; and determining causes and finding means of
preventing accidental poisoning and injuries by consumer
products.

The Poison Prevention Packaging Act (84 Stat 1670), enacted in
1970, is designed to protect children from accidentally eating
toxic substances by requiring special packaging designed so
that children under five have trouble opening the package
while adults do not.

Federal Hazardous Substances Act   This was originally known as
the Federal Hazardous Substances Labeling Act (FHSA) of 1960
(74 Stat 372). This is currently administered by the Bureau of
Product Safety of the FDA. The Act covers all categories of
household products, including toys, but not the raw materials
from which they are manufactured.

The Act is based on recognition of the potential hazards of
some consumer products and on the belief that certain of these
hazards may be minimized or prevented by cautionary labeling.
Under the Act's statutory policy, those types of substances
subject to its provisions must be identified by labeling. The
hazards these substances pose and also the penalties for
violation or omission of the act also must be stated on the
label. The labels must include the signal words "Danger" for

highly toxic substances, and "Warning" or "Caution" for all other hazardous substances.

Domestic cleaning products are subject to these requirements when one or more of their formulation characteristics or individual components are considered hazardous enough to create the risk of illness or injury under conditions of normal handling or use. Tests for acute toxicity following accidental swallowing, and for eye and skin irritation or toxicity, are provided for in the Act and defined in the regulations. The Act also provides that hazardous detergents must be conspicuously labeled with a statement which must include specific identification of each ingredient substantially contributing to the hazard and a description of the nature of the hazard.

The Act also provides (Sec. 2 (p) (1)) that a product can be banned if it is so dangerous that the user cannot be adequately protected by cautionary labeling. This provision, however, is highly restrictive and has yet to be invoked against any household detergent. In fact, only three household products have ever been banned under the Act (114).

## Federal Insecticide, Fungicide, And Rodenticide Act (FIFRA)

FIFRA (7 USC 135-135K) regulates the marketing, in interstate commerce, of "economic poisons and devices," which includes insecticides, rodenticides, herbicides, and household disinfectants. The Act, which is now administered by the Environmental Protection Agency, requires registration, appropriate labeling, and in some cases coloring of pesticide products in attempts to protect the user and handler.

## Food, Drug And Cosmetic Act

This act (21 USC 301 et seq.) gives extensive regulatory authority to the FDA. Its provisions and limitations, with particular reference to problems of product safety, are discussed in detail in Vol. 2 in relation to food additives, pesticide residues in food, feed additives, drugs, and cosmetics.

## The Delaney Amendment To The Food, Drug And Cosmetic Act

The Delaney Amendment, enacted on September 6, 1958 (P.L. 85-929), prohibits the use of any carcinogenic chemical as a food additive. Specifically, the law states:

"That no additive shall be deemed safe if it is found to induce cancer when ingested by man or animal, or if it is found, after tests which are appropriate for the evaluation of the safety of food additives, to induce cancer in man or animal...."

The Delaney Amendment applies only to intentional food additives. Unintentional or accidental "additives," such as DDT and other pesticides residues, are excluded from its requirements.

The philosophical and scientific basis for the Delaney Amendment largely derives from a meeting of the International Union Against Cancer in 1954. At this meeting, sharp distinctions were made between reversible and irreversible effects of chemicals. For chemicals inducing reversible toxic effects, such as acute and chronic toxicity per se, it was agreed that threshold levels, below which human exposure would be safe, could be reasonably determined. However, for chemicals inducing irreversible and possibly cumulative effects, such as cancer, threshold levels could in no way be defined.

This fundamental distinction was further emphasized at a symposium of the International Union Against Cancer two years later (115), all participants of which unanimously recommended that:

"...as a basis for active cancer prevention, the proper authorities of various countries promulgate and enact adequate rules and regulations prohibiting the addition to food of substances having potential carcinogenicity."

The Amendment invoked immediate strong opposition, exemplified by the statement of Dr. William Darby (116), Chairman of the NAS Food Protection Committee, that "adequate protection would be afforded by the law without the inclusion of the Delaney Clause."

At the same hearings, HEW Secretary Arthur Fleming (39) vigorously defended the scientific basis of the Delaney clause and rebutted the criticisms leveled against it by industrial representatives (see Insensitivity of Test Methods, above). Fleming stated that,

"The rallying point against (the Delaney Clause) is the catch phrase that it takes away the scientist's right to exercise judgment. The issue thus made is a false one, because the clause allows the exercise of all the judgment that can safely be exercised on the basis of our present knowledge... It allows the Department and its scientific people full discretion and judgment in deciding whether a substance has been shown to produce cancer when added to the diet of test animals. But once this decision has been made, the limits of judgment have been reached and there is no reliable basis on

which discretion could be exercised in determining a safe
threshold for the established carcinogen."

For the third time since its passage in 1958, the Delaney
Amendment is now again under attack. In hearings on the
hazards of color additives in 1960, in the wake of the
cyclamate ban in 1969, and now after the ban on the use of the
feed additive diethylstilbestrol in 1972, the Delaney
"anticancer" clause has been subjected to vigorous attack by
those who claim its strict prohibition against the deliberate
addition of chemical carcinogens to food is too rigid and
arbitrary. In each of these instances, the food and chemical
industry has claimed that the clause, if continuingly enforced,
will substantially hamper production of food by modern
scientific technology. It is perhaps no coincidence that the
attacks on the Delaney Amendment are mounting at a time when
the food chemical industry is poised for a major expansion.
The chemical industry predicts that sales of chemical additives
are expected to grow from $485 million in 1970 to $750 million
by 1980.

A wide range of other criticisms have been and still are
being leveled against the Delaney Amendment. All such
criticisms have emerged from industrial groups, trade
associations and their consultants, and from groups that are
clearly identified with protection of industrial interests
(117). The FDA has associated itself with this position in
several public statements by senior agency representatives. In
a statement as FDA Commissioner, Charles Edwards (Assistant HEW
Secretary since April, 1973) urged U.S. consumers to revoke or
radically modify the "controversial" Delaney Amendment, which
he described as "outstripped by current scientific knowledge."
(118)

It is of interest that as of July 1973 no similar criticisms
have emerged from qualified independent experts in
carcinogenesis, including those from the scientific staff of
the National Cancer Institute (NCI), from the membership of
the International Union Against Cancer, or from the American
Cancer Society.

In a workshop on the scientific basis of the Delaney
Amendment, held on January 15-16, 1973, by the New York
Academy of Sciences and attended by over 100 scientists and
lawyers, there was unanimity among all experts and authorities
on chemical carcinogenesis that the Delaney Clause should be
maintained inviolate (119). Detailed scientific rebuttals of
standard criticisms of the Delaney Amendment also were

presented at the meeting (120). Additionally, strong
recommendations were made that the Delaney concept should be
extended to carcinogens in air, water, and the occupational
environment. Of particular interest is a statement by Mr.
Eugene Lambert (120), a lawyer with the Washington-based firm
of Covington and Burling which represents many leading food
industries, including the National Canners Association:

"On the basis of the evidence presented at this meeting,
I don't see any practical basis for a change in the Delaney
Clause at this time."

A clear lay interpretation of the Delaney Law, with
particular reference to its importance in the prevention of
human cancer, has been recently developed by a leading
Washington-based public interest group (121).

Consumer Product Safety Act   This Act (P.L. 92-573) creates
a Consumer Product Safety Commission, which preempts
regulatory authority of the FDA Bureau of Product Safety, as
an independent federal regulatory agency to police the entire
consumer product field and to upgrade safety. This legislation
was enacted into law on October 28, 1972.
     This new Commission now deals directly with the Congress on
legislative and budgetary requests and is designed to be
relatively "insulated" from outside pressures. The Act allows
for individual initiative in government and also permits
individual consumers to force the Commission to set standards
for hazardous products.

## Regulatory And Legislative Needs

### Enforcement Of Existing Regulations And Legislation
Approximately 680 food additives, many of which have never been
adequately evaluated, are now on the FDA's Generally Recognized
as Safe (GRAS) list. Both the toxicological properties and
legal status of these additives is questionable. A strict
enforcement of the 1958 Food Additive Amendment would probably
have precluded the inclusion of the majority of these chemicals
in the GRAS list.
     Prior to 1958, the criterion for inclusion on the GRAS list
was safety; this was assessed to be either by formal scientific
evaluation or by experience of common usage in food. After
1958, scientific evaluation was the only allowable criterion.
     Apart from the 680 GRAS additives, manufacturers have
hitherto reserved the right to determine whether or not a food

chemical is safe without filing petitions. The result is that some chemicals are currently being illegally used in food.

Under the 1958 Amendments, the onus of safety evaluation of food chemicals supposedly was placed on the manufacturer. However, when such testing is performed by the FDA, for example at their Pine Bluff, Arkansas laboratory, the burden and cost is shifted to the taxpayer. Similarly, actions to reimburse cyclamate manufacturers for losses suffered when cyclamates were banned from interstate commerce implies that industry found guilty of violating laws -- in this case the Delaney Amendment -- should be protected at the taxpayers' expense from the economic losses incurred as a consequence of their violations.

Criteria And Standards To Be Met Prior To Introduction Of Innovative Products Into Commerce  In recent testimony before the Senate Government Operations Subcommittee (122), it was recommended that before a new product is introduced into interstate commerce, certain questions should be posed as to its efficacy, safety, and identity. Similar questions also may be asked about many products, such as GRAS additives, already in use.

The first obvious question is: Does the product achieve its stated objectives in narrowly defined FTC terms? An additional question is whether, allowing for possible bias or special value judgments, the product serves a socially and economically useful purpose for the general population; Sen. Gaylord Nelson (D.-Wisc.) has used the term "necessary" to describe such a purpose (2). If not, why introduce the product and accept potential hazards without matching benefits? Such considerations are relevant to the use of monosodium glutamate in baby foods, and cyclamates for the public at large. The need for efficacy, now contained in federal drug law, should be extended to all categories of consumer products. These concepts were emphasized at a 1969 White House Conference on Nutrition, where it was recommended that food additives be excluded from products unless they either significantly improve the quality or nutritive value of the food, or lower its cost, as well as being safe (12).

Questions on safety should be particularly rigorous for products with persistent chemical ingredients which are environmentally mobile and lipophilic and likely to accumulate in the food chain (122). Questions on identity can be partially resolved by establishing uniform requirements for disclosure, by appropriate labeling, of all ingredients in chemical consumer products. In this regard, synthetic chemicals and

their concentrations should be clearly labeled and identified
in drugs, cosmetics, foods, pesticides, household cleaning
agents, and other chemical products. Beside clear
identification of chemicals in the product in question,
information on their chemical and pyrolytic products,
metabolites, and contaminants should be made available to
appropriate regulatory agencies, whose staffs will then
anticipate adverse effects and monitoring the levels of the
chemicals and products in question in the environment, animals,
and man.

After the criteria of efficacy, safety, and identity have
been satisfied, the new product may be registered for commerce.
Still, the possibility of error, due to the insensitivity or
inappropriateness of toxicological and environmental testing,
must be recognized. Attempts to minimize such a contingency
can be developed post hoc by ecological, monitoring, and
epidemiological studies.

Need For Periodic Review Of Registration  Registrations for all
chemical products should be periodically reviewed against any
further evidence that may have developed with regard to human
and environmental safety (122). Additionally, such review
should include a critical examination of any new data on
efficacy for established applications and for altered patterns
of usage and application.

Development Of National Data Banks On Synthetic Chemicals
Standards for drugs are maintained in most countries and by
the World Health Organization in the International
Pharmacopoeia. Similar national and international
standardization and registration would be desirable for other
categories of chemical products. Data on safety, efficacy, and
identity could then be collated and distributed nationally and
internationally.

Quality Of The Data Base  The significant influence of economic
and related constraints on expert advisory committees, both
federal and nongovernment, is being increasingly appreciated
(122). In addition to constraints on the generation of
objective data, constraints on the evaluation and interpretation
of these data by regulatory agencies also may influence the
reading of the data base (123).

There is a growing consensus that there is a need for
legislation to ensure impartial and competent testing of all
products for which human exposure is anticipated. The present
system of direct, closed-contract negotiations between

manufacturing industries and commercial and other testing
laboratories is open to potential abuse and creates obvious
mutual constraints.

One possible remedy would be the introduction of a
disinterested advisory group or agency as an intermediary
between manufacturers and commercial and other testing
laboratories (122). Proper legal and other safeguards could be
developed to minimize potential abuses and conflicts of
interest. Manufacturers could notify the intermediary group
when safety evaluation was required for a particular product.
The advisory group would then solicit contract bids on the
open market. Bids would be awarded on the basis of economics,
quality of protocols, and technical competence. The progress
of testing would be monitored by periodic project site visits,
as is routine with federal contracts. At the conclusion of the
studies, the advisory group would comment on the quality of
the data, make appropriate recommendations and forward these
to the concerned regulatory agency for routine action.

This approach appears more consistent with general industrial
practice than is the secret award of unbidded contracts.
Additionally, quality checks during testing would ensure the
high quality and reliability of data, and minimize the need to
repeat studies, thus reducing pressure on federal agencies to
accept unsatisfactory data on a post hoc basis. This approach
not only minimizes constraints due to special interests, but
would also upgrade the quality of testing in commercial and
other testing laboratories.

Additionally, the development of independent nonprofit
research centers, concerned with problems of consumer,
occupational, and environmental safety, should be encouraged
in an effort to develop constraint-free research. Universities
represent such a potential resource, but the requisite concept
of interdisciplinary mission-oriented research is relatively
novel to most universities, which are still structured on
classical departmental lines. The AEC's National Laboratories
also represent a source of research potential but, under
existing charter, they cannot be directly responsive to
industrial needs.

Need For Promulgation Of Protocols  Industry, commercial
testing, and other laboratories should be provided with
unambiguous guidelines as to what tests are required, the
necessary protocols, and principles of interpretation. Concerned
parties should be given the opportunity to comment on such
protocols before their final promulgation in the Federal
Register. Reflecting this viewpoint, the EPA has recently

proposed specific toxicological guidelines for evaluating the safety of pesticide residue tolerances (123).

Such procedures would provide a clearer definition as to the relative responsibilities of industry and regulatory agencies in safety evaluation and minimize existing mutual constraints in these areas. Industry thus will know what tests are required, and hence be able to predetermine their approximate costs, before deciding whether to proceed with further product development.

Public Access To Data   Further legislation concerning public access to data is needed (122, 124). All formal discussions between agencies, industry, and federal and nongovernment expert committees on all issues relating to human safety and environmental quality, and data relevant to such discussions, properly belong to the public domain. Indeed, under the 1967 Freedom of Information Act (P.L. 89-487), all federal records are intended to be open to the public except for specified exceptions, such as trade secrets.

In a major policy shift announced May 4, 1972, by FDA General Counsel Hutt, it was proposed to make available for public inspection "most of its files and correspondence." (125) Prior FDA policy gave most of the agency's documents confidential status. Under the new policy, all but about 10 percent of the data would be open for inspection. Specifically excluded would be trade secrets, investigations in progress, and internal correspondence.

The FDA proposals are regarded as "cosmetic" by consumer advocates, especially as only manufacturers' summaries of data on safety and efficacy of new drug publications will be made public. As Anita Johnson of the Health Research Group, Washington, D.C., commented:

"The summaries will be perfectly useless. No competent scientist trying to assess the safety or efficacy of a drug would rely on summarized data." (126)

Another consumer advocate, James S. Turner, appeared equally unimpressed with Hutt's new regulations:

"All he has done is eliminate some of the FDA's more outrageous restrictions." (126)

Demands for access to federal agency data are now being extended to internal memoranda and documents, and to quasi-governmental bodies, such as the NAS, which are generally

considered to be exempt from the requirements of the Freedom
of Information Act. Recent impetus to these demands has been
additionally provided by the "leak" of an internal FDA
memorandum (128). This memorandum made it clear that the FDA
is not performing its statutory duties in that it has allowed
and are still allowing use of a wide range of carcinogenic
feed additives for cattle, poultry, swine, and sheep, in the
absence of practicable analytic methods which could be used
to exclude any residues in animal foods. The memorandum also
emphasized major deficiencies in FDA screening programs for
other feed additives, such as antibiotics and pesticides. The
author of the memorandum unambiguously stated that

"Unless the FDA resolves this drug residue problem, we will
soon be in direct confrontation with Congress and the
consumers defending an untenable position. For FDA to ignore
this problem would be disastrous." (127)

The implications of this memorandum for the safety of the
nation's food supply was discussed at a March 1973 hearing of
the Senate Commerce Committee (124).
Incidents of this kind have resulted in not only a greater
militancy of demands by consumer and public interest groups
for unrestricted access to data, on the basis of which
decisions may be made critically affecting public health and
welfare, but also for demands for public interest involvement
in decision-making processes, to ensure that the rights and
welfare of consumers are adequately perceived and appropriately
balanced against industrial interests in a socially acceptable
manner.

The "Public Interest"  In addition to open access of data on
all issues of product safety, public health and welfare, and
environmental safety, it is important that the consumer and
public interest be adequately represented at the earliest
stages of the decision-making process and agency-industry
discussions (122). Decisions by agencies on technological
innovations or on new products after closed discussions of
data which have been treated confidentially are unacceptable;
similar considerations obtain for products already established
in commerce with relation to data on safety and efficacy. The
consumer and public interest apart, such decisions are contrary
to the long-term interests of industry, which should be
protected from perforce  belated objections. While there is a
growing, if late, acceptance by industry of the legitimacy of
demands for representation by public interest groups, formal

mechanisms for this purpose have not yet been developed in the FDA. However, in January 1972, senior agency officials initiated informal monthly meetings with leading consumer advocates and representatives.

Reflecting these concerns for a more formal representation of the public interest in the regulatory process, two legislative proposals to establish a Consumer Protection Agency (CPA) were introduced in the 93rd Congress. One (H.R. 21) was introduced by Rep. Chet Holifield (D.-Calif.) on January 3, 1973, and the other (S. 707) by Sen. Abraham Ribicoff on February 1, 1973. The Ribicoff Bill is viewed as stronger. The Holifield Bill has been criticized by consumer advocates, as it limits the proposed CPA to a reactive role with insufficient power to effectively represent the consumer (128).

While concerns for consumer safety were instrumental in developing congressional initiatives for the Consumer Product Safety Commission, established on October 28, 1972 (P.L. 92-573), the Act made no provision for the earlier proposed direct consumer and public interest representation in the decision-making processes of the Commission that would be served by the CPA. Additionally, the rights for individual initiative in asking the Commission to issue, change, or revoke a product-safety rule are not effective until December 1975 (129). While the Commission may well exert a powerful impact on consumer product safety, it is likely that the public- and consumer-interest lobby will stimulate additional congressional initiatives to complement and supplement the activities of this new agency.

References

1.   Gandevia, B. and Mitchell, C., "The Dangers of Proteolytic Enzymes to Workers." Med. J. Austral., 1:363 (1971).

2.   U.S. Senate, 93rd Congress. S. 3163, Section 410 (c) (1972).

3.   National Academy of Sciences, National Research Council. "Task Force on Prescription Drugs." Second Interim Report and Recommendations, Washington, D.C. (Aug. 30, 1968).

4.   Staff Report. "Diminishing Returns." Environment 11:6 (1969).

5.   Bosch, R., "Pesticides: Prescribing for the Ecosystem." Environment 12:12 (1970).

6.   Coon, D. W. and Fleet, R. R., "The Ant War." Environment 12:28 (1970).

7.   "Report of the Advisory Panel on Carcinogenicity of Pesticides, p. 459. Report of the Secretary's Commission on Pesticides and Their Relationship to Environmental Health." U.S. Department of Health, Education, and Welfare. (December, 1969).

8.   Anon., "Eclipse of the Stinging Fire Ant." Nature 235:353 (1972).

9.   Epstein, S. S., Testimony on "Potential Biological Hazards Due to Nitrates in Water and Due to the Proposed Use of Nitrilotriacetic Acid Detergents."
     Hearings before the Subcommittee on Air and Water Pollution, Committee on Public Works. U.S. Senate. 91st Congress (May 6, 1970).

10.  Epstein, S. S., "Perspectives on Benefit-Risk Decision Making." Report of a Colloquium conducted by The Committee on Public Engineering Policy, National Academy of Engineering, Washington, D.C. (April 26-27, 1971).

11.  Oberle, M. W., "Lead Poisoning: A Preventable Childhood Disease of the Slums." Science 165:991 (1969).

12.   Kendall, D. M., A Summary of Panel Recommendations: "Report of a Panel on Food Safety to the White House Conference on Food Nutrition and Health." 19 (November 22, 1969).

13.   Earnes, J. M. and Denz, F. A. "Experimental Methods Used in Determining Chronic Toxicity." Pharmac. Rev. 6:191 (1954).

14.   Paulson, G. and Dubos, R. Unpublished data (1971).

15.   Epstein, S. S. Testimony on "Teratogenic Effects of 2,4,5-T Formulations."
      Hearings before the Subcommittee On Energy, Natural Resources and the Environment, Committee on Commerce, U.S. Senate. 91st Congress.

16.   Epstein, S. S. "Teratological Hazards Due to Phenoxyl Herbicides and Dioxin Contaminants." In Pollution: Engineering and Scientific Solutions. Pub. Plen. Corp., New York, N. Y. (1973).

17.   National Academy of Sciences, National Research Council. "Report on Nonnutritive Sweeteners" (November, 1968).

18.   Epstein, S. S., "Toxicological and Environmental Implications on the Use of Nitrilotriacetic Acid as a Detergent Builder." Report to Senator J. Randolph, Chairman, Committee on Public Works, U.S. Senate. Committee Print. 91st Congress (December, 1970).

19.   Hayes, W. J., "Clinical Handbook on Economic Poisons," Dept. of HEW, PHS Publication  No. 476 (1963).

20.   Shubik, P. and Sice, J., "Chemical Carcinogenesis as a Chronic Toxicity Test: A Review." Cancer Res. 16:728 (1956).

21.   Clayson, D. B., "Chemical Carcinogenesis." Chapters 3-4. Pub. Little, Brown, Boston (1962).

22.   Hueper, W. C. and Conway, W. D. "Chemical Carcinogenesis and Cancers." Pub. Charles C Thomas, Chicago (1961).

23.   "FDA Advisory Committee on Protocols for Safety Evaluation." Toxicol. Appl. Pharmacol. 20:419 (1971).

24.   Della Porta, G., "Use of Newborn and Infant Animals in Carcinogenicity Testing." Food Cosmet. Toxicol. 6:243 (1968).

25.   Epstein, S. S. et al., "Carcinogenecity Testing of
Selected Food Additives by Parenteral Administration to Infant
Swiss Mice." Toxicol. Appl. Pharmacol. 16:321 (1970).

26.   Innes, R. et al., "Bioassay to Pesticides and Industrial
Chemicals for Tumorigenicity in Mice: A Preliminary Note."
J. Nat. Canc. Inst.  42:1101 (1969).

27.   Preussman, R., Druckrey, H., Ivankovic, S. and Von
Hodenberg, A., "Chemical Structure and Carcinogenicity of
Aliphatic Hydrazo, Azo and Azoxy Compounds and of Triazenes,
potential In Vivo Alkylating Agents." Ann. N. Y. Acad. Sci.
163:697 (1969).

28.   Herbst, A. L., Ulfelder, H. and Poskanzer, D. C.
"Adenocarcinoma of the Vagina: Association of Maternal
Stilbestrol Therapy with Tumor Appearance in Young Women."
New Engl. J. Med. 284:878 (1971).

29.   "Report of the Advisory Panel on Teratogenicity of
Pesticides, pp. 655. Report of the Secretary's Commission on
Pesticides and their Relationship to Environmental Health."
U.S. Dept. HEW, Washington, D.C. (December, 1969).

30.   Epstein, S. S., "Environment and Teratogenesis," in
"Pathobiology of Development." Pub. Williams & Wilkins Co.,
Baltimore, Md. (1973).

31.   "The Mutagenecity of Pesticides, Concepts and Evaluation."
Epstein, S. S. and Legator, M. S. Pub. MIT Press, Cambridge,
Mass. (1971).

32.   "Chemical Mutagens: Principles and Methods for their
Detection," Vols. 1, 2. Ed. A. Hollaender, Plenum Press,
New York, London (1971).

33.   "Reports of the Advisory Panels of Carcinogenicity,
Mutagenicity and Teratogenicity. Report of the Secretary's
Commission on Pesticides and their Relationship to Environmental
Health." U.S. Dept. HEW, Washington, D. C. (December, 1969).

34.   Epstein, S. S. et al., "Wisdom of Cyclamate Ban." Science
166:1575 (1969).

35.   King, C. J., "Antihistamines and Teratogenicity in the
Rat." J. Pharm. Exp. Therap.  147:991 (1965).

36.   Yerushalamy, J., and Milkovich, L., "Evaluation of the
Teratogenic Effects of Meclizine." Amer. J. Obstet. Gynecol.
93:553 (1965).

37.   Kalter, H., "Teratology of the Central Nervous System."
University of Chicago Press (1968).

38.   Hueper, W. C., "Occupational and Environmental Cancers of
the Urinary System." University Press, New Haven (1969).

39. Fleming, A., "Hearings on Color Additives," Committee on
Interstate and Foreign Commerce, House of Representatives.
Eighty-sixth Congress. Second Session, 501.

40.   Sinhuber, R. O. et al., "Dietary Factors and Hepatoma in
Rainbow Trout (salmo gairdneri). 1. Aflatoxins in Vegetable
Protein Feedstuffs." J. Nat. Cancer Inst.  41:711 (1968).

41.   Bingham, E., and Falk, H. L., "Environmental Carcinogens.
Modifying Effect of Carcinogens on the Threshold Response."
Arch. Env. Health  19:779 (1969).

42.   Montesano, R., Saffiotti, U. and Shubik, P., "The Role
of Topical and Systemic Factors in Experimental Respiratory
Carcinogenesis, pp. 353. In "Inhalation Carcinogenesis."
U.S. Atomic Energy Commission (April, 1970).

43.   Bateman, A. J. Personal Communication (1970).

44.   National Safety Council, "Accident Facts," pp. 80-84
(1969 ed.).

45.   U.S. National Center for Health Statistics. "Types of
Injuries; Incidences and Associated Disability, U.S." July,
1965-June, 1967, p. 29. Series 10, No. 57 (Oct., 1969).

46.   "Final Report of the National Commission on Product
Safety." Final Report Presented to the President and Congress,
G.P.O. Washington, D.C. (June 1970).

47.   Gardner, J., "Consumer Report: Congressional Battle over
FDA Control focuses on Product-Safety Legislation." National
Journal  4(24) 987-997 (June 10, 1972).

48.   American Cancer Society, "Cancer Facts and Figures"
(1973), Quoted in Report of the National Panel of Consultants

on The Conquest of Cancer, for the Committee on Labor and Public Welfare, Senate (November 1970), p. 31.

49.   National Health Education Committee, Inc., New York (June 22, 1970), quoted in Report of the National Panel of Consultants on The Conquest of Cancer, for the Committee on Labor and Public Welfare, Senate  (November, 1970), p. 31.

50.   "Report of the National Panel of Consultants on the Conquest of Cancer." Prepared for the U.S. Senate Committee on Labor and Public Welfare (November, 1970).

51.   Epstein, S. S., "Control of Chemical Pollutants." Nature 228:816 (1970).

52.   World Health Organization, Technical Report No. 276. "Prevention of Cancer." Report of WHO Expert Committee (1964).

53.   Higginson, J., "Present trends in Cancer Epidemiology." Proc. 8th Canadian Cancer Res. Conf. (1969).

54.   Boyland, E., The Correlation of Experimental Carcinogenesis and Cancer in Man. Ed. Homberger & Karger. In "Experimental Tumor Research" (1964).

55.   Dunham, L. J. and Bailar, J. C., "World Maps of Cancer Mortality Rates and Frequency Ratios." J. Nat. Cancer Inst. 41:155 (1968).

56.   U.S. Dept. HEW, "Smoking and Health." Report of the Advisory Committee to the Surgeon General of the PHS. PHS Publication 1103, Washington, D.C. (1964).

57.   Hammond, E. C. and Horn, D., "Smoking and Death Rates." J.A.M.A.  166:1159, and 1294 (1950).

58.   Clemmesen, J. "Bronchial Carcinoma - A Pandemic." Can. Med. Bull. 1:37 (1954).

59.   "Particulate Polycyclic Organic Matter," p. 213. National Acad. of Sciences, Washington, D.C. (1972).

60.   Hueper, W. C. "Environmental Carcinogenesis in Man and Animals." Ann. N.Y. Acad. Sci.  108:963 (1963).

61.   Oettle, A. G., "Cancer in Africa, Especially in Regions South of the Sahara." J. Nat. Cancer Inst.  33:383 (1964).

62.   Kraybill, H.F. and Shimkin, M. B. "Carcinogenesis related to Foods contamination by Processing and Fungal Metabolites." Adv. Cancer Res.  8:191 (1964).

63.   Miller, R. W. "Environmental Agents in Cancer." Yale J. Biol. Med.  37:487 (1965).

64.   Schmal, D., "Exogenic Factors in Human Carcinogenesis and Methods for their Detection." Neoplasma  15:273 (1968).

65.   Higginson, J., "Present Trends in Cancer Epidemiology." Proc. 8th Canadian Cancer Res. Conf. (1969).

66.   Kmet, J. and Mahboubi, E., "Esophageal Cancer in the Caspian Littoral of Iran: Initial Studies." Science  175:846 (1972).

67.   Lijinsky, W. and Epstein, S. S. "Nitrosamines as Environmental Carcinogens." Nature  225:21 (1970).

68.   "Aflatoxin. Scientific Background, Control and Implications." Ed. Goldblatt. L.A., Academic Press, New York and London (1969).

69.   LaQuer, G. L. et al., "Carcinogenic Properties of nuts from Cycas Circinalis indigenous to Guam." J. Nat. Cancer Inst. 3:919 (1963).

70.   Keen, P. and Martin, P., Trop. Geogr. Med.  23:44 (1971).

71.   WHO, Liver Cancer, IARC - WHO Scientific Publications No. 1 (1971).

72.   McGlashan, N. D., Walters, C. L. and McLean, A. E. M. "Nitrosamines in Africa Alcoholic Spirits and Oesophageal Cancer." Lancet 2:1017 (1968).

73.   McGlashan, N. D., "Oesophageal Cancer and Alcoholic Spirits in Central Africa. Gut  10:643 (1969).

74.   Salyamon, L. S., "Carcinogenic Activity of Some Drugs Used in Practice." Vopros. Onkologii 9:22 (1963). Quoted in Federation Proc. 23:T. 136 (1964).

75.  Proceedings of the European Society for the Study of Drug Toxicity, Lausanne  (January, 1964).

76.  Roe, F. J. C., "The Relevance of Preclinical Assessment of Carcinogenesis." Clin. Pharm. Ther. 7:77 (1966).

77.  Napalkov, N., Shabad, L. and Truhaut, R., "On the Possible Risks of Carcinogenesis of Some Drugs." Chemotherapia 12:47 (1967).

78.  Bonser, G. M., "Cancer Hazards of the Pharmacy." Brit. Med. J. 4:129 (1967).

79.  Eckhardt, R. L., "Industrial Carcinogens." New York, Grune and Stratton (1959).

80.  Hueper, W. C., "Environmental Cancer Hazards." J. Occup. Med. 14:150 (1972).

81.  WHO, IARC, Monograph on the "Evaluation of Carcinogenic Risk of Chemicals to Man." Geneva (1972).

82.  American Public Health Association Annual Meeting. "Symposium on Occupational Carcinogenesis " (November, 1972).

83.  "Bladder Cancer." Ed. Lampe, K. F. Pub. Aesculapius Pub. Co., Birmingham, Alabama (1967).

84.  Hueper, W. C., "Occupational and Environmental Cancers in the Urinary System." New Haven (1969).

85.  Hueper, W. C., "Occupational and Environmental Cancers of the Respiratory System." New York, Springer-Verlag (1966).

86.  Laskin, S. et al., "Tumors of the Respiratory Tract Induced by Inhalation of bis-(chloromethyl)ether." Arch. Env. Health 23 (1971).

87.  Lloyd, J. W., "Long-term Mortality Study of Steelworkers. V. Respiratory Cancer in coke plant Workers." J. Occup. Med. 13:53 (1971).

88.  "Asbestos, The Need for and Feasibility of Air Pollution Controls." National Academy of Sciences, Washington, D.C. (1971).

89. Selikoff, I., Hammond, E. C. and Seidman, H., "Cancer Risk of Insulation Workers in the United States." Presented at the Meeting of the Working Group to Assess Biological Effects of Asbestos, Lyons, France (October 4, 1972).

90. Li, F. P., et al., "Cancer Mortality Among Chemists." J. Nat. Cancer Inst. 43:1159 (1969).

91. Report of the Advisory Panel on Mutagenicity, pp. 565. Report of the Secretary's Commission on Pesticides and their Relationship to Environmental Health. U.S. Dept. HEW, Washington, D.C. (December, 1969).

92. Crow, J. F. "Chemical Risk to Future Generations." Scientist and Citizen 10:113 (1968).

93. Lederberg, J. pp. X, in "The Mutagenicity of Pesticides: Concepts and Evaluation." Eds. Epstein, S. S. and Legator, M., M.I.T. Press, Cambridge, Mass. (1971)

94. Ethyl Corp. Technical Publication ICC 4 Ethyl Ignition Control Compound 4.

95. Hinkamps, J. B. and Warren, J. P. Ind. Eng. Chem. 50:251 (1958).

96. Epstein, S. S., "Mutagenicity of Trimethylphophate in Mice." Science 168:584 (1970).

97. Adler, I. D., Ramaro, G. and Epstein, S. S., "In Vivo Cytogenetic Effects of Trimethylphosphate and of TEPA on Bone Marrow Cells of Male Rats." Mutation Res. 13:263 (1971).

98. Roush, G. (Medical Director, Ethyl Corp.). Personal Communication (March 6, 1970).

99. Mullineaux, R. D. (General Manager, MTM-R & D, Shell Oil Co.). Personal Communication (December 15, 1970).

100. Report, "Working Conference on Health Intelligence for Fuels and Feed Additives." Environmental Protection Agency, Durham, North Carolina (January 7, 1973).

101. Mullineaux, R. D. (General Manager, MTM-R & D, Shell Oil Co.). Personal Communication (January 26, 1971).

102. Slomka, M. D., "Facts about No-Pest DDVP Strips." Shell Chemical Co., 18 pp. (1970).

103. Gillett, J. W. et al., "Evaluation of Human Health Hazards on Dichlorvos, Especially in Resin Strips," A Task Force Report of the Environmental Health Science Center, Oregon State University, Corvallis, Oregon 97331 (January 29, 1972).

104. Bridges, B. A., "Mutagenicity of Dichlorvos and Methyl Methanesulphonate for E. coli WP2 and Some Derivatives Deficient in DNA Repair." In Press (1973).

105. Lofroth, G., "Alkylation of DNA by Dichlorvos." Naturwiss 57:393 (1970).

106. Lofroth, G. Personal Communication (1972).

107. Miller, J. A., "Carcinogenesis by Chemicals: An Overview." Cancer Res. 30:559 (1970).

108. Schwetz, B. A., Sparschu, G. L. and Gehring, P. J., "The Effect of 2, 4-dichtophenoxyacetic acid (2,4-D) and Esters of 2,4-D on Rat Embryonic, Foetal and Neonatal Growth and Development." Fd. Cosmet. Toxicol. 9:801 (1971).

109. Wade, N., "Dow Redefines Word it Doesn't Like." Science 176:262 (1972).

110. Miller, R. W., "Relation between Cancer and Congenital Defects in Man." New Engl. J. Med. 275:87 (1966).

111. Herbst, A. L. Personal Communication (1972).

112. Shubik, P. and Hartwell, J. L., "Survey of Compounds which have been Tested for Carcinogenic Activity," Supplement 2. U.S. Dept. of HEW (1969).

113. Huseby, R. A. Proc. Amer. Assoc. Canc. Res. 3:29 (1959).

114. Council on Environmental Quality. "Toxic Substances." (April, 1971).

115. _____, Acta. Unio. Internat. Contr. Cancrum. 13:169 (1957).

116. Darby, J. W., "Hearings on Color Additives." Committee on Interstate and Foreign Commerce, House of Representatives. Eighty-sixth Congress. Second Session, 501 (1960).

117. Epstein, S. S., in "The Scientific Basis of the Delaney Amendment." Ed. Selikoff, I., Pub. Academic Press. In Press.

118. Address by Commissioner Edwards, as The Louis Mark Memorial Lecturer before the American College of Chest Physicians, December, 1972. Quoted in Hospital Tribune (December 18, 1972).

119. Selikoff, I., Ed., "The Scientific Basis of the Delaney Amendment." Pub. Academic Press. In Press.

120. Saffiotti, U., Schneiderman, M., and Epstein, S. S. Ibid.

121. Johnson, A., "Cancer Prevention and the Delaney Clause." Pub. Health Research Group. Washington, D. C. (1973).

122. Epstein, S. S., Testimony on "Adverse Human Effects due to Chemical Pollutants" before Subcommittee on Executive Reorganization and Government Research, Committee on Government Operations. United States Senate. 92nd Congress (April 6, 1971).

123. EPA. "Pesticide Chemical Safety. Proposed Toxicology Guidelines." Fed. Reg. 37:183, 19383 (September 20, 1972).

124. Epstein, S. S., Testimony on "The Federal Food Inspection Act of 1973, and on Deficiencies in Current Procedures for Monitoring Animal Food for Carcinogenic and Toxic Residues of Animal Drugs," before the Committee on Commerce, U.S. Senate. 93rd Congress (March 21, 1973).

125. Federal Register 1, 37:9128 (May 5, 1972) (21 CFR Parts 1, 2, 4, 8, 121, 135, 146, 191).

126. Quoted by Nicholas Wade, in "FDA General Counsel Hutt: A Man Trying to Serve Two Masters." Science 177:498 (1972).

127. Johnson, K. R. (Director of Division of Veterinary Medical Review of the Bureau of Veterinary Medicine). "Review of Veterinary Drug Residues and Drug Residue Monitoring Program for Food Producing Animals." Memorandum to Dr. C. D. Van Houweling (Director, Bureau of Veterinary Medicine) (September 27, 1972).

128. Gardner, J. "Consumer Report: Factions in Prolonged
Controversy Gird for Showdown on Strong Consumer Agency."
National Journal 5(9):312-320 (March 3, 1973).

129. Cottin, J., "Consumer Report: Powerful Product Safety
Commission to have Far Reaching Impact on the Marketplace."
National Journal 5(14):481-488 (April 7, 1973).

# 3

## TOXIC SUBSTANCES

Richard D. Grundy, Hanno C. Weisbrod,
Samuel S. Epstein

CONTENTS

## Introduction

Addressing the future, a 1966 study commissioned privately by
Imperial Chemical Industries (ICI) of Great Britain expressed
the view that the development of chemicals without regard to
the long-term environmental consequences, would soon be a
"luxury" of the past. It predicted that most nations would,
either singly or in concert, pass legislation in the "near
future" establishing policies requiring that all new technology
be subjected to evaluation and testing to assure that it will
not adversely affect human health or the environment. The ICI
study also warned that those industries that do not adjust
their planning and operation to this new fact would be likely
to be forced out of business.

In light of the events that have since taken place, that
warning may not have been far off the mark. With 12,000 toxic
chemicals now in use in industry (1) and some 500 new chemical
compounds being introduced annually into commercial use (2),
the situation can only become further aggravated.

Many types of adverse effects can be induced by metals,
their compounds, and by synthetic (man-made) and natural
inorganic and organic chemicals. Possible toxic human effects
include induction of cancer (carcinogenicity), genetic
mutations (mutagenicity), and birth defects (teratogenicity).

Many synthetic organic chemicals are of special concern
because frequently they are structurally alien to the
environment. As their numbers and varieties reaching natural
ecosystems grow, the capabilities of these systems to disperse,
sequester, or otherwise render them harmless begin to approach
their limits. Furthermore, as a result of only cursory
evaluative studies -- and sometimes of their complete
omission -- environmental contaminants from industrial sources
continue to surprise us by reaching man either in dangerous
concentrations and/or by unanticipated routes.

The gross environmental problems of the past have been far
more recognizable than the subtle but real hazards associated
with many of today's contaminants. The thick palls of smoke
that hung over cities in the first half of the century have
been replaced by smog, and, in general, the most obvious water
pollutants are no longer the main cause of the degradation of
waterways. Today we have to deal with a great variety of
environmental contaminants that frequently are not detectable
by our unaided senses, but are no less, and possibly even more,
hazardous to human health than are the "classical" pollutants.
Furthermore, some of the more exotic new chemical pollutants
are often pervasive, not being confined to local or even
regional distributions. For example, radioactive fission

products and chlorinated hydrocarbons can be found on every
continent and in every ocean.

Industrial Sources  Industrial sources of environmental
contaminants encompass an enormous variety of processes and
chemicals. The attempt to categorize or even count the variety
of industries and their products and effluents that are
relevant to this discussion is a formidable task. The
agricultural industry, for example, involves a number of
polluting activities, from growing food and fiber to
processing, packaging, and transporting. Likewise, the metals
industry is a source of large volumes of pollutants from a
diverse range of activities from mining and smelting to
processing and plating. The same is true for almost any
industry: chemical, petroleum, lumbering and paper production,
power generation, cement production, manufacturing of consumer
durables, plastics, clothing, building materials and
transportation, just to name a few outstanding examples.

It has been established that about 30 percent of all water
pollution in the United States (3) and about 20 percent of all
air pollution (4) (excluding pollutants emitted by electric
generating plants) originate from industrial processes.

Air Pollutants  The following is a list of the major industrial
polluters and their annual contributions to air pollution in
the United States (4).

Petroleum refining:
8.4 billion pounds of particulates, sulfur oxides, hydrocarbons,
and carbon monoxide.

Smelters (aluminum, copper, lead, zinc):
8.3 billion pounds of particulates and sulfur oxides.

Iron Foundries:
7.4 billion pounds of particulates and carbon monoxide.

Kraft Pulp and Paper Mills:
6.6 billion pounds of particulates, carbon monoxide, and sulfur
oxides.

Coal Cleaning and Refuse:
4.7 billion pounds of particulates, sulfur oxides and carbon
monoxide.

Coke Production:
4.4 billion pounds of particulates, sulfur oxides and carbon
monoxide.

Iron and Steel Mills:
3.6 billion pounds of particulates and carbon monoxide.

Grain Mills and Grain Handling:
2.2 billion pounds of particulates.

Cement Manufacturing:
1.7 billion pounds of particulates.

Phosphate Fertilizer Plants:
624 million pounds of particulates and fluorides.

While these are surely impressive figures, for the most
part they represent pollutants which have long been recognized
as serious problems and as such have a long history of
attempted regulatory control.

Water Pollutants  The situation existing in the nation's
surface waters is equally serious. In 1968, manufacturers
discharged directly into water systems enough organic wastes to
consume 29.7 billion pounds of oxygen, as measured by the
five-day BOD (biochemical oxygen demand) test, twice the amount
discharged in 1957. In addition, a survey conducted for the
U.S. Environmental Protection Agency (EPA) showed that 2.7
million tons of waste acid, 560,000 tons of refinery wastes,
330,000 tons of pesticide wastes, 140,000 tons of paper mill
wastes, and 940 tons of other materials were dumped into the
coastal waters of the United States in 1968 (5).
Inorganic wastes were largely contributed by the producers
of alkalies and chlorine, industrial gases, inorganic pigments,
paints, fertilizers (not including ammonia and urea),
inorganic insecticides, and explosives. Together, in 1968,
these industries discharged 1,178 billion gallons of water
laden with a variety of inorganic chemical wastes (5).

Perspectives  The above is by no means an adequate inventory of
pollutants originating from industrial sources. Just as
important as the large volume discharges -- and this may perhaps
be more significant -- are an almost endless variety of
synthetic organic chemicals released into the atmosphere and
into water systems in lesser amounts. There is a remarkable
paucity of data on the potential adverse human and ecological
effects of these chemical pollutants. Adequate research and
regulatory controls are usually not forthcoming except in
belated response to disaster situations.
There are several federal laws available for regulating
potentially toxic substances in consumer products and in the
environment; however, before discussing this aspect of the

problem, we will review its scientific aspects, with particular reference to two major categories of toxic substances -- synthetic organic chemicals and heavy metals.

## Synthetic Organic Chemicals

Synthetic organic chemicals are of special interest for several reasons. First, the industry is growing at a phenomenal rate (6). Worldwide production of synthetic organic compounds increased from 7 million tons in 1950 to 63 million tons in 1970, and it is estimated that production will climb to 250 million tons by 1985. This represents an annual growth increment of about 15 percent (2).

Secondly, many of these chemicals do not occur naturally in the environment and it is therefore difficult to predict their metabolic or physical pathways and the natural processes that might degrade them to their naturally occurring precursors or constituents. This has already been seen in the case of such chemicals as DDT and related chlorinated hydrocarbon pesticides.

### Classes Of Synthetic Organic Chemicals

In 1968, there were some 9,000 synthetic organic chemicals in commercial use (2). The potential number is to all practical intent unlimited. The Chemical Abstracts Service Registry Number System has registered some 1.8 million chemical compounds and the list is growing by 250,000 each year (2).

Synthetic organic chemicals in commercial use can generally be classed as shown in Table 1. They are obtained from coal, crude petroleum, natural gas, wood, vegetable oils, fats, resins, and grains. The manufactured products are formed by such processes as thermal decomposition, synthesis, catalytic cracking, distillation, absorption, or fermentation.

Dyes and pigments, which are used to impart color to other substances, number about 1,000 (2). As such, they come in direct contact with consumers and enter the environment from either manufacturing operations or the ultimate disposal of consumer products.

Another major class of synthetic organic chemicals are plastics and their associated resins and additives (2). Plasticizers, such as the polychlorinated biphenyls, are organic chemicals added to synthetic plastics and resin materials to improve their workability during fabrication, to extend or modify the natural properties of these resins, or to develop new, improved properties not present in the original resins (2).

As plastics are increasingly used to replace other materials, their production is expected to grow from about 8.9 million tons

Table 1   U.S. Production of Synthetic Organic Chemicals, 1968
(2)

| Chemical | 1968 Production (millions of pounds) | Percent Increase over 1967 |
|---|---|---|
| Intermediates | 25,014 | 20.3 |
| Colorants: | | |
| Dyes | 226 | 9.7 |
| Pigments | 54 | 1.9 |
| Flavors and perfumes | 117 | 4.5 |
| Plastic Products: | | |
| Plastics and resins | 16,360 | 18.6 |
| Plasticizers | 1,331 | 5.4 |
| Rubber products: | | |
| Processing chemicals | 313 | 13.6 |
| Elastomers | 4,268 | 11.6 |
| Surface active agents | 3,739 | 7.5 |
| Miscellaneous | 67,525 | 13.1 |
| Totals | 118,947 | 15 |

Note: This table includes some data taken from several
successive steps of the manufacturing process and therefore
some values may be high. Public disclosure in the U.S. Tariff
Commission Review is not permitted by the data-collecting
agency when only one manufacturer produces a chemical. Products
are not included if production was below 1,000 pounds, or
sales were below $1,000. Medicinals and pesticides are not
included.

in 1968 to over 25 million tons by 1980, or about 10 percent annually (2).

Rubber products can be manufactured from synthetic organic chemicals (elastomers) which are formulated with properties similar to those of natural rubber. Products made from natural rubber also may contain synthetic organic chemical additives. These types of synthetic organics are commonly found in numerous products including toys, tires, rain coats and shoes, carpet backing, garden equipment, and tools.

Surface-active agents are another category of synthetic organic chemicals. They are employed to reduce the surface tension of water or other solvents and are used chiefly in detergents, dispersing agents, emulsifiers, foaming agents, and wetting agents (2). A major portion -- about 550 million pounds -- is used for household and industrial detergents (2). The remainder is employed in the processing of textiles and leather and in the manufacture of agricultural sprays, cosmetics, elastomers, lubricants, paints, pharmaceuticals, and many other products.

In practice, synthetic organic chemicals can be tailored in their structure and properties to fit almost any conceivable function (2). Many such tailored chemicals fall in the miscellaneous category listed in Table 1. Their number is legion, totaling more than half of all the synthetic organic chemicals manufactured. This category includes halogenated hydrocarbons, used as solvents in drycleaning and as refrigerants; aerosol propellants for hair sprays, paints, and deodorants; alcohols; nitrogen compounds; acids and alhydrides; aldehydes; and ketones (2).

Concurrent to the massive direct use of synthetic organic chemicals, the biosphere is subjected to the discharge of a myriad of potentially toxic substances as wastes. Unfortunately, the toxicological and ecological data on the potential impact of the majority of these synthetic organic chemicals is meager. Further, the legislation and implementation of regulatory control of their intentional discharge or accidental release into the environment has been largely ignored. Only in emergency situations with regard to specific individual pollutants is there sufficient interest to provoke control actions. Unfortunately, such actions often are based on statutes without sufficient flexibility to meet the needs of similar situations. Clearly, preassessment of the scope and nature of potential problems inherent in large-scale use of such chemicals, while complicated, is preferable to present ad hoc approaches.

Agricultural poisons, for example, are often sprayed
directly onto crops. Later, they partition into various parts
of the ecosystems depending on their stability, the stability
of their degradation or pyrolytic products, the amounts used,
and their ability to migrate from the intended original site
of their application. Information on such partitioning has
been obtained (at least in part) for many agricultural poisons
before their widespread use. This is not the case, however, for
many other classes of synthetic organic chemicals. For the
most part, furthermore, the identity of most compounds reaching
the environment from industrial sources is poorly known. In a
recent survey (7) of 496 organic chemicals suspected of
contaminating fresh water, only 66 had been identified. Of
those identified, industrial sources were responsible for the
largest number and variety of structural chemical types.

In a more recent study (8), 33 different organic compounds
were identified and only seven of these were included in the
survey of 496 fresh water pollutants (7). The study further
revealed the discharge of what its author called "unexpected
compounds" which would not have been anticipated from lists
of raw materials and products supplied by the manufacturers
whose effluents were analyzed.

In order to better understand the overall issues it is
useful to review several illustrative case studies.
Polychlorinated Biphenyls  Probably no other class of organic
chemicals in industrial use more clearly illustrates the need
for effective environmental control of industrial chemicals
than the polychlorinated biphenyls (PCB's). While PCB's have
a history of use (9) dating back to 1929, it was not until
1966 that they became suspect as widespread environmental
contaminants. Since then, PCB's have been discovered as
contaminants in food (10), wildlife and fish (11), marine and
fresh water, and in human tissues (12). They now appear to be
one of the most widely dispersed and abundant environmental
contaminants.

While it is clear that PCB's are widely dispersed in the
environment, it is less clear how it happened. Given their wide
application in industry, the pathways through which they can
reach the environment are numerous. Although no quantitative
source data are available, the following appear to be the most
important (13): open burning and incineration of industrial and
municipal wastes; vaporization from paints, coatings, and
plastics; municipal and industrial sewers; accidental spills;
disposal of sewage sludge; and migration from surface coatings
and packaging materials into foods and feeds. It also is very
likely that a significant amount of PCB's used in "closed"

systems such as capacitators, transformers, and hydraulic
systems have been released, either by inadvertent leakage from
such devices, by disposal directly into sewer systems, or by
migration from land fills where spent devices containing PCB's
have been buried.

It has been estimated that over the past 40 years about
30,000 tons of PCB's have been lost to the atmosphere, 60,000
tons to water systems, and 300,000 tons to dumps (14). These
estimates are crude, and a recent report adds an element of
confusion. It has recently been suggested that DDT can be
converted to PCB's by irradiation with ultraviolet light of
wavelengths found in the lower atmosphere (15). If these
observations are confirmed, estimates of the total amount of
environmental PCB's may be drastically changed.

Because of their unusual properties -- stability at high
temperature, nonflammability, cooling and insulating capacity --
PCB's are now alleged to be essential or (at least for the
time being) nonreplaceable in the electrical industry.
(Although the silicones do appear to be possible substitutes.)
This fact, together with a lack of adequate biological and
ecological information about PCB's, has made dealing with them
on an ad hoc basis even more difficult. Their value to the
electrical industry can be detailed at length, while the
"externalized" costs of those uses, especially in terms of
human health, is at present unclear.

The most extensive adverse human experience with PCB's
began in Japan (16). In October 1968 an outbreak of a peculiar
skin disease known as chloracne was reported in Fukuoka
Prefecture. Shortly after, twenty other prefectures in western
Japan reported the disease and by August 1971 some 1,057 cases
had been reported.

The initial signs and symptoms of the disease are swelling
of the upper eyelids and eye discharge, acneiform skin
eruptions, follicular accentuation and skin pigmentation,
disturbances of digestive functions, and numbness and other
neurological disorders. No sex differences in the distribution
of the disease were noted, but it seemed to occur within
particular families. For instance, 325 patients examined in
Fukuoka Prefecture between October 1968 and January 1969
belonged to 112 families.

Soon after the epidemic became evident, a study group
composed of staff members of various faculties at the University
of Kyushu was formed to determine the cause of the epidemic and
to find means to control it. A thorough case study was
undertaken of 121 patients and 121 healthy controls, matched
by age and sex, in which individuals were asked 60 questions

concerning their occupation, medical backgrounds, health status, diets, and other personal habits.

It was discovered that the only significant difference between the patient's and the control's habits was the fact that a greater number of patients reported eating fried foods or tempura nearly every day. A further test matched 69 households with patients against 207 households without patients; 96 percent of the patients' households reported using a brand of rice oil designated as "K rice oil," while only 31 percent of the control households reported such use.

It was eventually established that the source of the disease (now called Yusho) was a supply of rice oil produced by a single company and shipped between February 7 and 10, 1963. The oil had become contaminated with as much as 3,000 ppm of PCB's during the process of heating the oil at reduced pressure to remove unwanted odors. It is believed that the PCB's leaked from the heating pipe and contaminated the oil.

In the summer of 1970, a mass clinical examination of Yusho patients was conducted. About 50 percent of the patients showed some improvement, despite the fact that no cure is known for the disease; the remaining 50 percent of the patients showed no improvement, with 10 percent of this group apparently deteriorating.

Ironically, six months before the outbreak of Yusho, parts of western Japan were affected by an outbreak of a disease in chickens as a result of which 400,000 birds died. This outbreak was eventually traced to feeds in which "dark oil" was used as an ingredient. It was further discovered that the "dark oil," which was contaminated with 1,300 ppm of PCB's, was purchased between February 6 and 27 from the same company that produced K rice oil.

While the United States fortunately has been spared the suffering associated with a massive outbreak of Yusho, there have been numerous cases paralleling the outbreak in Japanese chickens. Some of these incidents are rather bizarre and clearly indicate the need for overall regulation of toxic materials.

In one case, the state of New York placed three counties under quarantine when surveillance data collected by the Campbell Soup Company indicated excessive PCB levels in chickens raised in those counties (13). The federal Food and Drug Administration (FDA) advised the State and the United States Department of Agriculture (USDA) that the distribution of poultry containing less than 5 ppm of PCB's would be acceptable, implying of course that anything exceeding that level would be subject to confiscation. Apparently all parties, including the producers, agreed to this arrangement. On the basis of subsequent analyses performed by the State of New York, 140,450 chickens had to be slaughtered. It is interesting to speculate on the outcome of the situation had the producers been less cooperative. It is certain that the rationale for allowing PCB concentrations of no more than 5 ppm in chickens would be difficult to defend on scientific grounds. It is just as certain that defending the harmlessness of this level of PCB's would be equally difficult. The source of PCB's in this case was thought to be plastic bakery wrappers, as stale bakery goods were ground up, wrappers and all, and used as chicken feed.

In another case (13), an estimated 12,000 tons of fish meal were contaminated with PCB's by a leaky heating system in a fish-meal pasteurization plant at Wilmington, North Carolina, between April and July of 1971. Of this, about 2,000 tons were recalled from the market. Samples of the meal indicated PCB contamination ranging from 14 to 30 ppm. Not only did this result in the recall of fish meal, but it also affected the hatchability of eggs in at least one large poultry operation that used the meal as a poultry ration. Furthermore, one broiler chicken producer had to destroy 88,000 birds, also the result of contaminated rations. In these incidents, all actions were based on the FDA's 5 ppm guideline.

Further incidents involved poultry in Oklahoma, Minnesota, Mississippi, and California; milk in West Virginia, Ohio, Florida and Georgia; and meat meal in Illinois. The source of milk contamination in Ohio, Florida, and Georgia was thought to be from a PCB-containing sealant used in silos (13).

Because of these unexpected incidents, the FDA has initiated an extensive national surveillance program to monitor animal feeds and milk on a state-by-state basis.

Aside from the direct contamination of consumer products with PCB's, there are the longer-range environmental effects. Because of the stability of PCB's, even a total shutdown of all sources of environmental contamination would not result in an immediate decrease in PCB levels. Here the picture is even less clear than it is with immediate human health problems. While laboratory studies indicate a number of potentially adverse effects of PCB's, such as microsomal enzyme induction, estrogenic activity, and immunosuppression (17), there is a noteworthy sparcity of toxicological data; moreover, the eventual effect of even the present burdens of PCB's on the environment is far from clear.

In light of the aforementioned experiences, the Monsanto Chemical Company, the sole producer of PCB's in the United

States, has agreed to voluntarily limit the distribution of
PCB's to those uses which are considered "closed systems."
However, PCB's are now also manufactured in Great Britain,
France, Germany, the USSR, Japan, Spain, Italy, and
Czechoslovakia.

What is clear, as will be subsequently discussed, is that
existing federal authority is inadequate to restricting more
PCB's from entering the environment. Additionally, the federal
authority cannot at present control the importation of PCB's
manufactured in foreign countries. The result is that in the
United States there exists an almost universal presence of
PCB's in the environment which, under existing authority, can
be controlled only on a piecemeal basis.

Phthalic Acid Esters   Another group of chemicals to gain
recent attention of environmentalists (18) are the phthalic
acid esters (PAE's). Attention was first drawn to PAE's when,
following a widely publicized report in 1970, they were found
as a contaminant in whole blood stored in polyvinyl chloride
transfusion bags (19). Before long, other scientists began to
report the occurrence of PAE's in a diversity of environmental
samples: water taken from the Charles River in Massachusetts
(20), fish tissue from the Great Lakes (21), and heart tissue
from cows (22).

The mechanism by which PAE's enter the environment is
unclear. A very small amount of the total production is
applied directly to the land in the form of pesticide carriers;
evaporation from plastics is another source; and some PAE's
are probably released during the manufacturing process. A
number of reports indicate that some PAE's also are produced
naturally by a few species of plants, fungi, and bacteria.
These reports, however, are now open to question since
contamination of laboratory equipment during analysis has been
common.

Phthalates are incorporated into polyvinyl plastics to give
the end product its desired pliability. Oddly, however, the
plasticizer does not actually combine chemically with the
polymer resin, but simply acts to "lubricate" the polymer
molecules in such a way as to allow them to be flexible. The
plasticizer materials can sometimes account for as much as
50 percent of the entire weight of a plastic product. These
phthalate plasticizers are able to migrate from the plastic
into either the air or a surrounding liquid.

PAE's are one of the most widely used plasticizers. In 1968,
there were at least 10 different phthalate compounds in
production, totalling 715 million pounds (23). This is not
total production, however, because information about many

phthalate compounds is proprietary information. Therefore the actual substances are not identified; these unidentified PAE's account for another 125 million pounds annually (23).

The PAE's generally have been found to be of very low toxicity, when administered orally or by injection. When some eight phthalates were examined (24), their acute LD$_{50}$, when injected into the peritoneum, ranged from 1.58 grams per kilogram of mouse body weight to 14.19 grams per kilogram. In other words, by this route these compounds were virtually nontoxic from the standpoint of immediate effects. In the same study, however, some observations were made on more sensitive indices of subacute toxicity (24).

A factor complicating toxicological research on phthalates has been the difficulty in their precise chemical characterization (25). It was found, on careful analysis, that besides commercially prepared medical-grade plasticizer [di(2-ethylhexyl)phthalate (DHEP], several other related chemicals also were found in blood stored in plastic bags (25). The other contaminating chemicals were thought to be closely related compounds (homologues) of the plasticizer that became incorporated into the product during the production process. Most of the homologues were about as toxic as their plasticizing relatives. Special note was made of the fact that specially synthesized pure di-n-decyl phthalate was not toxic, while a commercial preparation was extremely toxic to mice. In conclusion, the authors stated (25) that:

"A pure plasticizer may have no demonstrable toxic response, but the presence of related homologues and isomers could add toxic potential to the plasticizer. To this possibility one must also include potential toxic effects from degradation products present or forming in the plasticizer during manufacture of a plastic device, or occurring after the device had been stored under various conditions for undetermined amounts of time."

More recent experiments have indicated that some PAE's were teratogenic (causing birth defects) following administration to laboratory animals (26). Eight different PAE compounds were injected into pregnant rats (at doses of 0.3 to 10 milliliters per kilogram of body weight) on the fifth, tenth, and fifteenth day of gestation. Among the effects induced were fetal death, decreased fetal size, and abnormalities such as twisted hind legs, fused ribs, and absence of eyes or tails.

Two PAE compounds were also tested for mutagenic (causing genetic damage) effects in male mice (26). A single dose of

DHEP was injected into male mice prior to mating. Litters from females mated to DHEP-treated males showed a significantly higher percentage of fetal deaths at all dosages tested. These results indicate that PAE's induce dominant lethal mutations.

Here again, as with PCB's, is a case in which a group of chemicals have become widely dispersed in the total environment before they were recognized as a potential hazard. Only minimal control has been exercised over the use of PAE's and those controls only apply to situations where the material comes in direct contact with food (27). It is likely that exposures from other sources, especially consumer products made from polyvinyl chloride plastics, are of much greater significance. Automobiles, for example, whose interiors are lined with plasticized materials, are probably a major source of inhaled PAE's and data on inhalation exposures are absent from the available toxicological literature.

Freons   Another class of synthetic organic chemicals, in widespread use before it came under careful examination, is the fluoroalkanes (Freons). These chemicals are almost universally used as the propellant in aerosol products. Yet they are now under strong suspicion. Since the 1950's, there has been a steady increase in the numbers of sudden deaths among asthmatics that is closely related to the increased use of pressurized aerosol bronchodilators. At present, the precise cause of these sudden deaths is unclear, but evidence is accumulating that they may be the result of cardiac arrhythmias (28). A recent FDA report indicated that 11 sudden deaths have been associated with the use of one of these products (29).

Optical Brighteners   Another category of chemicals, in wide use in industry and in consumer products which also may merit careful examination, is the optical brighteners.

The most recent method for producing good "whites" in the washing as well as the manufacture and processing of textiles is by adding optical brighteners, also referred to as optical bleaches, whitening agents and fluorescent bleaches. These optical brighteners do not interact chemically with impurities in the fabric, but rather compensate optically for these impurities' yellowing effects. They operate to convert some of the invisible ultraviolet portion of sunlight (300-400 millimicrons) into visible blue light (400-500 millimicrons). The net effect is to whiten the materials by increasing the level of blue light reflected relative to that of yellow light. In addition to whitening yellow materials, optical brighteners make materials appear brighter by increasing the total amount of reflected light.

Optical brighteners are used in soaps (0.01 to 0.03%),
detergents (0.02 to 0.5%), bleaches (0.02 to 0.2%), blueings,
fabric softeners (1%), and acid sours (1%). Other applications
are in textiles (0.05 to 1%), paper in mill operations (0.1 to
0.3%), plastics (0.001 to 0.5%), and toothpaste (0.05 to 2%),
as well as cosmetics, shampoos, waxes, varnish, and lacquer
coatings.

The estimated annual world production of optical brighteners
is now over 44 million pounds (Table 2), of which 60 percent
are used in washing compounds, 25 percent for paper, 10 percent
for textiles, and 5 percent for plastics and other purposes.
It also is estimated that there are over 200 chemically
different optical brighteners commercially available. Those
optical brighteners manufactured in the United States are
listed in Table 3.

By far the commonest class of optical brighteners are the
sulfonated aminostilbenes. The core of the molecule is
structurally related to the potent human carcinogen
diethylstilbestrol, and to a variety of other well-known
"animal" carcinogens.

Table 2  Estimated Production of Optical Brighteners (in
millions of lbs. per year)

| Year | World Production | U.S. Production |
| --- | --- | --- |
| 1958 | - | 5.9 (a) |
| 1962 | - | 11.8 (a) |
| 1964 | - | 16.7 (b) |
| 1965 | 25.0 (c) | - |
| 1969 | - | 39.8 |
| 1970 | 44.0 (d) | - |

(a) Chemical Week, March 1966.
(b) U.S. Tariff Commission Reports.
(c) Stensby, P.S., Detergent Age, 3:20 (1967).
(d) Jegrelius, G. Personal Communication.

Table 3  Optical Brighteners Manufactured in the United States

| Grade Name | Manufacturer | Uses |
|---|---|---|
| Tinopal | Geigy | Plastics, synthetic fibers, emulsions, varnishes, lacquers, plastisols, organosols, waxes |
| Uvitex | Ciba | Textile finishing, detergents, paper, synthetic fibers, plastics |
| Calcefluor | American Cyanamide | Plastics, fibers |
| Blancophor | General Aniline and Film (Bayer) | Detergents |
| MDAC coumarin derivatives | Carlisle | |
| Leucophor | Sandoz | |

In spite of the massive usage of these stilbene brighteners, there is only sparse information available in the literature with regard to their fate in water, or in regard to the nature of their associated degradation products. A recent industry-sponsored study (30) concluded that:

". . . most FWA's (fluorescent whitening agents) in waste water are removed in sewage treatment facilities. Since these materials are poorly biodegraded, it is presumed that they are removed by adsorption. In either case, effluent treatment greatly reduces their potential for any environmental influence."

While this report does not define "environmental influence," it does state that:

". . . The generation by metabolism of carcinogenic or other toxic compounds from the FWA's currently in use has not been demonstrated. These results, although reassuring, do not clear the FWA's of carcinogenic potential through metabolites, and the results of chronic oral studies now in progress will be required before this safety concern can be totally assuaged."

This clearly represents another situation where a consumer
product is being massively used although there is inadequate
information as to their fate in the environment and their
potential adverse effects on man. It was considerations of
this nature that led to voluntary discontinuance of the use
of nitrilotriacetic acid (NTA) as a substitute for phosphates
in detergents.

Metals
Out of the 105 known elements that form the basis of all
matter, 77 can be classified as metals because of their
ductility, malleability, luster, and good conductance of heat
and electricity (2).

Heavy Metals  The quantities used annually for commercial and
industrial purposes vary from millions of tons of iron to only
thousands of ounces for iridium (2). Nevertheless, some 52
elemental metals can be considered "economic metals." Adverse
environmental and/or health effects have been observed for
about one-fourth of these (2). Many of the more toxic of these
are the "heavy metals," e.g., lead and mercury (see Table 4).
     After extracting metals from the earth, man reintroduces
them into his environment in a wide variety of new forms; the
list of metal-containing consumer products is almost endless.
As new applications are developed in manufacturing and consumer
products the potential for human exposure increases. For
example, irridium, once only a laboratory curiosity, is now
used to make jeweler's platinum and to manufacture electric
instruments, pen points, surgical instruments, and needles (2).
Mercury  Mercury achieved world-wide notoriety as a major
environmental pollutant following two outbreaks of poisoning
in Japan (31). Between 1953 and 1960, some 110 people, near
Minimata Bay, on the Island of Kyushu, were seriously disabled,
and 43 died, as a result of eating fish heavily contaminated
with methylmercury (31). Not long afterwards, in the mid-1960's,
the Swedish government took steps to eliminate domestic uses of
mercury (32).
     It was 1970, however, before North Americans were alerted to
the possibility of widespread mercury pollution. A report (33)
to the Canadian government indicated that fish in Lake St.
Clair, on the U.S.-Canadian border, were contaminated with
levels of mercury approaching those associated with previous
serious illness in Japan.
     Since 1970, numerous lakes and rivers in the United States
and Canada have been found to be contaminated with significant
levels of mercury. In most cases, the sources have been

Table 4   Estimated U.S. Consumption of Selected Metals,
1948 and 1968 (2)

| Metal | Total Estimated Consumption (a) (tons) | | Percent Increase, 1948-1968 |
|---|---|---|---|
|  | 1948 | 1968 |  |
| Arsenic (AS$_2$O$_3$) | 24,000 | 25,000 | 4 |
| Barium (barite) | 894,309 | 1,590,000 | 78 |
| Beryllium (beryl) | 1,438 | 8,719 | 507 |
| Cadmium | 3,909 | 6,664 | 70 |
| Chromium (chromite) | 875,033 | 1,316,000 | 50 |
| Copper | 1,214,000 | 1,576,000 | 30 |
| Lead | 1,133,895 | 1,328,790 | 17 |
| Manganese (ores 35% or more Mn) | 1,538,398 | 2,228,412 | 45 |
| Mercury | 1,758 | 2,866 | 63 |
| Nickel | 93,558 | 159,306 | 70 |
| Selenium | 419 | 762 | 82 |
| Silver (b) | 3,611 | 4,938 | 38 |
| Vanadium | N.A. (c) | 5,495 | --- |
| Zinc | 1,200,000 | 1,728,400 | 44 |

(a) Includes stocks released to the open market by the Federal
Government and imports; does not include exports.
(b) Consumption by industry and arts; monetary consumption not
included because much was stockpiled.
(c) Figures not available between 1946 and 1955; consumption
in 1946 was about 748 tons, in 1955 about 1,700 tons.

industrial effluents. The consequence of these discoveries was economic disaster for many whose livelihood depended upon commercial and sport fishing. For example, the State of Alabama prohibited commercial fishing in 51,000 miles of waterways (33); commercial fishing was stopped in Lake St. Clair; and tuna and swordfish meat which was found to exceed the hastily established interim guideline level of 0.5 ppm was condemned.

The long period that passed between the Japanese epidemic and the realization in North America that mercury poisoning is a serious threat here as well as in Japan, may have been partly because the fate of mercury in aquatic ecosystems was completely misunderstood.

Metallic mercury, the form in which most mercury reaches the environment, has not been considered toxic when ingested. Vapors of metallic mercury, however, had long been recognized as toxic and serious outbreaks of poisoning had occurred in industries in which workers were exposed to these vapors (33).

In the Japanese cases, however, methylmercury, a highly poisonous form of organic mercury, was being discharged directly into the waters of Minimata Bay, as a waste product from a plastics manufacturing plant. Fish populations in the bay, in turn, were biologically concentrating the material. Thus, fishermen around the Bay brought home daily fresh catches heavily contaminated with methylmercury.

While most mercury entering the environment is the liquid-metallic form, large amounts of methyl and phenylmercury have been used as agricultural fungicides; over the years an estimated 400 tons of organomercury compounds have been used in agriculture alone, in the United States (34). This probably accounts for the contamination of wildlife species far removed from industrial sources. However, in most countries that had previously used mercury fungicides, steps have been taken to curtail and even eliminate their use (34).

Although in 1968 the United States placed restrictions on the use of and direct discharge of methylmercury into water, subsequently the entire emphasis of concern changed. In that year, it was reported that inorganic mercury could be converted to methylmercury by "methanogenic bacteria" living in the bottom mud of lakes and streams (35). Thus, it now appears possible that inorganic mercury stored in lakes and stream sediments may serve as continuous source for the production of methylmercury.

In the past, the pathways of mercury into the environment have been numerous. Aside from agricultural use, the pulp industry has been a major source of organic mercury, where

these compounds have been used to control slime formation in
pulping processes. Paint, dental amalgams, and drugs are minor
sources; however, the chloralkali industry and fossil fuel
usage are additional major sources. Canadian statistics alone
show that in 1969 then existing chloralkali plants ordered
195,000 pounds of mercury to replace process losses. About
65 percent of this lost mercury went directly to sewers, 25
percent to the atmosphere, and the remaining 15 percent adhered
to walls and floors of the plants (36). Coal-fired power plants
also emit mercury to the atmosphere, because mercury is a
trace contaminant in coal (37). For example, annual estimates
range from 450 pounds to 5,300 pounds of mercury from
central-station generating plants in the State of Illinois
alone.

Although no epidemic of mercury poisoning has been reported
in the United States, the conditions for such an event to take
place have, at times, been dangerously approached. It may even
be said that our eating habits, i.e., the low per capita
consumption of fish, have been a mitigating factor. Only little
is known about the effects of chronic intake of low levels of
organic mercury compounds (38).

Cadmium   Another metal that has become a significant
environmental contaminant and which may pose an even more
serious hazard than mercury is cadmium. Wastes from cadmium
mining have been shown to be responsible for an outbreak of a
severe degenerative bone disease in an area of northern Japan
(39).

The signs of this disease include softening and fracturing
of bone. The accompanying pain is so severe that the Japanese
refer to it as itai-itai (ouch-ouch) disease.

The source of the cadmium was eventually traced to zinc and
lead mining operations; for years waste waters had been
discharged into a nearby river that was being used downstream
to irrigate rice and soybean crops. Over the years, cadmium
levels in the soil had built up to the point that crops became
a toxic source of cadmium.

In the United States, a statistical survey of 28 cities
suggested a positive correlation between levels of airborne
cadmium and deaths caused by high blood pressure and
arteriosclerotic heart disease (40). Cadmium also has been
incriminated as a cause of lung, kidney, and bone damage, and
anemia in workers exposed to airborne cadmium (41).

Elevated and widespread environmental levels of cadmium, as
with mercury, are the direct result of its increased use in
industrial processes. In 1968, it was estimated that some 4.6
million pounds of cadmium were released into the atmosphere;

about 2.1 million pounds from the refining and processing of
cadmium-bearing ores in the zinc, lead, copper, and cadmium
industries. The United States consumed about 90 percent of the
cadmium produced, about 13 million pounds, in electroplating,
paint pigments, plastics, metal alloys, and batteries (41).
Another 2 million pounds was used in the manufacture of
polyvinyl chloride plastics. Cadmium compounds also are used
as plastic stabilizers (to prevent discoloration during the
manufacturing process and when the product is exposed to
ultraviolet light) and, like the PAE's, are able to leach out
of the plastics.

Probably the most serious evidence of a general increase in
cadmium levels is a study by the U.S. Geological Survey (41).
An analysis of 720 surface water samples for cadmium revealed
that 33 (4 percent) had concentrations above the USPHS's 10
microgram per liter maximum allowable concentration for
drinking waters. All samples exceeding this standard were from
urban watersheds  near major industrial complexes; on the
other hand, none of the samples taken from undeveloped drainage
basins exceeded the standard.

Consumer products also have been implicated in incidents
of cadmium poisoning. On several occasions acidic beverages and
foods stored in cadmium-plated ice trays have been responsible
for episodes of mild cadmium poisoning. For example, on one
occasion 29 school children suffered vomiting and nausea for
a short period after eating popsicles containing as little as
13 to 15 ppm of cadmium (42).

## Federal Controls

Overview  Several control mechanisms are available to the
Federal Government to deal with toxic substances (see Table 5).
However, in general, they have been inadequate to the tasks
described herein. Existing federal controls over the
introduction of toxic substances into interstate commerce, and
eventually, into the environment, are of two major types:

First, there is control over the initial production of a
substance and its distribution; this is referred to as a
"product"-oriented approach. For example, under the Federal
Insecticide, Fungicide, and Rodenticide Act (FIFRA), a
manufacturer must register a pesticide with the EPA before it
can be marketed in interstate commerce. FIFRA has been used by
the EPA to prevent the use of PCB's in formulations of
pesticides. On October 29, 1970, the EPA's Pesticide Regulation
Division (PRD) ordered pesticide manufacturers, formulators,
and distributors to eliminate the use of PCB's in pesticide

Table 5  Federal Laws and Regulations Concerning Handling,
Transportation and Disposal of Toxic and Hazardous Materials

| Law | Department Administering | Coverage |
|---|---|---|
| Atomic Energy Act (42 U.S.C. 2011 et seq.). Regulations: 10 CFR 1 et seq. | AEC | Authorizes the Atomic Energy Commission to set standards regulating the possession and use of nuclear materials including the granting of licenses; also authorizes AEC to cooperate with the States |
| Clean Air Act (42 U.S.C. 2011 et seq.). Regulations: 42 CFR pts. 75, 76, 77, and 81 | EPA | Authorizes the establishment of national air quality standards, performance standards for new and modified stationary sources, hazardous emission standards for new and existing stationary sources, emission standards for new motor vehicles and aircraft emission standards |
| Federal Aviation Act of 1958 (49 U.S.C. 1421-1430, 1472H). Regulations: 14 CFR pt. 103 | DOT | Regulates the transportation of hazardous materials by air |
| Federal Hazardous Substances Act (15 U.S.C. 1261-1273). Regulations: 21 CFR, pt. 191, subch. D | HEW | Requires precautionary labeling for products defined as hazardous in containers intended as suitable for household use; authorizes the banning of toys or articles where a child may secure access to the hazardous substances and provides for the banning of a hazardous substance where necessary for health and safety |

Table 5 (cont.)

| Law | Department Administering | Coverage |
|---|---|---|
| Federal Insecticide, Fungicide, and Rodenticide Act (7 U.S.C. 135-135h). Regulations: 7 CFR pt. 362 | EPA | Requires registration of economic poisons (pesticides) with the Administrator, EPA; requires submission of proof of safety and efficacy of product and label to be used; also authorizes Secretary to establish specific coloration requirements for certain products |
| Federal Water Pollution Control Act (33 U.S.C. 466-466n) as amended by 84 Stat. 91. Regulations: 18 CFR pts. 601, 602, 606, 607, and 620 | EPA | Provides for federal-State standards covering the quality of interstate and coastal waters. Recently, the 1899 Refuse Act, which requires federal permit to discharge effluents other than municipal sewage, has been used to maintain and improve water quality |
| Food, Drug and Cosmetic Act (21 U.S.C. 301 et seq.). | HEW | Authorizes the regulation of food labeling, food additives, drugs, some medical devices, and cosmetics |
| Hazardous Cargo Act (46 U.S.C. 170) (49 U.S.C. 1421-1430, 1472H). Regulations: 33 CFR pt. 126, 46 CFR pts. 38, 39 | DOT | Regulates the transportation of hazardous materials by air |

Table 5 (cont.)

| Law | Department Administering | Coverage |
| --- | --- | --- |
| Nonmailable Material (18 U.S.C. 1716). Regulations: Post Office Services Transmittal Letter 113, June 29, 1962, pts. 124, 125 | Post Office | Makes nonmailable certain poisons and other materials and provides for the regulation of certain permitted articles by the Postmaster General |
| Occupational Health and Safety Act of 1970 | HEW/ Labor | Labor sets standards based upon criteria developed by HEW. This statute preempts occupational safety standards promulgated under such statutes as the Welsh-Heeley Act, Construction Safety Act, and the Longshoremen and Harbor Workers' Compensation Act |
| Protection of Navigable Waters (33 U.S.C. 407. Regulations: 19 CFR pt. 23, S. 23, 32 | Army | Makes it unlawful to deposit from a ship or from the shore any refuse matter into any navigable water of the United States, other than that flowing from streets and sewers |
| Transportation of Explosives Act (18 DOT U.S.C. 831-935). Regulations: 49 CFR pts. 171-179, pts. 290-297 | DOT | Regulates the transportation of hazardous materials by land and by water |
| Armed Services Explosives Safety Board (10 U.S.C. 172) | DOD | Establishes board to advise the Secretary of Defense on Safety matters |

formulations within six months. This regulatory action was
designed to eliminate the small amount of environmental PCB's
from such sources.

Second, there is the capability to control air and water
pollution from various sources; this is referred to as a
"media"- or "effluent"-oriented approach. Such federal
authority derives primarily from the Clean Air Act and the
Federal Water Pollution Control (FWPC) Act. Under the FWPC Act
the EPA is authorized to enforce federally approved State water
quality standards and emission standards; however, the problem
is that standards for potentially hazardous materials must be
established on a substance-by-substance basis either by the
Federal or State governments. This presents a major undertaking.
Thus federal authority, under current EPA practices, is
restricted to control over accidental spills of toxic
substances such as PCB's and metals.

Under the Clean Air Act, the Federal Government sets ambient
air quality standards for classes of contaminants; the States
then set emission standards or more stringent ambient air
quality standards. In the case of hazardous substances,
natural emission standards can be established on a case-by-case
basis; however, enforcement depends on limiting the emissions
of a substance from a given source. For example, theoretically
the Clean Air Act could be used to prevent a substance such as
PCB's from entering the atmosphere as a result of refuse
burning. On the other hand, it would be almost impossible to
prevent PCB's from entering refuse, a goal that could only be
obtained by stringent control over the use of PCB's.

In theory, media-type authorities can be used to control
toxic substances; however, the current federal emphasis is on
contaminants which occur in large quantities. Control of
minute quantities of toxic substances also is difficult with
media-based authorities, in part because of the difficulty of
even detecting their presence in air or water, let alone
measuring their levels.

In addition, most toxic substances are not exclusively air
or water pollutants, but can be found in varying quantities in
air, water,  soil, food, and industrial and consumer products.
The multiplicity of ways by which man can be exposed to these
substances makes it difficult for the media-oriented authorities
to consider the total exposure of an individual to a given
substance. Yet this consideration is essential to the
establishment of adequate comprehensive environmental standards
(2).

Product Control  As mentioned, one approach is to control a product and its uses, including a total prohibition of a product. Several federal statutes can be applied to the manufacture and distribution of drugs, food and feed additives, consumer products, pesticides, and radioactive materials.

Under FIFRA, pesticides are regulated to protect users and handlers by requiring registration, proper labeling, and in some cases coloring of pesticide products. FIFRA regulates the marketing in interstate commerce of "economic poisons and devices," which includes insecticides, rodenticides, plant defoliants, and household disinfectants.

Under the Food, Drug, and Cosmetic Act, the FDA can regulate food labeling, food additives, food containers, drugs, and cosmetics. The FDA has used this authority to support its seizure of adulterated food in interstate commerce. This Act also has been used by the FDA to prevent PCB-contaminated food from entering retail markets. However, in the case of toxic substances, this authority is for the most part restricted to control after-the-fact. Moreover, enforcement relies heavily on knowing how and where to concentrate sampling efforts. The Act was primarily designed to see that registered food additives are used properly.

Under the Atomic Energy Act of 1954, as amended (42 U.S.C. 2011 et seq.), the Atomic Energy Commission (AEC) regulates almost the entire spectrum of activity associated with the handling, transportation, and disposal of radioactive materials. Specifically, the AEC licenses and maintains continuing surveillance over facilities utilizing, processing, or disposing of radioactive materials. It also prescribes procedures and standards for the packaging and shipping of such materials.

Other federal statutes that might be used include the Egg Products Inspection Act, the Wholesome Poultry Products Act, and the Wholesome Meat Act.

Effluent Control  There are two major federal statutes based upon the media approach that are available for controlling the release of pollutants directly into the environment -- the FWPC Act (33 U.S.S. 466 et seq.) and the Clean Air Act (42 U.S.C. 1857 et seq.).

Under the FWPC Act, provision is made for establishment of federal-State water quality standards for "navigable waters" and contiguous zones. These standards basically cover general parameters of the water -- such as oxygen content, temperature, and turbidity -- rather than specific substances in the water.

Although the standards may be enforced directly by the Federal
Government, primary responsibility for enforcement rests with
the States.

The obvious limitation of effluent controls is that they
generally deal with a problem only _after_ it is manifest. They
do not provide for obtaining information on potential
pollutants before obvious adverse effects have occurred.

More subtle but more serious limitations of effluent
controls arise from their focusing on the media -- air or
water -- in which the pollution occurs. This approach has
several consequences.

First, it leads to concern with those substances found in
air or water in the greatest quantities (2). Although gross
quantity is a valid indicator, it tends to disregard the
degrees of danger of the various pollutants. Trace amounts of
some substances can cause serious effects, but media-oriented
programs tend to overlook their importance (2).

A second consequence of the media approach is that it
cannot deal effectively with the fact that many, perhaps most,
toxic substances find their way into the environment through
several media (2). These substances cannot be strictly
characterized as water pollutants or as air pollutants, for
they are found in air, in water, and often in soil, food, and
elsewhere in the environment. The characteristic pervasiveness
of toxic substances makes it difficult for the media-oriented
programs to engage in adequate and efficient research,
monitoring, and control activities for such substances (2).

In turn, the Clean Air Act provides for a system of
federal-State establishment of air quality standards. However,
the Clean Air Amendments of 1970 (P.L. 91-604) require the
Federal Government to establish national air quality standards
and the States to submit emission standards for individual
pollutants for EPA approval. Further, the Amendments require
federal establishment and enforcement of emission standards
for certain classes of new industrial pollutants and for
hazardous air pollutants.

In addition to air and water pollution control, there is
the Solid Waste Disposal Act of 1965 (42 U.S.C. 3251-3259),
as amended by the Resource Recovery Act of 1970 (P.L. 91-512).
The Resource Recovery Act requires the formulation of a plan
for a system of national disposal sites for the storage and
disposal of hazardous wastes.

Hazardous Substances  Existing federal law is not entirely
void of authority to deal with toxic or hazardous substances.
Toxic substances are specifically dealt with in the Hazardous

Substances Act (15 U.S.C. 1261-1273), the FWPC Act Amendments
of 1972 (P.L. 92-500), the Clean Air Amendments of 1970
(P.L. 91-609), and the authorities of the Department of
Transportation relating to transportation of hazardous
substances.

The Hazardous Substances Act covers household products and
toys, but not the raw materials from which they are
manufactured (see Chapter 2). Thus, it does not deal directly
with most of the toxic substances discussed herein. The
statute, in effect, authorizes the Secretary of Health,
Education, and Welfare only to require how a product should be
labeled. Although the Act does provide a mechanism by which
extremely hazardous products can be banned from interstate
commerce, the definition of a "hazardous substance" is quite
restrictive, stating that a substance may be banned only if
special labeling or packaging is found ineffective in
preventing a hazard.

The FWPC Act (Section 311) authorizes the President to
designate hazardous substances and to recommend methods and
means for their removal from water. Under the section,
"hazardous substances" are limited to

"such elements and compounds which, when discharged in any
quantity into or upon the navigable waters of the United States
or adjoining shorelines or the waters of the contiguous zone,
present an imminent and substantial danger to the public
health or welfare, including, but not limited to, fish,
shellfish, wildlife, shorelines, and beaches."

The section is generally aimed at accidental discharges of
such substances and thus does not cover either continuous
discharges into water or release of hazardous substances into
other media.

The 1972 Amendments dealt with this issue in part, however.
The EPA was empowered to designate a list of toxic substances
for which effluent standards, including a prohibition, could
be established (43).

A broad definition was provided for "toxic pollutants" (44)
as

"Those pollutants, or combinations of pollutants, including
disease-causing agents, which after discharge and upon
exposure, ingestion, inhalation or assimilation into any
organism, either directly from the environment or indirectly
by ingestion through food chains, will on the basis of
information available to the Administrator, cause death,

disease, behavioral abnormalities, cancer, genetic mutations, physiological malfunctions (including malfunctions in reproduction), or physical deformations in such organisms or their offspring."

At the time, concern was mainly for arsenic, cadmium, mercury, and beryllium, as well as for certain chlorinated hydrocarbons. Significantly, this authority extends to national pretreatment standards for the discharge of toxic substances into public owned waste-water treatment facilities.

The Clean Air Amendments of 1970 (P.L. 91-604) also dealt with hazardous substances which were defined [Section 112(a)(1)] as

"...an air pollutant to which no ambient air quality standards is applicable and which in the judgment of the Administrator may cause, or contribute to an increase in mortality or an increase in serious irreversible or incapacitating reversible illness."

Under this authority, the EPA administrator can designate hazardous substances for which he then must establish national emission standards.

Additional federal authorities include the Department of Transportation's regulation of interstate transportation of hazardous substances under several authorities, including the Department of Transportation Act (49 U.S.C. 1651 et seq.), the Transportation of Explosives Act (18 U.S.C. 831-837), and the Hazardous Cargo Act (46 U.S.C. 170).

## Inadequacy Of Authorities Recognized

Prelude To Reform   Throughout this discussion an emphasis has been placed on the broad character of the issues attendant to the control of toxic substances. The key feature of this issue, as cogently expressed (2) by the Council on Environmental Quality, is the need to consider

"...the total human exposure to a substance and its total effect on the environment. The focus must be on a particular pollutant and all the pathways by which it travels through the ecosystem."

A significant early step toward the eventual control of toxic substances was Secretary John W. Gardner's establishment, in November 1966, of a Task Force on Environmental Health and

Related Problems. When the Task Force's report emerged in
June, 1967, the recommended Consumer Protection Goal was to
initiate by 1970

"...a comprehensive program for the identification of health
and safety hazards associated with the use of appliances,
clothing, food, hazardous substances, and other consumer
products and for the control of such products which fail to
meet consumer protection standards." (45)

This recommendation, however, tended to fade into history
until, in the 91st Congress (1969 to 1970), consumer and
environmental issues achieved stature as public-interest
movements. During this period, the Final Report of the
National Commission on Product Safety (46) concluded that
federal authority to protect the consumer against hazardous
products was inadequate. The Commission went on to say that
the "limited federal authority as does exist is scattered
among many agencies."

Moreover, existing laws were deemed difficult to enforce.
This was attributed to the influence of affected industries
both on the initial legislative process and on the federal
agencies administering the final statutory policies (46).

Many of the statutes contain provisions establishing
administrative and judicial appeal procedures, thus preventing
final enforcement for as long as an issue is kept in the
courts. Similarly, many statutes provide the regulatory
agencies with inadequate investigatory power necessary for
vigorous enforcement. An outstanding example of the
difficulties encountered in hurdling these obstacles is
provided in the legislative history of the Toxic Substances
Act.

Before discussing the Toxic Substances Act, it is useful to
briefly review the manner in which legislative proposals are
introduced and handled. There are various forms in which bills
are introduced. First, there are the so-called private bills
developed by individual members; second, legislation introduced
on behalf of others, such as the Executive Branch; and, third,
proposals developed by Congressional committees  and their
respective professional staff members.

In general, particularly in instances where major
legislative proposals are involved, the Congress appears to
react slowly and in a piecemeal fashion. While the Congress as
a whole seems reluctant to enact legislation, a flurry of
activity usually occurs as individual congressmen introduce

legislation to serve as an indication of their interest in
and concern for particular problems.

Where concern is for the hazards of a particular substance,
a common pattern has been that, after initial publicity on the
adverse effects of a particular substance, several congressmen
hurriedly introduce bills to ban the offending product. Thus,
a spate of bills was introduced late in the 91st Congress, and
some reintroduced at the beginning of the 92nd Congress,
banning the use of polyphosphates in detergents. Similarly,
early in 1971, following the findings of high mercury
concentrations in fish, numerous congressmen either introduced
or cosponsored bills banning or controlling the use of mercury.
Likewise, after the discovery of high concentrations of PCB's
in chickens, legislation was introduced to prohibit the
introduction into commerce of the chemical compound known as
polychlorinated biphenyl.

The primary motive for the introduction of such bills often
is to cash in on their publicity value and the issues
surrounding the discovery of the adverse effects of the
substance. The usual procedure is for one or more congressmen
to instruct their staffs to develop a bill which would deal
with the specific offending substance. Once completed, the
bill is introduced, the congressman also may ask a few
entrusted friends to join him in the initial introduction of
his bill, thus giving them the jump on the publicity and
possible national newsmedia coverage. Generally, this is
followed by a "Dear Colleague" letter asking others to join in
the reintroduction of the bill. Depending on the energy and
ambition of the staff member handling the collection of names
and/or the interest of other congressmen, the number of
cosponsors may increase substantially.

The number of cosponsors, however, is not necessarily an
indication of good prospects for easy passage of the bill.
It may mean merely that the various congressmen sent out press
releases to the media of their home district as a notice that
their representative in the Congress is doing something about
the problem.

Press releases do not move a bill through the Congress,
however. In general, a bill has to be forcefully called to
the attention of the chairman of the committee to which it has
been referred. Such pressure may come from the Executive
Branch, from special interest groups, or from other influential
congressmen. It also may originate with committee staff members
who take a direct interest in legislation, and who can get the
attention of one or more members of the relevant legislative

subcommittee. The latter, to a large extent, was the case for the Toxic Substances Control Act.

The 91st Congress, 1969-1970   As the 91st Congress began its work in 1969, a major order of business was the Water Quality Improvement Act, which had been lost during the closing days of the 90th Congress. When enacted in April 1970, the Act directed that a report be submitted to the Congress relative to

"...the need for, and desirability of, enacting legislation to impose liability, including financial responsibility requirements, for the cost of removal of hazardous substances discharged from vessels and onshore and offshore facilities. It specifies further that an accelerated study be conducted to include, but not be limited to, the method and measures for controlling hazardous substances to prevent such discharge, the most appropriate measures for enforcement, and the recovery of costs if removal is undertaken by the United States." (P.L. 91-224)

Against this background, in December 1969, the House Government Operations Subcommittee on Conservation and Natural Resources, chaired by Rep. Henry S. Reuss (D.-Wisc.), convened hearings on "Phosphates in Detergents and the Eutrophication of America's Waterways." On April 14, 1970, the Committee on Government Operations, whose chairman was Rep. William L. Dawson (D.-Ill.), recommended that

"...the phosphate content of detergents be reduced in phases, starting immediately, and that all phosphorus be eliminated from detergents within 2 years."

Thus, after a major campaign by environmentalists against detergent phosphates for their effect in accelerating the eutrophication of America's inland lakes and rivers, the detergent industry geared up to produce an alternative detergent builder, nitrilotriacetic acid (NTA), in massive quantities. The aim of the major detergent manufacturers in mid-1970 was to partially replace phosphates with NTA (about a 50 percent substitution) as fast as production could be expanded.

At this time, the Senate Public Works Subcommittee on Air and Water Pollution was actively engaged in water pollution legislative hearings. The question was raised by the

Subcommittee staff as to whether this action by the detergent
manufacturers might not result in the simple substitution of
an unknown for a known environmental problem. For advice the
Subcommittee staff turned to Dr. Samuel S. Epstein, who two
years earlier had been called as an expert witness on the
chronic health effects of chemical air pollutants. Thus, on
May 6, 1970, Dr. Epstein again testified before Senator
Muskie's Subcommittee -- this time to raise a number of then
unanswered questions regarding NTA's potential toxicologic
and environmental implications (48). Subsequently, Senator
Jennings Randolph (D.-W. Va.), Chairman of the Committee on
Public Works, requested Dr. Epstein to prepare a more detailed
analysis for the Committee.

While this report was in preparation, the National Institute
of Environmental Health Sciences (NIEHS) instituted tests (49)
which suggested that NTA combined with heavy metals such as
lead and chromium to form toxic chelates which caused birth
defects in laboratory animals. It also was believed that the
cadmium chelates might find their way into the drinking-water
supplies throughout the nation because of the common presence
of cadmium in water pipes. Thus, it was suspected that if
NTA were used widely as a substitute for phosphates, then a
human health hazard might be substituted for the environmental
effects attributed to phosphates.

In response to Nixon Administration pressures and out of a
desire to preempt the release of Dr. Epstein's report by the
Senate Committee on Public Works, the detergent manufacturers
reluctantly agreed to a voluntary termination in the
substitution of NTA for detergent phosphates, in December
1970, pending further exhaustive study. Concurrently, several
other possible NTA hazards were comprehensively detailed in
Dr. Epstein's report to the Committee." (50)

Although the original NIEHS tests were not subsequently
confirmed, in May 1972, HEW Secretary Duval still restated
the restriction on NTA on the basis of an Ad Hoc Advisory
Committee Report (51). In substance, this new report agreed
with Dr. Epstein's warning that use of NTA as a phosphate
substitute might result in "jumping from the ecological frying
pan into the toxicological fire." (50)

In summary, NTA was withdrawn from the market; however,
this occurred only after industry had spent almost $1 billion
for research and NTA production. This difficult situation arose
largely because there was no federal requirement for premarket
testing of substances to determine their potential long-range
impact on human health and the environment. For the most part,
testing under existing statutes (see Table 3) is restricted to

"acute toxicity" to ascertain their safety during handling in manufacturing. However, extensive mandatory testing is done for those substances intended for human or animal consumption. Other substances when determined to be hazardous must be labeled accordingly. In effect, existing statutory testing requirements were designed to protect the consumer against direct injury. Additionally, the nature of research on NTA by industry, by commercial testing houses under contract to industry, and by their consultants appears to have been responsive principally to short-term marketing interests rather than to an in-depth analysis of its potential long-term human and ecological implications under intended circumstances of massive use.

The 92nd Congress, 1971-1972  In recognition of the need for a more comprehensive approach to the regulation of environmentally hazardous manufactured products, Sen. Muskie, in the opening days of the 92nd Congress, introduced legislation (S. 573) to require premarket testing of new substances. Speaking of recent events Senator Muskie stated (52):

"I am convinced from our experience with phosphates and nitrilotriacetic acid (NTA) in detergents, with lead, and mercury, with pesticides, and with other hazardous substances that we must have a system to deal with these problems before they reach crisis stage...

We no longer can depend upon either special legislation for each dangerous product or upon voluntary cooperation among the manufacturers to deal with these problems. These approaches have produced only uncertain and haphazard decisions in the environmental policy."

Written as an amendment to the Clean Air Act and the FWPC Act, Senator Muskie's measure was referred to his Public Works Subcommittee on Air and Water Pollution. A significant feature of the bill was its statement of the congressional finding that (1) many manufactured products may contain substances which adversely affect the health of our people and the quality of air and water; (2) the control of such adverse effects may not be feasible or preferable at the points where the products are discharged into the environment; and (3) the Congress believes air and water quality must be protected by regulating the use of such dangerous substances at the point of manufacture and by seeking information about environmental effects before products are put on the market.

The Administration's Proposal  Concurrently, the Nixon
Administration was drafting its own legislative proposal
governing chemical substances not otherwise federally
controlled. This proposal was transmitted to the Congress with
President Nixon's March 1, 1971 environmental message (53).

At the Administration's request, Sen. Warren G. Magnuson
(D.-Wash.), Chairman of the Committee on Commerce, introduced
its bill (S. 1478), which was referred back to his Committee.
An identical measure (H.R. 5276) was introduced by Rep. Harley
Staggers (D.-W. Va.), Chairman of the House Interstate and
Foreign Commerce Committee.

Immediately, several Senate and House aides on affected
legislative committees began their analysis of the
Administration's legislation. Independently, the conclusion
was reached that the bill was not only weak in several
respects but it was weaker than an earlier draft prepared by
the staff of the Council on Environmental Quality (CEQ).

The original CEQ draft was prepared by a staff scientist
and, reportedly, contained a tough premarket clearance system
similar to that proposed later by Sen. William Spong (D.-Va.)
and Rep. Peter H. B. Frelinghuysen (D.-N.Y.). However, the
draft bill went through a "clearance process" before being
transmitted to the Congress. At that time, CEQ's draft bill
was not well received either by the Department of Commerce or
by the White House. Staff at both places felt the bill was too
strong and would arouse intense opposition from the chemical
industry.

In order to better understand the effect of the draft
measure on the chemical industry, their comments were
channeled through the office of John C. Whitaker (Deputy
Assistant to the President for Domestic Affairs). The White
House staff then incorporated industry's arguments into their
official critique of CEQ's draft bill. The return memorandum
from Whitaker's office to CEQ made it clear that their revised
draft was the best effort that the Administration would support
for controlling toxic substances, against expected opposition
by the chemical industry. When the Department of Commerce
transmitted almost identical objections, CEQ had little
alternative but to transmit the weakened version to the
Congress as the official Administration response to a generally
admitted need for legislation.

What is often overlooked is that the National Environmental
Policy Act (P.L. 91-190) requires that bills transmitted from
the Executive Branch to the Congress be accompanied by an
environmental impact statement. Such a statement was indeed
required to be sent by CEQ in connection with the Toxic

Substances Control Act. An Executive Order directs that such environmental impact statements be made public in a timely manner, and with a view towards providing "the public with relevant information, including information on alternate courses of action." The Executive Order also specifies that government agencies involved "have a responsibility to insure the fullest practicable provision of timely public information and understanding of Federal...programs." However, CEQ's environmental impact statement on the Toxic Substances Control Act had several shortcomings.

First, the environmental impact statement prepared by CEQ, the official "keeper of our environmental conscience," (53) considered only the two alternative extremes of either not submitting any legislation or requiring the registration of all chemical substances. There was no analysis of possible alternatives in between these two extremes. Second, the statement lauded the Administration bill as "carefully drawn to prevent unnecessary interference with technological development," yet there was no evaluation of the degree of regulation necessary to curb environmental degradation brought on by unfettered technological development. An immense assist would have been provided the legislative process had the bill attempted to provide criteria for weighing public benefit vs environmental risks.

Congressional Counter-Proposals  Dissatisfied with the Administration's proposal, several congressmen directed their respective aides to draft counterproposals. For example, several Senators  on the Committee on Commerce  encouraged staff members Michael B. Brownlee and Leonard Bickwit, Jr., of Sen. Phillip A. Hart's (D.-Mich.) Commerce Subcommittee on the Environment to draft a tougher bill. Concurrently, on Sen. Jennings Randolph's (D.-W. Va.) behalf a staff member of his Committee on Public Works, Richard D. Grundy, also was drafting a bill to reflect Sen. Randolph's concern over the events surrounding the substitution of NTA for phosphates in detergents. For this effort, Sen. Randolph's aide sought the assistance of Professor Samuel S. Epstein and other Committee consultants. On the House side, several staff members of consumer-oriented representatives, working together, incorporated suggestions for avoiding the shortcomings of the Administration bill, and wrote the House counterproposal.

Only two of these bills were ever introduced. On July 27, 1971, Sen. Spong introduced Michael B. Brownlee's effort as Amendment 388 to S. 1478, the Administration bill. This amendment was drafted as a substitute for the Administration bill. Thus both Sen. Spong's amendment and the Administration

bill were considered by the Senate Commerce Committee. About
this time, Sen. Randolph decided not to introduce the draft
prepared by Richard Grundy and Professor Epstein because of
other commitments to lung legislation and energy issues, as
well as to a 1972 reelection campaign. However, this draft
legislation was subsequently made available to Sen. Spong and
the Commerce Committee staff. Meanwhile, Sen. Muskie's bill,
S. 573, still was pending before his Subcommittee.

On the House side, Rep. Frelinghuysen introduced a separate
Toxic Substances Bill on September 23, 1971. The bill (H.R.
10840) was subsequently reintroduced by him twice more (H.R.
11148 and H.R. 11266), gaining a total of 44 cosponsors. An
identical bill also was introduced separately by Rep. John S.
Monogan (D.-Conn.).

About this time, beginning on August 3, 1971, Sen. Hart's
Commerce Subcommittee on the Environment convened hearings on
the Toxic Substances Control Act. These hearings were chaired
by Sen. William B. Spong (D.-Va.), because Sen. Hart was
involved elsewhere in an intensive investigation in his capacity
as Chairman of the Judiciary Subcommittee on Anti-Trust. Thus,
Sen. Spong was able to play a key role in the evolution of the
formulation of the bill later reported by the Committee.

At this point, a brief comparison of the two bills
considered by the Senate Commerce Subcommittee would be
helpful. The Administration bill, S. 1478, would have provided
the EPA discretionary authority to:

- require manufacturers to report, inter alia, the name,
chemical identity, categories of use, and amounts of chemicals
manufactured;

- set standards for test protocols of new chemical substances
and for the results to be achieved of such testing, as are
necessary to protect health and the environment;

- apply to the Attorney General to seek judicial limitations
on the use or distribution of a chemical substance in case of
imminent hazard;

- promulgate rules or regulations restricting or prohibiting
the use or distribution of chemical substances to the extent
necessary to protect health and environment;

- use administrative inspections to insure that regulations
issued under the Act are being complied with;

- establish a Toxic Substances Board, which would advise the
Administration on test protocols and restrictions (members
would be nominated by the National Academy of Sciences); and

- preempt, in large measure, State regulatory action once the
provisions of the Act have been applied.

Two principal differences between the Administration bill
and Sen. Spong's substitute subsequently were taken out after
vigorous denunciations by both government and industry
witnesses. The first was a strict premarket licensing for all
chemical substances. This would have required manufacturers
to test all substances and prove to the satisfaction of the
EPA Administrator that a substance was safe. The EPA
Administrator then would have issued a certification permitting
marketing of the substance. Instead, the final Senate version
contained a premarket screening provision.

The second major feature of Sen. Spong's substitute that
was deleted was a special excise tax to be imposed on the sale
of "certified" chemical substances. The tax was to be collected
by the Treasury and then paid out to the manufacturer to
recover his cost of testing. Subsequently, the tax would be
lifted when the costs of the test program and the certification
had been collected.

A major philosophic difference between the Administration
proposal and the Spong substitute was the mandatory duty on
the Administrator to carry out the provisions of the Act.
This survived the Hearings, the Executive Session of the
Subcommittee (March 6, 1972), and the Executive Session of the
18-member Senate Commerce Committee (April 11, 1972). Whereas
the Administration bill made liberal use of the phrase "the
Administrator may" the Spong substitute had employed the much
stronger and mandatory word "shall." In addition, the
substitute bill empowered the EPA Administrator to take
immediate and direct action in the case of "imminent hazard."
Under the Administration's bill the EPA Administrator would
have to request the Attorney General to petition a district
court to issue an injunction to prevent injury to health from
continued use or distribution of a chemical in an "imminent
hazard" situation. In Sen. Spong's substitute, the EPA
Administrator was required to issue a direct order

"When there is reason to believe that the manufacture,
processing, use, distribution or disposal of a chemical
substance will result in serious damage to human health or the
environment prior to the completion of an administration
hearing or proceeding under this Act." (emphasis supplied)

This compares with S. 1478 which required that the EPA
Administrator have evidence sufficient to show that

"A use or distribution creates a hazard to human health or
the environment (1) that should be corrected immediately to
prevent injury to health and (2) that should not be permitted
to continue while an administrative hearing or other formal
proceeding is being held." (emphasis supplied)

Sen. Spong's substitute empowered the EPA Administrator to
step in before damage occurred where he had "reason to believe"
that certain activities "will result in damage"; however, in
S. 1478, the damage had to occur before the EPA Administrator
could decide whether or not to apply for injunctive relief.

Another significant feature of Sen. Spong's substitute
was citizen suits to require a reluctant EPA Administrator to
enforce the mandatory provisions of the Act reflected in his
other amendment. Citizens also could sue either manufacturers
for violation of "use and distribution" regulations or
individuals for violation of "disposal" regulations. The Spong
Amendment also allowed civil and criminal penalties to be
assessed against consumers who knowingly failed to dispose of
toxic substances in accordance with label instructions. The
Administration's bill S. 1478 made no provisions for either
citizen suits or for civil penalties for such a violation of
disposal regulations.

Another major innovation of Sen. Spong's bill was the
requirement to publish all data received by EPA on a chemical
substance, except information which might contain or reveal a
trade secret. Even trade secret information, however, could be
released to the public if necessary "to protect their health
or safety." This would have been a far more sweeping
implementation of the Freedom of Information Act than is found
in any other regulatory legislation. The Administration bill,
on the other hand, gave the EPA Administrator discretionary
authority to keep confidential all the information obtained
from the manufacturer.

Senate Action   On August 5, 1971, Senate hearings opened
before the Commerce Subcommittee on the Environment (54).
Earlier, in the 90th Congress, the Subcommittee had held
hearings on the problems of several toxic chemicals not
controlled under existing federal authorities. For example,
in April 1970 testimony was received on the adverse effects of
mercury and other heavy metals (55). Concurrent with the
hearings on the Toxic Substances Control Act, the Subcommittee
under Sen. Spong was also receiving testimony on S. 2553, a
bill designed to control pollution by phosphates in laundry
detergents.

As the hearings proceeded, there were raised important philosophical principles that produced arguments and counterarguments by the various witnesses.

As is the practice, between the end of the formal Hearings and the Subcommittee "markup," considerable additional testimony was received for the record. Much of this represented amplification of or documentation for points raised in oral testimony before the Subcommittee. This general practice of receiving additional written materials into the record provides the committee members with an immense amount of usually excellent source material. It thus serves to improve the expertise of those staff members involved in formulating the technical and legal aspects of a particular piece of legislation.

Another important advantage of this practice is that this source material also becomes available to the public in the form of printed Hearings. Although in many instances the published Hearings are not available until shortly before passage of the legislation, there is nonetheless great utility in having the record available to the public and affected parties. Moreover, in the event the legislation does not achieve passage in one Congress, this record can then be drawn on again during subsequent considerations of similar legislation in later Congresses. An alert staff also will pass written statements submitted for the record by one party on to others for their comment.

One shortcoming of the printed Hearing transcript is that sometimes it does not represent a true verbatim record of what was said during the oral testimony. This stems from the practice of allowing witnesses to proofread and supposedly edit the verbatim transcript prepared by the committee stenographers. However, such corrections are not always limited to improving syntax and form; not infrequently, they extend to substantive alterations or even deletions. In the press of time, this may occur despite the best efforts by Committee staff to forestall such practices.

Another important legislative input that is not recorded is the personal contacts between committee members or their staffs and parties interested in affecting changes in legislation pending before a committee. Such contacts are seldom subject to public scrutiny, as they rarely come to light. The way this practice operates is for the representative of an "interest group" (e.g., the Administration, a "consumer advocate," or a trade association) to approach a senator, representative, or a key staff member who is known to be sympathetic to his general position. The potential congressional spokesman is then

asked to voice this position on specific amendments, which
would bring the pending bill more in line with the interest
group's vested interests -- whether industry or environmental.

For example, in the case of the Toxic Substances Bill, the
Department of Commerce and industry representatives sought out
Sen. Howard Baker (R.-Tenn.). Among other requests, he was
asked to oppose strongly the extensive premarket testing and
clearance requirements of Sen. Spong's Amendment. Later, in
the Subcommittee's final mark-up session, held on March 7,
1972, a compromise clause was adopted by majority vote that
required premarket screening of new chemicals only. This
compromise was a direct result of the intense behind-the-scenes
lobbying applied to Committee members and staff that occurred
after the Hearings were terminated. Similar efforts also were
being made by consumer advocates and by industrial interests
on this and other provisions of the bill. Such is the nature
of lobbying, which is hidden from public view, that opposing
interests often are unaware and thus unprepared or unable to
offer counterproposals. Thus, the members and their staff
often are besieged by advocates representing a wide spectrum
of economic and societal interests.

Another focus for special-interest-group pressures is the
full committee executive sessions, as distinguished from the
subcommittee sessions. Whereas the membership of a specialized
subcommittee usually is quite liberal or quite conservative,
the membership of the full committee often reflects the
opposite slant. For example, the Toxic Substances bill was
handled by a Senate subcommittee with a very liberal complexion.
Since the subcommittee members were generally unreceptive to
attempts to weaken the regulatory provisions of the bill,
chemical industry and Commerce Department representatives
concentrated their efforts on the more friendly members of the
full Senate Commerce Committee. Thus, at the first executive
session of the full Committee, on April 1, 1972, it was
apparent that Administration and chemical industry spokesmen
had succeeded in persuading several Senators to offer amendments
that would make the bill conform more closely to the original
version offered by the Administration. The Commerce Committee's
Chairman, Sen. Magnuson, concluded that the normally
expeditious approval of the Subcommittee's work might drag on
indefinitely and produce a weakened bill. Therefore, he
adjourned the Executive Session after ordering the Committee
staff to prepare compromise amendments for consideration by
the members. Thus at later mark-up sessions of the Committee
on April 17, 18, and 25, 1972, efforts to weaken the bill were
forestalled.

After much debate, the Senate Commerce Committee on May 5, 1972, unanimously reported the Toxic Substances Control Act of 1972 (56).

Senate consideration followed on May 30, 1972, with Sen. Spong serving as the floor manager; then he remarked that the bill's passage would represent

"...a major advance in this nation's efforts to halt the degradation of our environment.

Pesticides, drugs and food additives are all controlled at the point of manufacture.... Yet, this control technique currently applies only to a small portion of the total number of potentially toxic substances. Moreover, existing controls do not deal with all the uses of a substance which may produce toxic effects.

Without premarket testing and review, the regulation of chemical substances would in many cases deal with a problem only after that problem is manifest. We will not tolerate those conditions to exist with respect to pesticides, drugs and food additives. Neither should we tolerate similar threats with respect to other toxic substances." (57)

At this time, Sen. Baker reiterated his concern

"...over the dangers made possible by the broad language [of parts of the bill] which might have the result of depriving the public of the benefit of many new chemical products and of stifling development, particularly on the part of small chemical companies, of new products which may pose no hazard to health or the environment." (57)

Sen. Baker emphasized that he spoke

"...not in strenuous opposition to the purposes of the bill [for he had voted in favor of it being reported by the Committee, but rather] to emphasize that we are entering into a very delicate area of balancing the equities between environmental protection and the preservation of future technology." (57)

In recognition of his concern, Sen. Baker offered two amendments, which were rejected. The first required the EPA Administrator to issue regulations designating those chemical substances which were to be tested, because he specifically felt those might pose an unreasonable threat to human health or the environment. This amendment was rejected by a rollcall

vote of 29 to 43, with 24 Republicans and 5 Democrats voting
for its adoption (57).

Sen. Baker's second rejected amendment would have required
the EPA Administrator to complete a manufacturer's test data
within 90 days. The Committee's bill allowed a 90-day delay
in certain cases.

House Action   In the House, action was not initiated until
after S. 1478 was reported to the Senate (on May 5) by the
Senate Commerce Committee (56). The House Interstate and
Foreign Commerce Committee also has a Subcommittee on the
Environment, and an outsider logically would have expected
this bill to be referred there. However, since the
Administration's bill (H.R. 5276) was written as an Amendment
to the Hazardous Substances Act, by legislative precedent, it
was referred to the Subcommittee on Commerce and Finance.
This Subcommittee, chaired by Rep. John E. Moss (D.-Cal.) deals
with subjects of greater diversity than almost any other
committee in the Congress. Just prior to its consideration of
the Toxic Substances Act, the Subcommittee completed a study
of the securities industry and completed action on flammable
products, on automobile bumper reparability standards, and
on consumer product safety legislation.

In early 1971, both the House Committee and Subcommittee
were faced with a particularly full calendar. In fact, it
took the direct intervention of the EPA Administrator with
both Rep. Harley Staggers and Rep. Moss to arrange for the
Toxic Substances legislation to be squeezed into their Hearing
schedule. In five hours, over a period of two days, the Moss
Subcommittee received testimony from eight witnesses, covering
all pending versions of the bill. While this might seem to be
undue haste, it should be noted that the Senate had completed
action. Thus, the House committee could rely on the Senate's
extensive Hearing record rather than duplicate everything, for
the major policy issues had been clearly delineated already.

The major additions to the House Hearings that might have
received more exhaustive consideration were the alternative
bills, for example, H.R. 10840, introduced by Rep.
Frelinghuysen. This bill contained several new concepts, such
as the establishment of a national center for gathering
information on all new chemical substances, as well as a
clause specifying that the standards for long-range toxicity
testing set up under the bill would become the standards for
all federal agencies. However, when the House Hearings were
scheduled on very short notice, Rep. Frelinghuysen's staff
assistant principally responsible for the drafting of H.R.
10840, Dr. Hanno Weisbrod, was unavailable. Thus, aside from

some general remarks of support by Rep. John S. Monagan (D.-
Conn.), detailed supporting testimony on H.R. 10840 was not
presented to the House Subcommittee. This left only the
Administration's bill H.R. 5276 (and S. 1478 as passed by the
Senate) under active consideration by the Moss Subcommittee.

The crucial point at issue was what kind of procedure should
be used to prevent a hazardous substance from reaching the
market. At the hearings, the CEQ Chairman (Russel Train) argued
for the Administration's bill, H.R. 5276, as

"...an efficient mechanism for the comprehensive and systematic
control of hazardous substances in our environment. Under the
proposed bill, the administrator of the Environmental
Protection Agency would be empowered to restrict the use or
distribution, including a total prohibition, of a chemical
substance, if such restrictions were necessary to protect
health and the environment. In proposing such restrictions,
the administrator would be required to consider not only the
adverse effects of the substance but also the benefits derived
from the use of the substance as compared with the risks; the
normal circumstances of the use; the degree to which the
release of the substance or its byproducts to the general
environment is controlled, and the magnitude of the exposure
of humans and the environment to the substance or its
byproducts." (58)

Under the Administration's proposal manufacturers would be
required to test new chemicals in accordance with EPA
regulations and the tests would have to be completed before
marketing is initiated. However, the test results would not
have to be submitted to EPA unless specifically requested by
the Agency. The only mandatory reporting requirement was
limited to periodic surveys as to what substances were entering
the marketplace and in what quantities. In this regard, a
spokeswoman for Ralph Nader's Public Interest Research Group,
Judy Jackson, argued that neither bill provided an adequate
regulatory framework:

"The administration bill (H.R. 5276) is totally inadequate:

-  It does not provide for any preclearance or premarket
screening mechanism for toxic substances.

-  It provides for little or no public participation in
regulation or enforcement.

By failing to provide for administrative power to deal with
imminent hazards, it robs the [EPA] of one of its most important
means of protecting the public health and environment.

The Frelinghuysen bill (H.R. 10840) does contain some
provisions which the subcommittee should include:

- Recognition of a governmental role in testing.

- Creation of a national registry of chemical substances.

- Placing on the manufacturer the burden of proof that exported
chemicals will not endanger human health or the environment in
the United States." (58)

Meanwhile, then CEQ Chairman Train and EPA Deputy
Administrator Robert Fri reiterated that any more stringent
reporting procedures, involving premarket clearance, would
bog down EPA in a bureaucratic quagmire.
Concurrently, the Manufacturing Chemists Association, while
supporting H.R. 5276, was urging caution:

"It is important to recognize that the chemical industry
is presently subject to broad and sometimes overlapping federal
legislation. In view of the regulatory statutes already in
force, there is no need for sweeping new legislation. Existing
authorities may not give the Federal Government adequate
control over uses of chemical substances in all instances,
however. The EPA administrator should have specific authority
to deal with existing chemical substances that reasonably
could be considered a threat to health or the environment and
to require some premarket testing." (158)

In turn, the Subcommittee was faced with the task of
reporting a bill responsive to the problem. Chairman Rep. Moss
suggested a middle ground of requiring manufacturers to notify
EPA of new products ready for marketing. The EPA also would
develop a list of substances considered inherently dangerous
and therefore subject to premarket testing. In the same vein,
Rep. Eckhardt (D.-Tex.) suggested that prior restraint and
premarket screening be limited to cases where, first, the
Administrator has probably reason to believe that the substance
would be released in a dangerous degree into the environment;
and, second, the magnitude of such exposure is dangerous to
humans or to the environment. Thus, the burden of proof would
be placed on the EPA to show that a chemical substance was
dangerous, whereas the proponents of a strict premarket
clearance wanted the manufacturer to prove that a substance
was safe. This represented a major difference from the
Senate-passed version which would have required premarket
screening of all test results, except for substances which
a priori were considered safe. In turn, EPA Deputy Administrator

Fri objected to this procedure as creating "a fairly
substantial bureaucratic paper-processing machine that would
divert resources from the writing of test protocols and
research." (59)

From this and previous testimony, it was clear that the
Administration had no desire to be placed in the position of
reviewing all test results. However, the door had been left
open for Rep. Eckhardt's proposal that EPA establish a list of
classes of substances which were considered inherently
hazardous and thus subject to EPA's screening of any new
marketing applications. On the other hand, the Senate bill
specified that all existing and new chemical substances would
have to be screened; then, after EPA had collected sufficient
test data, it would all be evaluated and a list of substances
or classes of substances established where their manufacture,
processing, distribution, use, or disposal might pose
unreasonable threats to human health or the environment. In
other words, the lists would have to be established, on the
basis of test data, before certain categories could be
exempted from the screening procedure. Thus, a manufacturer
would have had to submit test data prior to putting an
existing substance to use in a new and untested application.

As in the Senate, the scope of the premarket screening
provision became the crucial issue in House Committee
deliberations. The House Commerce Committee thus adopted the
minimum premarket screening provision acceptable to EPA --
that EPA would propose test regulations only for those
substances, or classes of substances, which it considered
"likely to pose" substantial danger to health and environment.
Premarket screening was required only for substances falling
into those categories. However, even this relatively weak
requirement for premarket screening was still viewed as
anathema by some sectors of the chemical industry. Particularly
active lobbying was observable on the House side by
representatives from DuPont, Union Carbide, Kodak, and Dow
Chemical. In varying degree, all had opposed the concept of
premarket clearance or screening, and all felt that the
Senate version was excessive. However, after the House Committee
version was reported (60), only Kodak and Dow Chemical continued
to work behind the scenes for delay and defeat of the House
bill.

On the other hand, the official Administration position
was initially confused. Even though only the CEQ and the EPA
had been asked to testify on the legislation, it was well
known on Capitol Hill that the Department of Commerce was
opposed to any bill other than the Administration's original

version. It was not until the closing moments of the 92nd
Congress, in October, 1972, that the Administration uniformly
lined up behind the House version.

The procedural circumstances under which the House bill
was called up for consideration created a particularly
favorable situation for opponents of a stronger bill. The
Toxic Substances Control Act came up on the Suspension
Calendar; thus, a two-thirds majority of those present and
voting was required to bring the bill up for House
consideration. The opportunity thus existed for the
Administration to persuade the Republican minority to take
a hard-line stand. This forced Rep. Staggers to promise on
the House floor (as Chairman of the Legislative Committee)
that the passed House bill would not be subject to compromise
in any Senate-House conference to reconcile differences (61).
When the bill passed the House (240 to 61), the Senate was
faced with a take-it-or-leave-it situation.

On the following day, Sen. Moss, acting as the Senate floor
manager, chose not to accept the House version in toto.
Instead, he offered a motion to concur in the House version
with amendments dealing with new substances for which dangers
are unknown and thus did not fall into one of the EPA-
established classifications of substances that "are likely
to pose" danger (62). Sen. Moss then proposed to close this
loophole by also requiring premarket notification and
screening of test results for this class of substances (62).

A second major change suggested by Sen. Moss provided that
the EPA Administrator have the flexibility to choose from the
various laws as his disposal, including the Toxic Substances
Control Act, to regulate or eliminate a hazard to the
environment (62). This significant change of the House-passed
bill would have specifically prohibited the EPA Administrator
from taking action under the authority of this legislation
if any other statutes covered the situation. Thus, as Sen.
Moss pointed out, under the House measure the EPA might be
forced to act under the authorities of the Clean Air Act or
the Federal Water Pollution Control Act to control a toxic
substance; whereas under the Senate amendment the EPA
Administrator had the authority of the Toxic Substances Act
to regulate and to prohibit the substance from entering air
or water in the first instance.

Unable to resolve the differences between the Senate- and
House-passed measures, the legislation died in the closing
days of the 92nd Congress for lack of time to convene a
House-Senate conference.

The 93rd Congress, 1973-1974  In the 93rd Congress action was quickly initiated when, on January 18, 1973, Senators Magnuson, Hart, and Tunney introduced S. 426, the Toxic Substances Control Act of 1973. Upon receipt of the Administration's proposal, it was introduced as S. 888, on February 15, 1973, by Sen. Robert Byrd for Sen. Magnuson.

Meanwhile in the House, two bills immediately were taken up by Rep. Moss's Subcommittee on Commerce and Finance: H.R. 5087, the Administration's proposal, and H.R. 5356, introduced by Rep. Moss and others, which largely tracked the previously passed House measure.

Thus, the stage was immediately set for a renewed congressional effort, which produced early returns.

Renewed Senate Action  In the Senate, the principal difference between the two bills (S. 426 and S. 888) was primarily in the manner in which they dealt with new chemical substances prior to commercial production. In S. 426, all new chemicals except those which EPA excluded on the basis of no unreasonable effects would have to be tested in accordance with EPA procedures and the test results submitted to EPA 90 days in advance of their commercial production. Thus, the bills' emphasis was on those new substances posing an unreasonable threat to human health or the environment. On the other hand, S. 883 would require testing, but with no regulatory review prior to commercial production.

A significant turn of events was the introduction of three amendments to S. 426. The first, by Senators Magnuson and Hart, required the FDA to develop procedures for screening food for the presence of dangerous materials. The second, by Sen. Tunney, required EPA to submit to the Congress all proposed congressional testimony, budget requests, and legislative initiatives simultaneous with their submission to the President. Under existing Executive Branch procedures, this material requires approval of the Office of Management and Budget. The third, by Sen. Hart, was intended to insure that indemnities are not paid by the Federal Government as a result of EPA actions taken under this legislation and also would repeal the indemnity provisions of FIFRA.

The latter two amendments were included in the bill reported by Sen. Magnuson's Committee on Commerce on June 26, 1973 (63). The first proposed amendment was to be treated as a separate legislative matter. In summary, the Committee reported bill provides (63)

- that new chemical substances which may pose unreasonable threats to human health of the environment be tested by their

manufacturer prior to commercial production and that the test
results should be reviewed by the EPA prior to such production
and that notification be given to EPA prior to the commercial
production of all other new chemicals;

- that EPA will specify those existing chemical substances
which there is reason to believe may present unreasonable
threats to human health or the environment and that these
substances will be tested as well;

- a variety of tools to regulate toxic substances including
the authority to restrict use or distribution, to seize
chemical substances in violation of certain requirements of
the Act, and to take immediate action against the chemical
substances creating imminent hazards;

- that manufacturers and processers of chemical substances be
required to maintain certain records and reports to enable the
Administrator to properly determine hazards; and

- that citizens be allowed to bring suits to enjoin certain
violations of the Act and to require the performance of
mandatory duties of the Administrator of EPA.

Commenting on the pressing need for a systematic way to
deal with chemicals yet to be developed the Committee report
states that

"While it is obviously difficult to judge what threats may lie
in store for us in the future, past experiences with certain
chemical substances does illustrate the need for properly
assessing the risks of new chemical substances and regulating
them prior to their introduction. For example, it is only in
recent years that the hazards of mercury have been fully
documented. If this knowledge had been known at the time many
mercury containing products were introduced and had a regulatory
mechanism existed, there is little doubt that regulatory
officials would have curbed their use. The same could be said
for polychlorinated biphenyls, which were responsible for the
recent contamination of chickens in the southeastern United
States. Cadmium, asbestos, and other materials must also be
regulated. Not only must legislation to control toxic substances
be designed to gain knowledge about known chemicals but it must
also provide a mechanism for dealing with future 'mercuries'
before commercial production." (63)

In response to an expressed concern that every new product
would have to be subjected to expensive testing for safety,
the Committee's position was:

"Regarding existing chemicals, EPA could only require testing
of existing chemicals if there is reason to believe unreasonable
hazards may exist. EPA would first have to establish by
regulation a list of those chemicals about which there is
reason to be concerned. Thus, a very large number of the
existing chemicals and possibly most, would escape testing
altogether.

   With respect to new chemicals, it would seem important that
the Environmental Protection Agency have a mechanism of
gathering information of new chemical substances the
introduction of which could not have been predicted. It would
obviously be desirable to create a mechanism whereby all new
chemicals are not treated with the same broad brush so that
chemicals which may prove to be innocuous are not subjected to
extensive, costly testing." (63)

   Finally, after considerable effort on the part of the
Committee and its staff, the Toxic Substances Act of 1973
passed the Senate on July 18, 1973, by a voice vote (64). An
amendment was offered by Sen. Randolph as Chairman of the
Committee on Public Works and accepted without debate by Sen.
Tunney, the floor manager.

   Sen. Randolph's amendment was designed to preserve the
authority of the Clean Air Act and the Federal Water Pollution
Control Act for controlling substances in industrial effluents
or emissions (64). Thus, use of the Toxic Substances Control
Act for this purpose is restricted to situations where control
is more effective than under the two media-based statutes.
However, this would not preclude regulation under all three
statutes where needed. It is of interest to note that a
decision of the EPA Administrator for control of industrial
effluents under either the Clean Air Act or the Federal Water
Pollution Control Act would not be subject to judicial review;
however, use of the Toxic Substances Control Act for control
of a substance would be reviewable (64).

Renewed House Action   Not to be overshadowed by the Senate
Commerce Committee, Rep. Moss's Subcommittee on Commerce and
Finance had been hard at work and, after a remarkably short
two-day executive session, reported their marked-up bill to
full Committee on June 22, 1973. In turn, the House Committee
on Interstate and Foreign Commerce, on June 29, 1973, reported
H.R. 5356, a different version of the Toxic Substances Control
Act of 1973 (65). Supporting the need for the legislation the
House Committee emphasized the necessity for comprehensive and
systematic information on chemical substances and enunciated
two significant and essential principals when evaluating the
health effects of chemical substances:

"First, no threshold should be stipulated below which
exposure is harmless, absent evidence to the contrary [sic].
Human response is directly related to the concentration level
of a toxic material and the level of resistance of persons
exposed. For example, there may be no safe level of exposure
to carcinogens or it may be indeterminably low.

Second, the concept of total body burden should be the
significant indicator of exposure, not the burden acquired
from one or another part of the environment or from one or
another toxic material. Synergistic effects among two or more
substances, by which the combined effect is greater than the
sum of the separate effects, should be considered." (65)

When called up in the House on July 19, 1973, the day after
the Senate passed its bill, the House measure passed, 324 to
73.

In summary, the House version would (66)

- permit the Administrator of the Environmental Protection
Agency to require manufacturers, processors, or importers to
test chemical substances in accordance with prescribed test
protocols;

- direct the EPA Administrator to establish a list of chemical
substances which he finds are likely to pose substantial
danger to health or environment;

- establish a system for premarket screening of test data in
advance of the manufacture or distribution of a chemical
substance which has been listed as substantially dangerous;

- authorize the EPA Administrator to adopt rules which prohibit
or limit the manufacture, distribution or use of a chemical
substance or require labeling of such substance upon a finding
that these rules are necessary to protect against unreasonable
risk to health or environment;

- permit the EPA Administrator to apply to a U.S. district
court to protect the public from an imminently hazardous
chemical substance;

- permit the EPA Administrator to require manufacturers,
importers, or processors to submit reports giving the chemical
identity, molecular structure, categories of use, estimates of
amounts, and descriptions of byproducts of chemical substances;

- establish a Chemical Substances Board to advise the EPA
Administrator in his exercise of authority under the bill;
and

- permit administrative inspections and seizures of chemical substances or products containing them which have been manufactured or distributed in violation of the requirements of the bill or of agency rules.

Enforcement of the bill could be obtained through the court-injunctive process or through imposition of criminal and civil penalties.

Prior to House passage of H.R. 5356, the EPA expressed concern regarding several provisions. For example, the criteria for the EPA Administrator's action is that the substance "poses an unreasonable threat to health or the environment"; thus, there exists an uncertainty regarding the degree of threat posed which requires a weighing of the benefits and costs of any regulatory action. Because of the difficulties inherent in performing this assessment EPA Acting Administrator Fri strongly favored the criterion "protect health and the environment." (65)

A second EPA concern was the relationship of the full Committee's version of H.R. 5356 to other statutes, since, as drafted, the authorities of the Toxic Substances Act would be subordinate to EPA's other authorities. For the EPA Administrator would be prevented from exercising his authority under this Act to screen substances, to restrict the manufacture, use or distribution of substances found to pose an unreasonable risk to health of the environment, or to take action against an imminent hazard, if the risk posed by a given substance could be prevented or reduced "to a sufficient extent" by actions taken under any other federal law, including those presently administered by the EPA (65).

Thus a major thrust of the Act would be to restrict the EPA Administrator's ability to control toxic substances before they became environmental or public health problems. As pointed out by the EPA (65), if it can be shown that a substance will pose an unreasonable risk to health or the environment as it is used, manufactured, or distributed, it may be far more appropriate to control that substance early in its life and use rather than at the effluent stage or some later phase of its use. It was emphasized that the EPA Administrator, in his approach to a given problem, must have the flexibility to select that regulatory mechanism or combination of mechanisms that would provide for the most complete and effective protection of health and the environment with a minimum of adverse economic impact.

Nevertheless, the full House Committee's position prevailed over that of the Subcommittee's Chairman, Rep. Moss, and Representatives John B. Dingell (D.-Mich.), Bob Eckhardt (D.-Tex.), Bertram L. Podell (D.-N.Y.), and Henry Helstoski

(D.-N.J.), who filed dissenting views (65). These Committee
members argued that the full Committee's version would
effectively limit the EPA Administrator's use of the regulatory
authorities of the Toxic Substances Act to those situations
where no other federal law is applicable. It was pointed out
that

"The Federal Water Pollution Control Act, and the Clean Air
Act as amended, focus on toxic pollutants at the point which
they are released to the environment, either in the form of
discharges to water or emissions to the air, and allow the
Administrator to control the use or distribution of a substance
before it reaches the stage where an effluent or emission of
that substance could occur." (65)

Nevertheless, the full Committee's sentiments prevailed.
Thus, if this language prevails, the question of the EPA
Administrator's jurisdiction over a problem could be subject
to repeated challenges and litigation. In other words, any
rule proposed under the Toxic Substances Control Act would
have to be able to withstand the challenge that no other
authority or combination of authorities could prevent or
reduce to a "sufficient extent" the risk to health or the
environment associated with that chemical substance (65).

## Key Policy Issues
Besides the issue of federal controls, there are several
policy issues that deserve special mention: premarket testing;
confidentiality of information; citizens suits; quotas; and
standardization.

Premarket Testing  The crucial issue dividing government and
industry spokesmen from the public-interest and labor
witnesses is premarket clearance. As mentioned, in 1972 the
Administration vigorously opposed the concept on the grounds
that it would impose a "very substantial administrative burden
upon the government," which would weaken EPA's ability to deal
with other pressing matters of environmental concern (58).
Industry spokesmen charged that a compulsory registration
system for new chemicals would be a "major disaster for the
chemical industry and the future of chemical technology." (58)
The Manufacturing Chemists Association (MCA) argued (67)
that the costs and delays in a premarket clearance system
would be prohibitive. It was felt (67) that compulsory
laboratory animal experiments to test for chronic toxicity,
including carcinogenity, on every chemical substance could

delay production or marketing at least three to four years at
a cost "conservatively estimated, of about $200,000." The MCA
feared that (67) "all conceivable tests" would be frozen into
a stereotyped list that "would be applied to all candidate
chemicals," regardless of class or use by an EPA administrator
who wanted to play it super-safe under the mandatory
requirements of Sen. Spong's Amendment. In addition, industry
representatives claimed (67) that a premarket clearance system
would drive small chemical companies out of business. On the
other hand, Union representatives argued that

"All new technology, particularly chemical substances, must
be presumed guilty of potential environmental degradation and
adverse health effects until proven safe." (69)

In turn, a public-interest spokesman cited the history of
the problems with DDT, 2,4,5-T, NTA and phosphates as another
argument for preclearance, stating that

". . . once the technology is turned on and incorporated into
the Nation's commercial fabric, turning it off calls for
economic disruption, political strife, and governmental
vacillation." (70)

It was emphasized (70) that a preclearance procedure was
necessary to remind manufacturers that should environmental
concerns be preempted by commercial fait accompli, nevertheless,
they could be undone. The result could be the requirement for
major conversion, with widespread disruption. This sort of
situation arose following the detergent manufacturers'
acclerated introduction of NTA when threatened by an EPA
crackdown on phosphates as sources of river and lake pollution.
The economic disruption occurred when these plans were halted
overnight.

With regard to the House version of H.R. 5356, the EPA
commented on the issue of how to require sufficient submission
of information to the agency to render decisions, without, at
the same time, imposing unnecessary burdens on both the Agency
and the industries involved. On the other hand, the EPA opposed
any limited premarket screening provision as inefficient or
ineffective (65). Such a limited provision was viewed in 1973
as placing the nearly impossible burden of determining what
new substances are likely to be introduced into commerce in
the future, assessing their potential danger, and, by rule,
placing them on this list so that the "hazard" may be reviewed
prior to commercial production of the substance (65).

On June 18, 1973, the EPA wrote the Senate Commerce
Committee in recognition

". . . that some notification at an early date of test results
and certain other information would contribute to an orderly
regulatory process."

Accordingly, the EPA supported provisions which would
permit the government to obtain some important information at
an early stage (65). Such provisions were viewed as affording
an opportunity to make prior, but preliminary, judgments as to
any dangers which might be presented by the proposed
introduction of chemical substances into the environment (65).
  In the event that a substance is recognized as posing an
imminent hazard, the EPA supported provision for seeking
injunctive relief during this notification period as well as
retention of the other remedies already afforded by S. 888 (65).
  Meanwhile, the position of the Department of Commerce, on
April 9, 1973, was to oppose premarket clearance or screening
by EPA of new substances. Their view was that

". . . such premarket screening is unnecessary and would
represent a serious administrative burden both to EPA and to
the industries involved. It would result in delays not only
in the introduction of a new chemical substance into the
market, but even upon its manufacture preparatory to such
introduction." (65)

It also was the view of the Commerce Department that such
delays would be automatic, and would be incurred after the
chemical had satisfactorily passed all tests that the
Administration had prescribed (65). Further, during any such
period of delay, manufacturers would be unable to make
critical business judgments as to resource allocation, raw
material purchasing, and marketing strategy (65).
  In defense of the small entrepreneur, Rep. James M. Collins
(R.-Tex.) expressed concern for the capability to perform the
required premarket testing, stating:

"Many chemicals and compounds have been developed on a
shoe string by determined individuals working alone. In almost
every instance in recent times the process, once proven, has
been immediately bought out by established chemical producers...
How many of the great names of the past and the myriad unknowns
who have made truly great contributions to mankind through
their discoveries and developments in chemicals would have

bothered to fire up the bunsen burner? The list of drop-outs
would have been long and the loser would have been society."
(65)

Thus, the issue is more than just another intervention of
government into the supposed free market; it also overlaps
into the issue of small vs big business.

Confidentiality Of Information  Closely tied to the issue of
confidentiality of information and test data is the issue of
biases and constraints in their interpretation by both
government and industry. Repeatedly in congressional testimony
and in various scientific publications, Dr. Samuel S. Epstein
has argued strongly that any direct connection between the
manufacturer and the testing facilities be severed (71, 72,
73). These views were unequivocally endorsed at the 1972
Senate hearings by consumer advocate Harrison Welford from the
Center for the Study of Responsive Law (74). Under both Sen.
Spong's and the Administration's bills the producer of chemical
substances, whether in his own lab or by contract with an
independent laboratory, would have to arrange for the
necessary testing to satisfy EPA's safety criteria. As Welford
pointed out, the incentive and opportunities for abuse under
such an arrangement are obvious:

"The commercial laboratory, anxious to retain its industry
contracts, has the incentive to choose a testing methodology
which will reveal the least negative characteristics of the
chemical. The chemical company has the incentive  to avoid a
laboratory which is embarrassingly thorough in its tests." (74)

Moreover, if the test results are provided to the manufacturer
alone, he still retains control over how much of the test data
would be submitted to EPA.

In order to avoid such situations, several witnesses
suggested that EPA be authorized to inspect and certify
laboratories to do testing under their proposed protocols.
In order to "sanitize" the research money (as one witness
called it), it also was proposed that the EPA Administrator
issue the research contracts and the laboratories report their
results back directly to EPA. This procedure was embodied in
Rep. Frelinghuysen's bill (H.R. 10840), which also contained
a provision designed to allay the fear of manufacturers that
such governmental control of the research and evaluation
process would lead to intolerable bureaucratic delays.

The issue of delays is quite valid; nevertheless, the
Department of Commerce cautioned that to the extent that such
delays become substantial, there could be an incentive for
domestic manufacturers to locate their facilities for foreign
markets abroad, where screening provisions would not apply.
This, however, also raises the issue as to whether American
companies locating abroad should be required to conform to
"standards of good practice" at home.

A second possible major safeguard against bias,
falsification, or distortion of data by all parties involved
is public access to the data. Manufacturers generally have
opposed such policies strenuously on the grounds that they
compromise trade secrets. In our so-called free-enterprise
system this has been a powerful argument.

Federal regulatory agencies, in general, have supported
this position both for the sake of the principle per se, and
because it meant that public scrutiny of their activities also
was reduced. However, this latter situation has been partially
reversed upon enactment of the 1967 Federal Freedom of
Information Act.

On the other hand, the arguments in support of
confidentiality are engrained in our social policies and
ethics themselves. These were iterated by the Department of
Commerce:

"Conducting the tests that would be required under . . .
this legislation would be a lengthy and expensive process,
which would constitute a major part of the research and
development costs of a new product.

In our view, it would be inherently unfair and
anticompetitive for the proposed legislation to permit a
subsequent manufacturer or processor unilaterally to decide to
rely upon the results of tests previously performed by
another, or to authorize the Administrator to require this
result by allowing exemptions of subsequent manufacturers or
processors from the otherwise applicable testing requirements.
Such an approach would fail to recognize the heavy investment
represented by the performance of the required tests, and
the resulting financial and proprietary interest of the
performer in the data and results. It would operate as a
substantial disincentive to innovation and the development of
new products.

We strongly urge the Committee to recognize these
considerations . . . This would allow manufacturers or
processors voluntarily to undertake to pool their resources to

comply with testing requirements, upon such financial terms
and conditions of confidentiality as they may agree upon." (65)

Nevertheless, the Congress can be expected to permit some
degree of disclosure in the "public interest." The House
Committee restricted this to circumstances related to the
EPA's administration and enforcement activities (65). The
Senate measure reflects that body's more sympathetic response
to the "new consumerism," for the EPA Administrator is
authorized to disclose any information to the public in order
to protect their health, after notice and opportunity for
comment in writing or for discussion in closed session within
fifteen days by the manufacturer of any product to which the
information appertains (if the delay resulting from such notice
and opportunity for comment would not be detrimental to the
public health) (63).

Another aspect of public disclosure, however, is to give
citizens the power to bring civil suits against individuals
or government officials for violation of the law. In this
regard, witnesses from environmental groups and public interest
law firms strongly supported this section of Sen. Spong's
Amendment on Citizen Civil Action. Industry and government
witnesses, on the other hand, were notably unenthusiastic
about this provision. The reasons for these opposing sentiments
are not hard to understand. Environmentalists are using the
power given to them under recently passed environmental
legislation. They have stopped numerous major construction
projects and have obtained injunctions against some major
industrial polluters.

Citizen Suits  A major issue of continuing debate is provision
for access to the courts both for public officials and for
ordinary citizens on important environmental issues.
Alternatively, there is concern that the courts and
administrative agencies not be unduly burdened by citizen
suits on environmental matters.

Therefore, the actions of the Congress, in recent years, on
several major environmental statutes has restricted court
actions by citizens to enforcement of the law and to compelling
the EPA Administrator to perform actions mandated by law. Such
provisions authorizing citizen civil actions are found in the
Clean Air Amendments of 1970, the Federal Water Pollution
Control Act of 1972, and the Noise Control Act of 1972. In
addition, the Consumer Product Safety Act, enacted during the
92nd Congress, includes even more far-reaching provisions
authorizing citizen suits to bring to the attention of the

agency and the courts' failures to comply with the law or to perform a duty imposed by the Congress.

Endorsing inclusion of similar provisions in the Toxic Substances Control Act, then CEQ Chairman Train stated that

"With respect to citizen suits, our general position is that we would support a citizen clause to enforce mandatory duties of EPA. We would also approve of a citizen suit clause to enforce violations of regulations on use and distribution where such suits are brought directly against manufacturers or processors." (65)

With the Administration's support, Rep. Moss's Subcommittee included such authority in their bill. However, the full Committee deleted this provision, in opposition to Representatives Moss, Dingell, Eckhardt, Powell and Helstoski (65). Nevertheless, the Senate bill contained such a provision. Thus this issue remained for final resolution at the House-Senate Conference.

Opponents of this type of provision argue that such citizen actions impede the EPA's effectiveness and create delays; however, the history of the citizen action provision of the Clean Air Amendments of 1970 refutes such a contention. In the first three and one-half years following its inception, only 12 lawsuits were brought; 11 were against the EPA Administrator. In most cases the plaintiff prevailed, and the court directed a modification of EPA procedures or decisions to comply with the Act's requirements. At no time has the EPA suggested that the subject provision is anything other than helpful (65).

Quotas  A new twist was added to H.R. 5356 by the Committee, requiring the EPA Administrator to promulgate criteria for assigning quotas in any regulation limiting the amount of a substance which may be manufactured, imported, or distributed. The criteria for assigning such quotas were to take into account such factors as effects on competition, the respective market shares and production capacity of applicants, any emergency conditions and the effects on technological innovation. The EPA commented that such a requirement would be extremely unwise and would make the regulatory process vastly more cumbersome to administer. If the authority were retained, however, the EPA urged that it, at the very least, be made discretionary so that it could be employed only where such drastic and complex action might be warranted (65).

The Department of Commerce was even more disturbed about the proposed rule-making that would empower EPA with authority

" . . . for assigning production . . . or distribution quotas
to persons who wish to manufacture . . . or distribute the
substance. [This authority was viewed as creating] a serious
anticompetitive effect upon the industry, and would distort
the already complicated business judgments which must be made
before chemical substances may be manufactured or distributed.
It would establish in EPA an unprecedented, broad economic
regulatory authority over an entire major industry." (65)

Their opinion was that the other provisions of the H.R. 5356
provided adequate authority to prevent human or environmental
exposure to regulated substances directly, by restricting
their use or distribution (65).

Standardization  Another important issue is that of
standardization. Throughout the legislative history of the
Toxic Substances Control Act, chemicals now controlled by
existing statutes have been exempt from coverage. Unless a
substance poses an unreasonable threat to human health or the
environment, this exemption extends to pesticides, foods, drugs,
devices, or cosmetics subject to the Federal Food, Drug and
Cosmetic Act, the Federal Meat Inspection Act, the Egg Product
Inspection Act or the Poultry Product Inspection Act, to any
nuclear material defined in the Atomic Energy Act, to the
transportation of hazardous materials insofar as they are
regulated by the Department of Transportation, to intermediate
chemical substances unless the Administrator finds that the
Clean Air Act or the Federal Water Pollution Control Act can
not sufficiently regulate these substances, or any other
chemical substance that can be more effectively regulated by
the Clean Air Act of the Federal Water Pollution Control Act.
Laboratory reagents, which are generally small amounts of
chemicals used for research purposes, would not be covered
unless a reagent poses an unreasonable threat to human health
of the environment (63).
   Tobacco and tobacco products would likewise be exempted as
would the extraction of any mineral deposit governed by the
mining or mineral leasing laws of the United States, unless
that extraction poses an unreasonable threat to human health
and the environment which could not be effectively regulated
under other provisions of law (63).
   Thus, as in the past, each of the various federal agencies
can continue to set its own standards for testing and for
determining safety tolerance levels. Although interagency task
forces periodically have been assembled (there was one
functioning in late 1971) to recommend standardization, their

major recommendations have not been implemented. Thus, it
appears that such standardization will be brought about only
through legislative fiat.

Such an approval was written into Rep. Frelinghuysen's bill
(H.R. 10840); it provided that

". . . within two years of enactment the standards for test
protocols issued by the Administrator . . . shall be considered
minimum standards for all federal departments charged with
testing substances for human health or environmental impact."

It also would have required the various federal departments
to consult with EPA regarding actions to bring federal testing
regulations into conformity.

Rather, the House bill (H.R. 5356) required EPA to consult
with HEW when developing test protocols and premarket screening
of new chemical substances. A potentially significant step
toward eventual federal minimum standards is the Chemical
Substances Board contained in both House- and Senate-passed
bills. The 12-member Board is to be established by EPA. As is
the usual practice in the establishment of such boards, the
National Academy of Sciences (NAS) is to submit a list of
nominees for appointment. Thus, the board members would be
scientists drawn from the fields of chemistry, toxicology,
ecology, and public health. Far more important, however, is
the requirement for representation on the Board from broad
interest groups, as well as from the special scientific
disciplines. The NAS has been clearly unresponsive to such
requirements in the past and despite repeated claims of
internal reforms no mechanisms have yet been developed for
participation of duly qualified scientific and legal
representatives of public-interest and consumer-interest
movements in NAS leadership and committee activities; these
considerations are emphasized by the fact that NAS committees
have been exempt from the requirements of the Freedom of
Information Act.

## Conclusion

It is obvious that securing legislation to effectively restrict
or prevent toxic substances from entering the environment is a
complicated and arduous task. The combination of an extremely
complex body of scientific knowledge and an equally complex
Congressional procedure presents formidable obstacles to
obtaining responsive statutory authorities. On the other hand,
the continued introduction of toxic substances into the

environment makes it imperative that such legislation be
enacted with all due haste.

Existing legal authorities are inadequate to deal with toxic
substances that are pervasive or mobile in the environment.
Thus, toxic substances must be dealt with on a systematic and
comprehensive basis, rather than as contaminants in air, in
water, or on the land. Although not applicable to many existing
Federal programs, the Toxic Substances Control Act represents
the first major comprehensive attempt to deal with certain
chemicals as environmental contaminants, rather than on the
basis of the media in which they are introduced into the
environment. This approach, which is now inherent to the AEC's
regulation of radioactive materials, has now been proposed for
extension to toxic substances. The effectiveness of such
control will only be assured when it also is exercised at the
time of manufacture, rather than consumption, as an imperative
for preassessment of potential adverse environmental effects of
possible toxic substances.

Acknowledgment   The authors express their deep appreciation to
Kevin P. Shea, editor of Environment magazine (Saint Louis, MO
53130), for his able assistance in gathering some case material
in this chapter.

References

1.  U.S. Department of Interior, Federal Water Pollution
Control Agency, March 1970.

2.  Council on Environmental Quality, "Toxic Substances,"
Washington, D.C., April 1971.

3.  Environmental Protection Agency, "Cost of Clean Water,"
Vol. II, March 1971, Washington, D.C.

4.  Ross, R. D., Ed., Air Pollution and Industry, Van Nostrand,
Reinhold, 1972, 489 pp.

5.  U.S. Environmental Protection Agency, Solid Waste
Management Office, "Ocean Disposal of Barge Delivered Liquid
and Solid Waste from U.S. Coastal Cities," Pub. SW-19c.

6.  Iliff, N., "Organic Compounds in the Environment," New
Scientist, Feb. 3, 1972, pp. 263-265.

7.  Davis, T.R.A. et al., "Water Quality Criteria Data Book,
vol. I, Organic Chemical Pollution of Fresh Water," Water
Pollution Control Research Series 18010 (Dec. 1970).

8.  Keith, L. H., "Chemical Characterization of Industrial
Effluent," presented before the Division of Water, Air and
Waste Chemistry, American Chemical Society, Boston, Mass.
(April 1972).

9.  Risebrough, Robert with Brodine, Virginia, "More Letters
in the Wind," Environment, 12:1 (1970).

10. Berglund, F., "Levels of Polychlorinated Biphenyls in Food
in Sweden," Environmental Health Perspectives, 1:67 (April
1972).

11. Stalling, D. and Mayer, F.L., "Toxicities of PCB's to
Fish and Environmental Residues," Environmental Health
Perspectives, 1:159 (April 1972).

12. Yobs, A. R., "Levels of Polychlorinated Biphenyls in
Adiopose Tissue of the General Population of the Nation,"
Environmental Health Perspectives, 1:79 (April 1972).

13. Interdepartmental Task Force on PCB, U.S. Department of
Commerce, National Technical Information Service, "PCB's and
the Environment," ITF-PCB-72-1 (May 1972).

14. Nisbet, I.C.T. and Sarofim, A.F., "Rates and Routes of Transport of PCB's in the Environment," Environmental Health Perspectives, 1:21 (April 1972).

15. Maugh, T.H. II, "DDT: An Unrecognized Source of PCB," Science, 180:578 (1973).

16. Kuratsume, T., et al., "Epidemiologic Study on Yusho, a Poisoning Caused by Ingestion of Rice Oil Contaminated with a Commercial Brand of Polychlorinated Biphenyls," Environmental Health Perspectives, 1:119 (April 1972).

17. Vos, J.G., Toxicology of PCB's for Mammals and for Birds," Environmental Health Perspectives, 1:105 (April 1972).

18. Shea, K.P., "The New Car Smell," Environment, 13:8 (1971).

19. Jaeger, R.J. and Rubin, R.J., "Plasticizers from Plastic Devices; Extraction of Metabolism and Accumulation by Biological Systems," Science, 170 (3956): 460-461 (1970).

20. Hites, R.A., "Phthalates in the Charles and Merrimac Rivers," Environmental Health Perspectives, experimental issue no. 3 (Jan. 1973), p. 17.

21. Stallings, D.L., et al., "Phthalate Ester Residues - Their Metabolism and Analysis in Fish," Ibid., p. 159.

22. Nazir, D.J., et al., "Di-2-ethylhexyl Phthalate in Bovine Heart Muscle Mitochondria: Its Detection, Characterization and Specific Location," Ibid., p. 141.

23. U.S. Tariff Commission, "Synthetic Organic Chemicals, U.S. Sales and Production," Pub. no. 327 (1965).

24. Calley, D., et al., "Toxicology of a Series of Phthalate Esters," Journal of Pharm. Science, 55:158-162 (1966).

25. Nematollchi, Jay, et al., "Plasticizers in Medical Application I. Analysis and Toxicity Evaluation of Dialkyl Benzene-dicarboxylates," Journal of Pharm. Science, 56 (11): 1446-1453 (1967).

26. Dillingham, E.O. and Autian, J., "Teratogenicity, Mutagenicity, and Cellular Toxicity of Phthalate Esters," Environmental Health Perspectives, experimental issue no. 3 (Jan. 1973), p. 81.

27. Shibko, S.I. and Blumenthal, H., "Toxicology of Phthalic Acid Esters Used in Food Packaging Material," Ibid., p. 131.

28. Taylor, G.J. IV and Harris, W.S., "Cardiac Toxicity of Aerosol Propellants," Journal of American Medical Association, 214:no. 1 (Oct. 5, 1970).

29. Washington Post, June 22, 1973.

30. Arthur D. Little, Inc., "The Current Status of Human Safety and Environmental Aspects of Fluorescent Whitening Agents Used in Detergents," presented for the Minor Additives Committee of the Soap and Detergent Association. Contract No. 7483. March 1, 1973.

31. Grant, Neville, "Legacy of the Mad Hatter," Environment, 11:4, 18 (1969).

32. Lofroth, G. and Duffy, M.E., "Birds Give Warning," Ibid.

33. Grant, Neville, "Mercury in Man," Environment, 13:4, 3 (1971).

34. Novick, Sheldon, "A New Pollution Problem," Environment, 11:4, 3 (1969).

35. Wood, J.M., et al., Nature, 220:173 (1968).

36. Aaronson, Terri, "Mercury in the Environment," Environment, 13:4, 16 (1971).

37. An Environment Staff Report, "Mercury in the Air," Ibid., p. 24.

38. Grant, Neville, "Mercury in Man," Ibid., p. 3.

39. Christensen, F.C. and Olsen, E.C., "Cadmium Poisoning," Archives of Industrial Health, 16:8 (1957).

40. Carroll, R.E., "The Relationship of Cadmium in the Air and Cardiovascular Disease Death Rate," Journal of the American Medical Association, 198 (3):267-269 (Oct. 17, 1966).

41. McCaull, Julian, "Building a Shorter Life," Environment, 13:7 (1971).

42. Frant, S. and Kleeman, S., "Cadmium Food Poisoning," *Journal of the American Medical Association*, 117:86-89 (1941).

43. U.S. Senate. Committee on Public Works. 92nd Congress. Report on S. 2770. Senate Report No. 92-414 (October 28, 1971).

44. U.S. Congress. Federal Water Pollution Control Act Amendments of 1972 (P.L. 92-500).

45. Linton, Ron M., "A Strategy for a Livable Environment," A Report to the Secretary of HEW by the Task Force on Environmental Health and Related Problems (June 1967).

46. National Commission on Product Safety, Final Report, Washington, D.C. (1968).

47. U.S. Congress. House of Representatives. Committee on Government Operations, "Phosphates in Detergents and the Eutrophication of America's Waters." House Report No. 91-10004 (April 14, 1970).

48. Epstein, Dr. Samuel S., Testimony before the Subcommittee on Air and Water Pollution, of the Committee on Public Works, U.S. Senate, 91st Congress (Water Pollution - 1970, Part 2), May 6, 1970.

49. Chernoff, Dr. N., and Courtney, Dr. H.O., "Maternal and fetal effects of NTA, NTA and cadmium, NTA and mercury, NTA and nutritional imbalance in mice and rats." Progress Report, N.I.E.H.S., Research Triangle Park, North Carolina, January 18, 1970.

50. Epstein, Dr. Samuel S., "Toxicological and Environmental Implications on the Use of Nitrilotriacetic Acid as a Detergent Builder." Staff Report to the Committee on Public Works, U.S. Senate, December, 1970.

51. Assistant Secretary's Ad Hoc Group on NTA. "Final Report: Assessment of the Potential of NTA to compromise human health," Submitted April 19, 1972.

52. Muskie, Senator Edmund S., Press Release, February 3, 1973.

53. Nixon, President Richard M., "Program for a Better Environment," House Document No. 92-46 (February 8, 1971).

54. U.S. Congress. Senate. Commerce Committee. Hearings on the Toxic Substances Control Act of 1971 and Amendments (Serial No. 92-50), (Parts 1-3).

55. U.S. Congress. Senate. Commerce Committee. Hearings on the Effects of Mercury on Man and His Environment, 91st Congress (Serial No. 91-73).

56. U.S. Congress. Senate. Commerce Committee. Report on S. 1478, Senate Report 92-873 (May 5, 1972).

57. _____, Toxic Chemicals, Congressional Quarterly, June 3, 1972, p. 1298.

58. _____, Toxic Substances, Congressional Quarterly, June 3, 1972, pp. 1280-1281.

59. Fri, Robert, Hearings before the House Committee on Interstate and Foreign Commerce, U.S. Congress, May 18, 1972, p. 85.

60. U.S. Congress. House of Representatives. Report to accompany S. 1478. House Report No. 92-1477 (September 28, 1972).

61. Staggers, Representative Harley, Toxic Substances Control Act, Congressional Record, 118:H. 9925-9932 (October 13, 1972).

62. Moss, Senator Frank, "Toxic Substances Control Act of 1972," Congressional Record, 118:S. 18253-18262 (October 14, 1972).

63. U.S. Congress. Senate. Commerce Committee, Report on S. 426, Senate Report No. 93-254 (June 26, 1973).

64. Tunney, Senator John, "Toxic Substances Control Act of 1973," Congressional Record, 119:S. 13815-S. 13830 (July 18, 1973).

65. U.S. Congress. House of Representatives. Committee on Interstate and Foreign Commerce, House Report 93-360 (June 29, 1973).

66. Staggers, Representative Harley, Toxic Substances Control Act of 1973, Congressional Record, 119:H. 6467-6514 (July 23, 1973).

67. Shaffer, C. Boyd, Testimony before the Commerce Committee, Senate, 92nd Congress (Serial No. 92-50), November 5, 1971.

68. Derby, Roland, Ibid., November 5, 1971.

69. Mazzochi, Anthony, Chemical and Atomic Workers, _Ibid._, October 4, 1971.

70. Rodgers, William, Jr., Ibid., August 5, 1971.

71. Epstein, Dr. Samuel S., Testimony before the Subcommittee on Executive Reorganization and Government Research, Committee on Government Operations, Senate, 92nd Congress, April 6, 1971.

72. Epstein, Dr. Samuel S., Testimony before the Select Committee on Nutrition and Human Needs, Senate, 92nd Congress, September 20, 1972.

73. Epstein, Samuel S., "Environmental Pathology: A Review," _American Journal of Pathology_, 66:352 (1972).

74. Welford, Harrison, Testimony before the Committee on Commerce, Senate, 92nd Congress (Serial No. 92-50), November 5, 1971.

# 4

## RADIATION EXPOSURES FROM CONSUMER ELECTRONIC PRODUCTS

Richard D. Grundy

CONTENTS

## Introduction

In recent years, the consumer has been presented with an unprecedented variety of highly sophisticated electronic products. While these electronic devices aid us in our daily lives, many -- either in the course of their intended use or when improperly operated -- may emit unwanted and dangerous radiation. A significant public health challenge may well be the devising of ways to preassess and reduce the nonefficacious and accidental exposure of the consumer to ionizing and nonionizing radiation.

Although the Roentgen ray was discovered in 1895, concern for consumer radiation exposure is a relatively recent issue. The utility of X rays in diagnostic medicine was recognized as early as 1896 by surgeons in Vienna and Berlin (1). It is of interest to note, however, that the apparatus was considered so expensive, $100 and upward, that few surgeons could afford to offer Roentgen photography in their private practice. In light of the subsequent discovery of the adverse biological effects of ionizing radiation, this proved a blessing in disguise.

As a phenomenon of the "electronics age," consumer exposure to ionizing and nonionizing radiation from electronic products such as televisions and microwave cooking ovens has extended the potential public health hazard to the home. And new electronic devices are increasingly being introduced into commerce; if improperly used, many of these electronic devices could be dangerous to individuals and, if precautions are not taken, their widespread use could result in general environmental pollution. Yet the consumer is generally completely unaware of the associated radiation emissions, or of any precautions that might be employed to reduce the danger.

Radiation is energy, carried by waves or invisible particles moving through space or matter. Both ionizing and nonionizing radiation may be characterized in terms of wave length or energy (Figure 1).

There is potential for consumer exposure over the whole electromagnetic spectrum: from the shortest X rays, through ultraviolet, visible and infrared light, up to microwave and long radio waves. Studies indicate that eventually the entire spectrum may well be used for communications, energy transfer, and medical diagnosis and treatment.

Ionizing radiation such as X rays is defined as that which can strip electrons from atoms. The electrically charged ions thus created are capable of disrupting life processes; however, it is believed that any exposure to ionizing radiation can cause adverse biological effects. As discussed subsequently,

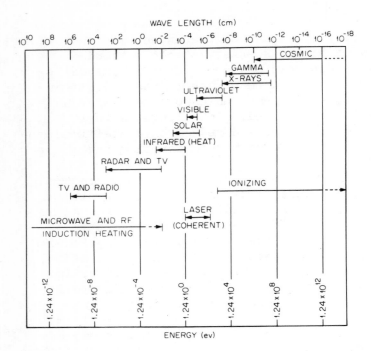

Figure 1. Electromagnetic (ionizing and nonionizing) radiation spectrum (2).

the extent of the health effects from ionizing radiation is believed to be linearly related to exposure. This means that both the risk and seriousness of radiation effects decline in direct proportion to the amount of exposure. But it also means that some effect can be anticipated no matter how small the exposure. In other words, there is no threshold or "safe" level of ionizing radiation exposure below which it can be stated that no adverse effect occurs.

On the other hand, it is common knowledge that there are apparently "safe" exposure levels below which no known short-term adverse effects or injury are known to occur. This complicates life for those individuals who are responsible for protection of public health. At issue is whether the goal should be zero exposure without regard to economic or societal costs or whether the allowable exposure should be based on a balancing of risks and benefits. The latter approach, in turn, raises the issue of who should decide the balance point and what should be the participation from those in our society who are likely to be exposed in their work or where they live.

Nonionizing radiation such as microwaves, although lacking the ability to create ions, also may adversely affect human

health. Knowledge of the biological effects of such radiation
is still in its infancy; however, sufficient knowledge has
accumulated so that the prudent approach here is also the
assumption of a linear relationship between exposure and
biological effect. The attendant issues can be expected to
become more prominent as microwave transmission of electric
power becomes more attractive.*

For both ionizing and nonionizing radiation, knowledge of
the long-term effects of single or repeated low-level exposure
is far from complete. This information is essential for the
effective application of benefit-cost or benefit-risk analyses,
which depend upon the clearest possible understanding of
radiation effects.

The electronic-products industry is expanding both in
number of manufacturers and in variety of products (3). In the
United States there were in 1971 approximately 5,400 plants
manufacturing an estimated 30,000 different types of electronic
products (Table 1). Many of these products may emit ionizing
or nonionizing radiation by design or inadvertence.

Past concern was principally for X-ray machines used in
medical and dental diagnosis. While the use of such machines
continues to grow, recent concern has focused on the potential
for significant consumer exposures to both ionizing and
nonionizing radiation from the other electronic products
listed in Table 1.

Color television sets still outnumber all other sources of
radiation that are generally available to the consumer. Recent
additions to the scene, however, include microwave ovens and
ultrasonic dishwashers, which are being increasingly marketed
for home use.

Medical diagnostic applications of ultrasound are being
promoted as replacements of some X-ray methods. Although such
equipment now represents only a small fraction of the total
medical-equipment market, the diagnostic and therapeutic uses
of ultrasound are expected to grow rapidly. A similar
expansion in markets is also anticipated for microwave and
short-wave diathermy.

---

*Serious proposals are being made to employ orbiting satellite
power stations to transform solar energy into microwaves that
are then beamed to large collection antennas on the earth.
Other proposals would transmit energy from one point to
another over microwave beams reflected from satellites in
synchronous orbit.

Table 1 Estimates of Selected Electronic Products In Use In The United States, January 1970 (4)

| Product | Estimated Total Number | Annual Production | Annual Growth (%) |
|---|---|---|---|
| X-ray machines | | | |
| Dental | 100,000 | | < 5 |
| Medical | 115,000 | | < 5 |
| Industrial | 15,000 | | < 5 |
| Accelerators | 1,200 | | -- |
| Color television sets (households) | 24,000,000 | 6,000,000 | ~ 25 |
| Electron microscopes | 500 | 200 | > 25 |
| Infrared ovens (commercial) | 15,000 | | |
| Microwave ovens | | | |
| Commercial | 45,000 | 12,000 | ~ 25 |
| Domestic | 50,000 | 4,000 | ~ 25 |
| Microwave heating (industrial) | 300 | 60 | ~ 25 |
| Microwave diathermy units | 15,000 | 700 | ~ 5 |
| Microwave communications transmitters | 66,000 | | |
| Radar | | | |
| Stationary | 5,500 | | |
| Pleasure boat | 7,500 | | |
| Transmitters | | | |
| Commercial AM | 4,300 | | |
| Commercial FM | 2,200 | | |

Table 1 (cont.)

| Product | Estimated Total Number | Annual Production | Annual Growth (%) |
|---|---|---|---|
| Transmitters (cont.) | | | |
| Educational FM | 400 | | |
| Commercial TV | 700 | | |
| Educational TV | 200 | | |
| Amateur | 300,000 | | |
| Citizens' | 3,000,000 | | |
| Aviation services | 200,000 | | |
| Industrial services | 1,700,000 | | |
| Transportation services | 500,000 | | |
| Marine services | 200,000 | | |
| Public safety services | 700,000 | | |
| TV translators and boosters | 2,200 | | |
| Laser | | | |
| HeNe | 10,000 | 5,000 | ~ 75 |
| Ruby | 2,000 | 600 | ~ 25 |
| Nd glass | 1,000 | 600 | ~ 50 |
| CO$_2$ | 1,500 | 1,000 | ~ 50 |
| Argon | 1,250 | 1,250 | ~ 50 |
| YAG | 1,000 | 1,000 | ~150 |
| Ultrasonic | | | |
| Medical diagnostic | 3,000 | | > 50 |
| Medical therapeutic | 3,000 | | > 50 |
| Welders | Few thousand | | > 50 |
| Cleaners | Tens of thousands | | > 10 |

The general communications market is also expected to
sustain substantial growth in areas such as microwave-relay
systems and radar and other navigational aids. The number of
microwave, television, and radio transmitters is increasing
rapidly; in 1968 alone, the Federal Communications Commission
(FCC) authorized 6,425,209 transmitting devices, exclusive of
military systems (3). Across the country small watercraft also
are being equipped with new, compact radars. In high school
and college classrooms, electronic radiation sources are being
utilized in increasing numbers. Public health concern should
thus extend to radiation hazards across the whole
electromagnetic spectrum (Figure 1), rather than being
narrowly focused, as it is now, on ionizing radiation.

At issue are not the benefits of these consumer products,
but whether or not the consumer's health is being endangered
by unnecessary or nonefficacious radiation exposure.

Prudence dictates that all unnecessary exposures to manmade
sources of radiation be avoided. This requires that the best
engineering design practices be utilized to reduce the
consumer's radiation risk from all sources -- including
products such as television receivers and microwave cooking
ovens as well as diagnostic X-ray equipment.

The most frequently reported adverse health effects
attributed to nonionizing radiation overexposures are eye and
skin damage (5). In some cases only short single exposures
were involved, while in other cases, individuals were exposed
for extended time periods. The effects included both short-term
reactions, such as skin irritations, and long-term effects,
such as cataracts and leukemia (3). Acute burns from lasers,
microwave generators, X-ray diffraction units, and ultraviolet
light sources also have been reported (3). Thus, virtually the
whole electromagnetic spectrum can produce undesirable effects
if exposures are large enough.

There is still a scarcity of systematically collected
information regarding biological injury from exposure to
electromagnetic or acoustical energy. Preliminary studies on
animals show that microwaves of sufficient intensity can induce
chromosomal abnormalities, cataracts, and alter atoms in
protein synthesis (3). Ultrasonic vibrations intense enough to
be of therapeutic value also have the potential to cause tissue
damage (3). This has not been shown, as yet, to be true for
diagnostic intensities. As the use of these sources increases,
it is essential that knowledge of the health implications of
such exposures be understood.

Insufficient knowledge of the health effects resulting from
consumer radiation exposure dictates that emphasis be placed on

providing adequate margins of safety in the formulation of
realistic standards. We should continue to follow the
radiation-protection philosophy adopted by the International
Commission on Radiological Protection (ICRP), the National
Council on Radiation Protection and Measurements (NCRPM), and
the Federal Radiation Council (FRC) (whose functions now
reside in the Environmental Protection Agency) that will be
summarized herein.

These three bodies uniformly agree that the prudent course
lies in the assumption of a linear relationship between
ionizing radiation exposure and adverse effects. This was
expressed by the ICRP as follows:

"The basis of the Commission's (ICRP's) recommendation is
the cautious assumption that any exposure to radiation may
carry some risk for the development of somatic effects
including leukemia and other malignancies and hereditary
effects. The assumption is made that down to the lowest levels
of dose the risk of inducing disease or disability increases
with the dose accumulated by the individual. This assumption
implies that there is no wholly safe dose of radiation." (6)

This statement does not imply either demonstrated proof of
a linear nonthreshold model; nor does it imply rejection of
the existence of a threshold. Rather, it advocates that the
most cautious and reasonable approach, until there is an
absence of proof to the contrary, is to assume that any
radiation exposure, whether ionizing or nonionizing, has an
accompanying biological risk. One must expect that very low
exposures may have biological effects even though the effects
are not detectable. It is also to be assumed, in the absence
of other evidence, that any actual effects will not exceed
those predicted under the linear assumption.

The modes of human exposure largely determine the types of
action that might be taken for man's protection, within the
following broad categories:

1. Personal radiation exposures resulting from social habits
(e.g., the use of television or microwave ovens). These
exposures can be controlled only by educating the consumer to
take precautionary steps to minimize his exposure.

2. Personal radiation exposures from medical and dental
diagnosis and treatment. These exposures can be controlled only
by the medical practitioner or the radiologic technologist
administering the radiation.

3. Exposures under occupational conditions. Occupational exposures can be altered by controlling the source of exposure (i.e., by using shielding or interlocks) or the movements and work habits of employees (i.e., operators of electron microscopes or particle accelerators).

4. Exposures of large or small segments of the general population from manmade or natural sources through no action of their own.

All four of these modes of exposure can be reduced by the application of enlightened equipment-performance standards and, in occupational situations, by use of operator-performance standards.

Some indication of the relative need for control in these four categories is provided by records (5, 7) of radiation incidents involving acute occupational and nonoccupational exposures (Figure 2). It is reasonable to assume that the FDA's Radiation Incidents Registry severely understates the actual incidence of radiation exposure; for notably under-reported and even omitted are nonacute short-term effects, chronic effects, and consumer effects in general.

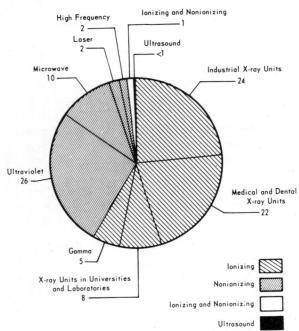

Figure 2. Percentage of persons reportedly exposed to ionizing and nonionizing radiation and ultrasound: Radiation Incidents Registry, December 1970. (7)

The preponderance of the reported incidents were of occupational origin in the following decreasing order: (a) engineering technicians, physical scientists, and miscellaneous professional services personnel; (b) persons employed in electrical-equipment industries; (c) hospital personnel; and (d) students performing experimental work in educational institutions (5). The most frequently reported injuries were eye and skin damage and various blood disorders (see Table 2). The largest fraction, 59 percent, involved ionizing radiation (X and gamma radiation); however, ultraviolet, microwave, laser, high frequency, and ultrasonic energy also were involved.

Industrial exposures accounted for 24 percent of the reported incidents, involving principally accelerators, such as electrostatic generators, linear accelerators, and, in one instance, a gradient synchrotron. Others involved industrial X-ray equipment including thickness gauges, fluoroscopic and radiographic units, diffraction units, and spectrographic units (5).

X-ray exposures from medical and dental units accounted for 22 percent of the reported incidents, involving high-voltage-therapy equipment, fluoroscopic and radiographic equipment, and electrostatic generators. The major causes of excessive radiation exposures were operator carelessness and failure of accelerator interlock systems.

The majority of nonionizing radiation exposures were occupational in origin; the principal sources being welding and ultraviolet equipment. Microwave-generating equipment, microwave ovens, radar, and diathermy equipment accounted for 10 percent of the reported incidents. Exposures to laser equipment in universities and laboratories accounted for 2 percent of the total number of persons exposed.

One report involved a high school student who constructed a ruby laser and also operated a borrowed helium-neon laser in his home. Although no injury was reported, this incident indicates that safety precautions are needed even at the high school level.

Obviously, the increased use of consumer electronic devices which emit radiation presents another whole class of potentially hazardous situations.

## The Congress Enunciates A Federal Policy

Initial congressional interest in electronic-product radiation was motivated in 1967 by an air of crisis. Some color television sets were found to emit X-rays in excess of the accepted safety limits previously established and voluntarily adopted by industry.

Table 2 Types of Exposure and Selected Characteristics of Incidents Reported to the Radiation Incidents Registry as of December 1970 (7) (excluding Workmen's Compensation claims)

| Type of Exposure | Number of Incidents | Number of Persons | | Type of Injury (a) | | | |
|---|---|---|---|---|---|---|---|
| | | Total | Injured | Eye | Skin | Blood | Other |
| All claims | 133 | 192 | 141 | 85 | 58 | 5 | 9 |
| Occupational | | | | | | | |
| Nonionizing | 71 | 84 | 77 | 64 | 12 | 2 | 7 |
| Ionizing (X-ray) | 47 | 69 | 38 | 7 | 34 | 3 | 1 |
| Nonoccupational | | | | | | | |
| Nonionizing | 7 | 16 | 14 | 14 | 1 | | |
| Ionizing (X-ray) | 7 | 22 | 11 | | 11 | | |
| Ultrasound | 1 | 1 | 1 | | | | 1 |

(a) Some persons had more than one injury.

Background   In the fall of 1966, the U.S. Public Health Service (USPHS) had undertaken research on techniques for the measurement and evaluation of potential consumer radiation exposures from television receivers. The Electronic Industries Association's (EIA) Ad Hoc Committee on X-ray Protection was relied upon as the prime source of industry-wide data. On January 26, 1967, the USPHS was informed by EIA that the NCRP's recommendations were then being observed by the television industry "in a very conservative way," (8) whatever that meant!

Yet the first indication of excess consumer radiation exposure also arose in January 1967. The New York State Department of Labor reported by telephone to the USPHS that the General Electric Company had informed the State that excessive X-ray emissions had been observed from some color television receivers being tested on a production line. The radiation exposures were found to be the result of a design change involving a shunt regulator tube.

As some color televisions were then designed, the voltage across the shunt regulator tube could be adjusted to be high enough to cause emissions of X rays. Normally such tubes were to be shielded; but in some sets the shielding was inadequate, so that there resulted external X-ray fields exceeding the industry standards.

Three months later, on April 10, 1967, G.E. requested federal assistance to deal with the problem of consumer radiation exposures from the receivers already sold. And on April 20, 1967, the USPHS requested information from the EIA for all domestically manufactured television receivers in order to evaluate if there was an industry-wide problem.

The first public disclosure of the problem came in May 1967. The USPHS announced that certain of G.E.'s large-screen color television receivers, produced between June 1966 and February 1967, might emit sufficient X rays to produce undesirable exposures. G.E. then instituted a program to recall and rework the units already in both dealers' and consumers' hands. By August 1967, seven months after the initial report, all but 1,877 out of some 112,374 television sets had been corrected, and in October 1968 the USPHS judged G.E.'s modification program to have been successful (9).

Meanwhile, on June 29, 1967, the EIA submitted to the USPHS the requested data for some 20 television manufacturers, representing 95 percent of industry sales. The EIA's expressed opinion was that, under normal operation conditions, all the sets came within the recommended standard. This opinion notwithstanding, the USPHS eventually decided that a problem existed, and that it was industry-wide in scope. On April 1, 1968, the USPHS estimated that from 5 to 10 percent of the 14 million color television sets in the United States could emit radiation in excess of the industry's voluntary standard (10).

Although the industry was capable of producing television sets within recommended emission limits, a 1970 survey demonstrated the need for further improvement (11). Television sets surveyed prior to sale were found to be in compliance, but about 3.4 percent of the units in home use emitted X rays in excess of the standards.

Several other unfortunate characteristics in the evolution of this issue serve to point up a public health policy which relies on voluntary standards that are established by other than regulatory bodies, and on voluntary enforcement.

First, in 1960, the NCRPM recommended (12) that X-ray emissions from television receivers should not exceed 0.5 mr/hr* at a distance of 5 cm from the screen. This level was estimated to result in a maximum consumer exposure of less than five percent of that due to the average natural background radiation. With slight revision, the NCRPM reaffirmed this standard five years later (in July 1965): the recommended standard was that the exposure rate averaged over an area of 10 cm$^2$ not exceed the stated 0.5 mr/hr at any external location 5 cm from the surface of the television receiver cabinet (13).

However, in 1967, seven years after the recommendation, the Underwriters' Laboratories (U.L.) was still utilizing for certification purposes their 1945 standard (revised in 1958) of 2.5 mr/hr. Although a revision of this practice was proposed at the January 24, 1967 meeting of UL's Industry Advisory Conference for Radio and Television Receiving Appliances, the Conference failed to approve the revised standard; and it was not until September 1967 that 0.5 mr/hr was adopted as UL's standard for prototype certification purposes.

Second, the suggestion was made that viewers should not sit closer than 6 feet from color television sets nor watch more than 2,000 hours per year (or about 6 hours per day). Yet it is quite likely that children, who cannot be totally controlled, will watch television for more than 5 to 6 hours and frequently at a distance closer than 6 feet (14).

---

*The roentgen (r) is the standard international measure of X or gamma radiation. It is a measure of the amount of ionization energy deliverable to a unit volume of space by the radiation. The milliroentgen (mr) is one-thousanth of a roentgen.

Third, the normal procedure for the U.L. is to certify prototype rather than production line models supplied by manufacturers. The limitations of this procedure for establishing compliance are revealed in the following G.E. episode.

For many years G.E. had utilized the same design for its color television sets. The U.L. engineers' procedure was to test standard television chassis designs. Thus, they did not consider it necessary to test the subject chassis on the basis of a new shunt regulator tube alone. The new design was certified on the basis of similarity to previously tested television receivers (15).

The unfortunate aspect of the G.E. episode was that it could have been avoided (16). Data on radiation emissions for various shunt regulator tubes was reported in the September-December 1964 issue of the Japanese Journal of Radiation Research, which indicated that the emission rate from shunt regulator tubes showed a remarkable spread due to large differences in the characteristics of the individual tubes (16). Some 15 percent of the regulators sampled had exhibited X-ray leakages greater than the advisory standard including some regulator circuit designs similar to those employed in the new G.E. receivers. The research was performed by the Matsushita Electric Industrial Company with whom G.E. had close technical, if not financial, relations. In other words, data which could have been used to estimate radiation emissions attendant to the G.E. chassis design was available to the company.

The legislative consequence of the G.E. episode was the Radiation Control for Health and Safety Act of 1968 (P.L. 90-602), discussed below.

Legislative History  Radiation hazards have always possessed greater news value than many other public health hazards, and the news about radiation emissions from television sets quickly attracted the attention of the press and the interest of members of both the Senate and the House of Representatives (17).

On June 13, 1967 (i.e., following closely upon the disclosure of the problem in May), Rep. John Jarman (D.-Okla.), Chairman of the Subcommittee on Public Health and Welfare of the House Committee on Interstate and Foreign Commerce, and Rep. Paul G. Rogers (D.-Fla.), the second-ranking majority member, cosponsored H.R. 10790, the Radiation Control for Health and Safety Act of 1967.

The purpose of the legislation was to assure that electronic products sold in interstate commerce would be designed and manufactured to meet federal performance standards for radiation emissions.

In a bipartisan stance, similar bills were introduced by Reps. David Satterfield (D.-Va.); L. H. Fountain (D.-N.C.); John Dingell (D.-Mich.); William Springer (R.-Ill.); Horace Kornegay (D.-N.C.); G. Robert Watkins (R.-Pa.); Clarence Brown (R.-Ohio); and John Murphy (D.-N.Y.).

A similar bill, S. 2067, was introduced in the Senate on July 10, 1967, by Sen. Bartlett, a leading member of the Senate Commerce Committee, and others (17). This legislation was referred to the Committee on Commerce where hearings were held at full Committee. This referral reflected the regulatory approach of the bill, which hinged on the Federal Government's Constitutional responsibility for interstate commerce.

Support for electronic-product legislation was voiced in President Johnson's January 1968 State of the Union Message and again in his February 6, 1968 Consumer Message. A bill similar to those already mentioned (S. 3211) was introduced by Sen. Lister Hill (D.-Ala.) on behalf of the Johnson Administration; however, this bill was intended to be a public health rather than a consumer-product measure. Consequently, the legislation was referred to Sen. Hill's Committee on Labor and Public Welfare, where it died.

Both House and Senate Committees, when reporting the Radiation Control for Health and Safety Act, emphasized that the measure covered all types of radiation and electronic products: color television sets, microwave ovens, lasers, and other electronic products. The enforcement mechanism was to rely upon establishment of performance standards designed for the protection of public health and safety. However, the standards were statutorily conditioned upon reasonableness, technical practicality, and appropriateness. And they were to be restricted, by definition, to electronic-product radiation or sonic-wave emissions.

Following passage by the House (March 20, 1969), the Senate Commerce Committee substantially strengthened the enforcement provisions. Inspection of manufacturing plants was authorized, as well as the investigation of manufacturers' records. Training requirements for radiologic technologists was also provided for in the Senate bill.

During Senate debate (October 2-3, 1968), a significant amendment by Sen. Paul J. Fannin (R.-Ariz.) was adopted exempting electronic products used by, or under the direction of, a licensed doctor, dentist, or hospital. This was intended

to meet the expected opposition from the medical profession
(18).

A second amendment by Sen. Hugh Scott (R.-Pa.) restricted
performance standards to the fully assembled product. A third
amendment by Sen. Ralph W. Yarborough (D.-Tex.) extended
coverage to persons engaged in the manufacture, installation,
maintenance, or repair of electronic products.

The Senate version authorized (1) a study of existing State
and federal programs for the control of health hazards due to
radiation from electronic products as well as from other
sources of radiation; (2) a study to determine the necessity
for the development of standards for the use of nonmedical
electronic products for commercial and industrial purposes;
and (3) a study of the development of procedures for the
detection and measurement of electronic-product radiation from
products manufactured or imported prior to the effective date
of any applicable standards.

The Congressional Quarterly credits a strong lobbying
effort against the stronger Senate-passed enforcement
provisions to former Postmaster General J. Edward Day, whose
work was financed by the EIA (19). This effort concentrated on
three or four major provisions. The final Senate inspection
provisions parallel almost exactly the FIA's desired language
(20), as we will now show.

First, a Senate provision authorizing court orders against
an electronic product found to be in violation of an
applicable standard was dropped. Second, the Senate floor
amendment extending protection to assembly line workers in
addition to the final consumer was dropped. Third, a weakened
inspection provision was adopted, permitting inspection only
if sufficient evidence existed to suggest that adequate
precautions to control radiation emissions were not being
taken. The fate of other provisions in the House-Senate
Conference were: fourth, modification of the Senate language
requiring a manufacturer to repair or replace a defective
product or refund the purchaser's payment; fifth, agreement to
Senate language requiring that performance standards apply to
components only in the context of the fully assembled products,
as was intended; sixth, deletion of the Senate provision
exempting electronic products used by, or under the direction
of, a licensed physician, dentist, or hospital; and seventh,
deletion of the Senate provision requiring the development of
advisory standards for the licensing and training of
radiologic technologists.

<u>Radiation Control For Health And Safety Act</u>  The outcome, the
Radiation Control for Health and Safety Act of 1968 (P.L. 90-
602, 42 U.S.C. 263b et seq.), was signed by President Johnson
on October 18, 1968. The evolution of this law serves as a
reminder that the Congress does not always wait for and depend
upon legislative recommendations sent from the Executive
Branch.

The 1968 Act amends the Public Health Service Act (42 U.S.C.
201 et seq.) to provide for a federal electronic product
radiation control program. The statute authorizes the Secretary
of Health, Education and Welfare to establish a program which
includes

- development and administration of performance standards for
X-ray and other radiation emission from electronic products;

- planning, conducting, coordinating, and supporting research,
development, training, and operational activities to minimize
the emission of and the exposure of people to unnecessary
electronic product radiation;

- maintaining liaison with and receiving information from
other federal and State departments and agencies with related
interests, professional organizations, industry and labor
associations, and other organizations on present and future
potential electronic product radiation;

- study and evaluation of emissions of, and conditions of
exposure to, electronic product radiation and intense magnetic
fields;

- development, testing, and evaluation of the effectiveness of
procedures and techniques for minimizing exposure to electronic
product radiation; and

- consultation and liaison with the Secretary of Commerce, the
Secretary of Defense, the Secretary of Labor, the Atomic
Energy Commission, and other appropriate federal departments
and agencies on (1) techniques, equipment, and programs for
testing and evaluating electronic product radiation and (2)
the development of performance standards to control such
radiation emissions.

During House hearings a spokesman for the EIA advocated
performance standards rather than design criteria. The EIA
advocated that the Congress provide statutory guidance to the
Secretary in this regard. An Advisory Committee on Radiation
Standards also was advocated.

During the House hearings criticism was directed by the
International Union of Electrical, Radio, and Machine Workers'

spokesman, David Lasser, to limiting regulations to
performance standards (16). Such standards were viewed as
being restricted to the overall performance of instruments
after manufacture and thus did not necessarily require
consideration of possible emissions at the design stage.
Criticism also was directed against inclusion of any specific
criteria for use in standard setting in the legislation
itself (16). The opinion was expressed that there was
insufficient knowledge at the time on radiation emissions from
electronic devices to set meaningful criteria; thus any attempt
to establish such criteria were viewed as possibly tying the
hands of the administering agency.

The Act directs the Secretary, when setting performance
standards for electronic products, to consult with appropriate
federal and State agencies and professional organizations
which would be affected by such standards.

Manufacturers also are required to certify, on a permanent
label or tag on the equipment, that the product conforms to
all applicable standards.

The federal performance standards are preemptive. In effect,
no other political authority may establish, nor continue in
effect, any standard which is not identical to the federal
standard. The legislation, however, does not affect the
long-recognized authority of States to regulate the use of
radiation and devices which produce or emit radiation. The
principal major gap in State authority is the statutory
preemption to the Atomic Energy Commission of the regulation
of radiation from nuclear powerplants, fission-product wastes,
and radioactive materials produced in nuclear reactors. On the
other hand, the AEC has entered into agreements with some
States for their regulation of the possession and use of small
quantities of fissionable materials and all reactor-produced
radioisotopes.

Performance standards can provide considerable control for
the safe use of electronic devices which emit radiation. When
electronic products are intended for medical, commercial, and
industrial uses, such standards can control conditions of use
such as location, facility design and shielding, safety
interlocks, warning devices, and proper radiation safety
procedures. Additional controls, not covered by the federal
standards, are adequate training as well as certification or
licensure of operators. State agencies also can play an
important role in inspections and surveys.

Radiation Protection Criteria And Standards
Usually when radiation is mentioned, attention focuses on such
sources of ionizing radiation as nuclear reactors, fallout from

nuclear weapons, and possibly, in a casual way, medical and
dental X-ray machines and perhaps sunbathing. However, with the
advent of the electronic age public health concern also has
extended to consumer exposures to sources of nonionizing
radiation such as infrared lamps and microwave ovens, and even
television sets, insofar as the latter involve the use of
microwave and radio frequency energy. These are just a few
examples of the new sources of radiation to which man is now
exposed in his daily life.

Consequently, there emerged the need to establish public
health policies for radiation protection which cover all these
sources of consumer exposure. These policies would be followed
in turn by the establishment of standards for nonionizing
radiation. As for other public health standards, judgments
must be made on the extent of known and suspected health
hazards and the risks to which society is willing to be
subjected in order to realize the known benefits of radiation
(21). In the past various scientific and professional groups
have performed these value judgments in the course of setting
advisory standards. The literature is laced with their
warnings that any final decisions should be made by society.
Thus far, however, our political institutions have not fully
come to grips with the complex task of balancing risks and
benefits. Consequently, by default, the consumer is left with
little more than an assurance by presumably knowledgeable
scientists that the risk is acceptable. This is an elitist
situation, incompatible with recent concepts of consumerism
which advocate public participation in policy decisions
affecting the health and welfare of the general population.*

---

*A distinction must be made between radiation exposure
standards governing the exposure of the consumer or the
population, and emission standards for radiation from
electronic products. The Radiation Control for Health and
Safety Act of 1968 (P.L. 90-602) is silent on the promulgation
of exposure standards. Such standards exist for ionizing
radiation but are yet to be established by any government body
for nonionizing radiation from electronic products. Rather
the Act provides for promulgation of emission standards for
radiation from electronic products. These latter standards are
justified as reducing human exposure to radiation even though
there may be an absence of definitive information on the
exposures associated with a given emission standard or on the
specific causal relationships associated with a given level
of exposure.

It is generally recognized that this approach for the
setting of standards relies on narrowly specialized groups.
While the members of such groups are competent to delineate
radiation risks, they are hardly qualified to decide what risks
are acceptable to society, nor are they constrained by public
accountability for their decisions.

Whether exposure risks are established by advisory groups
or by government, there still remains the difficult task of
balancing the benefits and risks attendant to establishing
radiation exposure standards (Table 3). In turn, the resultant
exposure standards must then be applied to the various sources
of consumer radiation exposure. Even here, there remains the
issue of who should perform this assessment.

Criteria and Standards for Ionizing Radiation   The adverse
effects of ionizing radiation have been observed since the
discovery of radium and of X rays. The effects included
radiation burns to X-ray machine users, bone cancers in
radium-watch-dial painters who had ingested radioactive paints,
and the incidence of lung cancers in uranium and pitchblende
miners. Among many physicians who pioneered in the practice
of radiology an increased incidence of leukemia and other
malignancies was observed.

In the ensuing years there has emerged an extensive
literature on the adverse biological effects of ionizing
radiation. The simplest unit for comparing ionizing radiation
exposure is the roentgen (r) (see footnote on page 184). The
roentgen, however, measures only relative ionizing power, and
not the actual biological effects of different radiations.
To better describe the effects on living tissue, two empirical
units, the rad and the rem, are employed. The rad (from
"radiation") measures the amount of absorbed ionizing
radiation. One rad corresponds to 100 ergs/gm for soft tissue.
The rem (for "radiation equivalent man") describes the
equivalent absorbed dose for the various types of ionizing
radiation, taking into account all causes of radiation in
their relative biological effectiveness.

The immediate somatic effects of large exposures to ionizing
radiation are generally understood and may include burns,
nausea, anemia, fatigue, and intestinal disorders, and loss of
hair. At very high levels of exposure to ionizing radiation
injury to the central nervous system and even death may occur.

There are also long-term effects of such exposure; these
may include cancers, including leukemia and cataracts, and a
decrease in the life span, even in the absence of other
symptoms. There is evidence that some inheritable genetic

Table 3   Consumer Benefit And Risks For Exposure To Radiation
(22)

| Benefits | Risks |
| --- | --- |
| Good health, entertainment, employment, modern convenience | Sickness and suffering, deformities and physical handicaps, life shortening, and early death |
| Medical X-ray<br>Treatment of diseases<br>Medical diagnosis | Cancer<br>Leukemia<br>Central nervous system cancer<br>Bone Tumor<br>Tyroid cancer<br>Lung carcinoma |
| Color Television<br>Educational programs<br>News<br>Entertainment | |
| | Eye Cataract |
| Nuclear Power<br>Cheap electricity<br>Reduction in air<br>pollution | Life Shortening |
| | Damage to Unborn Children<br>Mongoloidism<br>Microcephaly (abnormal<br>smallness of head)<br>Various forms of cancer |
| Industrial X-ray<br>Locate metallurgical<br>flaws<br>(prevent accidents) | |
| Microwave Ovens<br>Quicker preparation<br>of food | Genetic Mutations<br>Fetal and infant deaths<br>Deformities (physical and<br>mental) |
| Ultraviolet Radiation<br>Destroy bacteria in<br>operating rooms | |
| Radar<br>Improved and safer<br>air transportation | |
| Laser<br>Improved communications | |
| Radioisotopes<br>Medical diagnosis and<br>treatment, power source<br>for heart pump, etc. | |

defects can result from the exposure of reproductive tissue
to radiation.

Unfortunately, the effects of chronic ionizing radiation
exposure on man are not well understood. Yet the consumer is
subjected to such exposures from a variety of natural and
manmade sources (Table 4). One disconcerting uncertainty about
chronic and intermittent low-level exposure is the suggestion
that such exposures of the lens of the human eye may augment
or accelerate senile cataracts (24).

However, it is generally agreed that chronic exposures tend
to be cumulative. Although some repair may occur in exposed
organisms, the consensus is that any increase in exposure will
be accompanied by a commensurate increase in risk of injury
(3). Therefore, it is imperative that consumer and general-
population exposures to ionizing radiation be kept as low as
practicable: To wait for absolute proof of cause and effect
relationships or proof of the linear theory of radiation
effects before acting to reduce risks is to invite disaster.

The prudence in this approach to radiation protection is
reinforced by recognition of the presence of high-risk segments
of the population. A direct causal relationship exists between
X-ray exposure of pregnant women and later development of
malignant disease -- primarily leukemia and cancer of the
central nervous system -- in their prenatally exposed children
(25, 26). The relative risk of juvenile cancer is about 60
percent greater among those children whose mothers were
exposed than among those children whose mothers were not
exposed (26). The resultant risk over the first ten to fifteen
years of life amounts to about one juvenile cancer death per
2,000 children prenatally exposed (25). There also is evidence
of a similar increase in juvenile cancer among the children of
mothers who were X-rayed even years before pregnancy (26). This
attests to the existence of genetic damage due to X-ray
exposures.

Although not conclusively demonstrated, there even are
suggestions of susceptible subgroups among children. The
subgroups appear to be prone to develop leukemia following
X-ray exposures which have no apparent effect on other
individuals (27). There also are suggestions of racial
differences among prenatally exposed children. There has been
published preliminary, epidemiologic evidence indicating that
white children may be 40 to 60 percent more susceptible than
black children to adverse prenatal radiation effects (28).
Among the prenatally exposed white children mortality during
the first 10 years of life was almost twice that of the white
controls (nonexposed) for all causes of death except cancer

Table 4  Consumer Exposure to Ionizing Radiation in the United
States (22, 24)

| Source | Exposure (mrem/yr) |
|---|---|
| **Natural Background** | |
| Cosmic rays | 35 |
| External terrestrial | 50 |
| Internal terrestrial | 20 |
| **Medical and dental** | |
| Gonad (a) dose from diagnosis (1964) | 55.0 |
| Gonad dose from therapeutic use (1964) | 7.0 |
| Bone marrow dose from diagnosis (1964) | 125.0 |
| Thyroid dose from diagnosis (mostly dental) (1964) | 1000.0 |
| **Occupational exposures** | |
| Nuclear energy industry gonad dose (1970) | 0.8 (b) |
| All other occupational exposure gonad dose (1966) | 0.4 |
| **Weapons fallout** | 2.0 (c) |
| **Other manmade sources** | |
| Watches, television, shoe-fitting machines, radioisotope applications, etc., gonad dose (1966) | 0.1 |

(a) Testes and ovaries.
(b) Includes all occupational and environmental exposure from
all nuclear energy research and production operations.
(c) Gonad and total body dose from cesium-137 estimated to be
1.2 millirems in 1966, 0.68 millirem in 1967, and 0.54 millirem
in 1968. The average dose to bone marrow from strontium-90
estimated to be 3.6 millirems in 1966, 2.8 millirems in 1967
and 2.3 millirems in 1968.

(exclusive of leukemia), congenital malformations amo
and nervous system diseases among females (28). In the
leukemia the risk of death was about three times highe1
the exposed group than among the controls. In sharp con\_ \_st,
the mortality among the exposed black children was not greater
in any respect than among their control group (28).

A number of examples can be selected from a long list of
epidemiologic studies involving the diagnostic uses of X rays
which provide an indication of the subtle nature of the adverse
effects of ionizing radiation. The medical and dental benefits
of diagnostic X rays are well recognized; nevertheless,
diagnostic X rays do constitute the largest single source of
consumer radiation exposure. In the United States, X-ray
examinations account for about 95 percent of the population's
total exposure to manmade ionizing radiation (Table 4).

Non-Electronic Product Sources  Nuclear Power: In contrast to
the foregoing, normal operation of nuclear power plants
accounts for less than 1 percent of public exposure to ionizing
radiation. Nevertheless, proper concerns for the potential
adverse effects from disposal of radioactive wastes has impeded
the constructive use of atomic energy. However, the
preventative regulatory philosophy, that has characterized the
regulation of nuclear power over the last 25 years, may easily
prove to be its greatest asset, the problem now being largely
one of public education.

When the safety record of nuclear power generation and the
extreme precautions taken in handling the resultant nuclear
wastes have been demonstrated to the public's satisfaction,
they may well generally come to accept it, pending any major
accidents. The approach that has been taken toward
preassessment of the public health and safety implications of
nuclear energy is unique to the history of waste management and
disposal. In a very real sense, this development represents the
first deliberate attempt of government to understand and
control the hazards of an emerging large-scale industry before
it became a reality. This point was emphasized in a 1956 report
by the National Academy of Sciences (NAS), which stated:

"The use of atomic energy is perhaps one of the few major
technological developments of the past 50 years in which
careful consideration of the relationship of a new technology
to the needs and welfare of human beings has kept pace with
its development. Almost from the very beginning of the days of
the Manhattan Project careful attention has been given to the
biological and medical aspects of the subject." (29)

Consequently, atomic energy development in the United States has a record as one of the safest of industries, both from the standpoint of radiation hazards as well as ordinary industrial risks. However, issues still remain regarding occupational radiation exposure.

An optimist might suggest that man has learned something from this experience but, unfortunately, this is not the case.

The nuclear power industry was initially and remains monopolistic, and for all intents and purposes is nationalized. Initiated as a war measure, the industry also characterizes the waste management axiom: "the fewer the sources, the easier the solution."

There now remains the challenge of applying this radiation protection policy, predicated upon "prudence," to the regulation of the other environmental and consumer product sources of human radiation exposure. For man has, through changes in his life-style, actually increased his exposure to natural radiation sources.

Building Materials: Common building materials may emit small but measurable quantities of radiation -- not only the gamma rays (i.e., X rays) considered in this book, but also "particulate" radiation (e.g., alpha and beta rays), not considered here. Different materials emit different amounts of radiation. For example, radiation levels are lower in wood houses than in masonry buildings. A granite building may double the resident's background radiation exposure due to the radium and the thorium in the stone (30).

The radioactive content of aggregate, sand, and cement also varies widely. It is realistic to consider a two-thirds reduction in the radiation levels currently found in masonry buildings through a better selection of concretes and sealers to be used in construction.

Prime concern is for radon and thoron, natural radioactive gases, which are released from radium and thorium in building materials and escape into the air. Exposure to these gases, and their daughter products, can be reduced through improvements in ventilation systems; for these gases can be collected on commonly available filters.

Radon also occurs as a co-product of natural gas (31). Estimates are that under realistic conditions in poorly ventilated kitchens near a geological source of natural gas consumer exposure could conceivably reach maximum allowable exposure levels (31).

Food and Water: Radium and other naturally occurring radioactive materials are found in food and water. Decontaminating these sources offers another possibility for

reducing man's exposure to background ionizing radiation. The
easiest affect is the removal of radium from drinking water
through the use of home water softeners.

Some 900 community water supplies (serving approximately
3.8 million people in 20 states) were sampled by the USPHS in
1967 (32). Most of the water samples showed virtually zero
radium content: a number centered in the upper Mississippi
Valley and extending through southern Missouri, contained
significant radium levels. The highest levels were found in
Maine and New Hampshire.

Foods can be another source of radiation exposure.
Naturally occurring radioelements occur in fertilizers, or
make their way into food from the soil. An example is
radiophosphorus (33). Another example is tobacco when grown
with naturally radioactive fertilizers; some of the radioactive
materials become incorporated into the leaf and later appears
in inhaled smoke. Since tobacco is processed before being
formed into cigarettes, it is realistic to consider the removal
of such radioactive impurities, which include radium, lead-210,
and polonium-210, during the processing phase. Obviously this
is largely a matter of economics (33).

The foregoing examples dramatize the myriad of man's sources
of ionizing radiation exposure. Such natural sources are
significant since a reduction of only 20 percent in man's
exposure to natural sources of ionizing radiation would be
equal to the total reductions already accomplished, or sought,
through efforts to control manmade sources such as: nuclear
power, occupational exposures, and medical and dental
exposures.

Radiation Standard Advisory Committees   Although the benefit-
risk concept was applied to radiation protection in the late
1880's, the first formal effort was made in 1922 by the medical
profession -- then the principal users of radiation -- when the
American Roentgen Ray Society established a Radiation Protection
Committee. Until the 1930's their voluntary radiation standards
were primarily addressed to the users of ionizing radiation in
medicine, and to a lesser extent in industry. Little attention
was devoted to federal regulation: control of radioactivity
was regarded as inherent in the police powers of State and
local governments.

Consequently, even today, not all sources or uses of
ionizing radiation are covered by applicable federal or State
standards. For example, radium is not covered and at the
insistence of the medical profession the medical uses of
radiation were specifically excluded from recommended standards
or guidelines such as those of the FRC. These exceptions were

made on the premise that the risk-benefit equation for medical
exposures was best left in the hands of physicians. At the
time, however, the qualifications needed to perform this
assessment were unknown. This attitude of deference to the
medical profession has noticeably altered in recent years.

Medical Radiation standards have been largely the work of
three scientific bodies: the National Council on Radiation
Protection and Measurements (NCRPM), the International
Commission on Radiological Protection (ICRP), and the Federal
Radiation Council (FRC). The ICRP was established in 1928 by
the International Congress on Radiology, its membership
representing 14 countries. The National Committee on Radiation
Protection (NCRP) was formed in 1929, under the sponsorship of
the U.S. National Bureau of Standards, to work with the ICRP.
Later, in 1964, the NCRP was chartered and renamed by the
Congress as the "National Council on Radiation Protection and
Measurement" (NCRPM). Each of these advisory bodies was intended
to provide a mechanism that would make use of the combined
knowledge, experience, and judgment of the world's most
outstanding experts in such fields as radiology, radiation
biology, radiological physics, genetics, and human health.

In 1955, the NAS established a Committee on the Biological
Effects of Atomic Radiation (BEAR Committee) to conduct a
continuing appraisal of the effects of ionizing radiation on
living organisms (29). Supported by funds from the Rockefeller
Foundation, the BEAR Committee operated until 1963. Also in
1955, the United Nations established the U.N. Scientific
Committee on the Effects of Atomic Radiation (UNSCEAR).

In August, 1959, in response to concern for fallout from
nuclear weapons testing, President Eisenhower established the
FRC (Executive Order 10831), to "...advise the President with
respect to radiation matters, directly or indirectly affecting
health, including guidance for all federal agencies in the
formulation of radiation standards and in the establishment and
execution of programs of cooperation with States...." One month
later, the Congress endorsed the concept, providing a statutory
base for the Council in P.L. 86-373. The Council was chaired by
the Secretary of Health, Education and Welfare, and included
as members the Chairman of the AEC and the Secretaries of
Agriculture, Commerce, Defense, and Labor. Subsequently, in
1964, at FRC's request, the NAS-NRC established an Advisory
Committee to the FRC, to review and evaluate available
scientific evidence bearing on a variety of problems of
radiation exposure and protection.

In August 1970, as discussed subsequently, the FRC
contracted with the NAS-NRC to conduct a review of existing

ionizing radiation standards by their Committee on the
Biological Effects of Ionizing Radiation (BEIR Committee).
With the December 1970 federal environmental reorganization,
however, the FRC's functions, including responsibility for
this contract, were transferred to the then created
Environmental Protection Agency (EPA).

Since 1948, when the concept of a linear exposure (dose)-
effect relationship was introduced, the protection achieved in
any particular case has been viewed as a matter of degree and
judgment. However, this "benefit-risk" concept, now fundamental
to radiation protection standards, is often obscured in
radiation terminology.

A second significant step was the ICRP's attempt in the
1950's to assess the benefits and potential costs of exposure
to ionizing radiation. The difficulties inherent in the
application of this concept led the ICRP, in 1965, to state (6)
that

"...it is not yet possible to balance risks and benefits since
it requires a more quantitative appraisal of both the probable
biological damage and the probable benefits than is now
possible."

In other words, the setting of radiation standards, while
predicated upon the concept of balancing benefits versus risks
attendant to the use of radiation, still remained a matter of
judgment. This is true even today for consumer electronic
products, nuclear power, medical and dental X rays, and nuclear
medicine.

ICRP and NCRP: The Concept Of The Maximum Permissible Dose

Another concept to emerge from the application of benefit-risk
considerations to ionizing radiation was that of "maximum
permissible dose" for general population exposures (30). This
concept represented the first extension of the radiation
protection ethic beyond the previous limited concern for
specific groups (e.g., industrial workers) to the general
public. The inherent difficulty with this nomenclature was an
implied willingness to accept a predetermined, specific amount
of consumer radiation exposure for the whole population or any
portion thereof (30). The Congressional Joint Committee on
Atomic Energy, however, extended this concept one step further,
in 1957, by suggesting the need for a "population average
acceptable dose" (34). The Committee pointed out that such a
concept implied a willingness to accept a predetermined
specified quantity of radiation exposure in a population (34).
The idea that radiation protection policies, criteria, and

standards were of <u>central</u> importance to such matters did not
fully emerge until the spring of 1960, after extensive hearings
before the Joint Committee (35), when the Joint Committee
stated simply (36) that

"1. Development of the uses of atomic energy and other
sources of ionizing radiation will inevitably be accompanied
by the exposure of persons to manmade ionizing radiation.
    2. Enough is known about the biological effects on man...
to permit agreement (that the most reasonable working
assumption) is that all such exposures, however small, have
an associated biological risk...."

The Committee's Summary-Analysis further remarked that
"the state of our knowledge of the biological effects of
radiation compares very favorably with that of other hazards
to health..." and that the assumption which attaches some risk
of harm to every dose, no matter how low, is not unique for
radiation (36).
    At the time, the Joint Committee noted that the development
of radiation protection standards and criteria "...is based on
substantial scientific agreement as to the present state of
knowledge and the nature of its limitations." (36) Concerning
"the many points of view on balancing benefit versus risk,"
the Joint Committee stated that "...nowhere else in the
hearings can so much directly contradictory testimony...be
found." (36) The Committee also attempted to arrive at a
consensus but it immediately noted the "need for clarification
of concept," adding:

"If the need is not satisfied, the greater danger is not
that individuals or populations will be unnecessarily subjected
to radiation exposure -- at least not in the near future --
but rather the danger is that the developing military and
commercial applications of atomic energy will continue to occur
in an atmosphere of unnecessary governmental, commercial, and
public tension and confusion as to what is actually being done
for protection against radiation hazards." (36)

Thus, after several years of debate by all parties, two
radiation protection concepts emerged as the basis for
regulatory practices: first, that of a linear dose relationship,
or the absence of threshold effects; and, second, that all
radiation effects, both somatic and genetic, are additive.
After elaborate analyses of the genetic effects of radiation,
the NAS in this country and the Medical Research Council in

Great Britain both came to essentially the same conclusion:
that the genetic effects of ionizing radiation are cumulative
and more likely to be deleterious than beneficial.

FRC Radiation Protection Guides  Following the FRC's creation
in 1959, its working groups immediately undertook a review of
the available medical and scientific evidence on ionizing
radiation effects, principally, on man.

The first, and subsequent recommendations of the FRC
concerned exposures of radiation workers and the general public
originating from the nuclear-energy industry. The FRC's
guidance was not intended to apply to consumer product and
medical and dental exposures.

The recommendations of the FRC were developed with the
assistance of appropriate federal agencies: the NAS, the NCRPM,
and expert consultants. The FRC also carefully considered then
existing ICRP recommendations. After approval by President
Eisenhower, the recommendations of the FRC were published in
the Federal Register as guidance to federal agencies and so
became the basis for the AEC's regulations (10 CFR Part 20).

The first recommendations of the Council, approved by the
President on May 13, 1960, provided a general philosophy of
radiation protection that federal agencies could follow in the
conduct of their specific programs and responsibilities (37).
A second report (38) specifically on Radiation Protection
Guides was issued on September 20, 1961. When introducing the
term "Radiation Protection Guide (RPG)" the FRC stated that

"The term 'maximum permissible dose' is used by the NCRP
and ICRP for the radiation worker. However, this term is often
misunderstood. The words 'maximum' and 'permissible' both have
unfortunate connotations not intended by either the NCRP or
the ICRP. This report introduces the use of the term Radiation
Protection Guide (RPG)." (37)

Thus the basis for radiation standards was consciously
moved from the concept of maximum limits to the concept of
guides governing individual consumer radiation exposures. The
RPG's were defined by the FRC as

"...the radiation dose which should not be exceeded without
careful consideration of the reasons for doing so; every effort
should be made to encourage the maintenance of radiation doses
as far below this guide as practicable." (37)

The RPG's were intended to provide guidance for the control
and regulation of normal peacetime uses of nuclear technology.

As such, these guides were a balance between (1) the possible
risks to the general public that might result from exposures
from routine uses of ionizing radiation and (2) the benefits
derived from the activities causing the exposure. It cannot be
emphasized too often, however, that they were not intended to
establish an absolutely safe level of exposure to ionizing
radiation.

The Annual RPG for ionizing radiation for any individual in
the general population is a maximum exposure of 0.5 rem. As an
aid in the application of the advisory standard, a value of
0.17 rem per year, or one-third the maximum value, was
established as the RPG for the average member of the population
from all sources of ionizing radiation (37).

The RPG's were based on available medical and scientific
evidence and were considered to be below the level where
biological damage had been observed in man. The FRC's first
report stated that

"This staff report seeks to provide some of the required
radiation protection recommendations. These recommendations
are of an interim nature. Periodic review will be necessary to
incorporate new information as it develops. This staff report
includes recommendations for additional research which will
provide a firmer basis for the formulation of radiation
standards." (37)

The first report further stated that

"It is recognized that our present scientific knowledge does
not provide a firm foundation within a factor of two or three
for selection of any particular numerical value in preference
to another value. It should be recognized that the Radiation
Protection Guides recommended in this paper are well below the
level where biological damage has been observed in humans."
(37)

The report also recommended that every effort should be made
to encourage the maintenance of an individual's ionizing
radiation exposures as far below the RPG's as practicable.

At the time, the FRC also established Protective Action
Guides (PAG's) as "...the projected absorbed dose to individuals
in the general population that warrants protective action
following any contaminating event." (38) The PAG's were intended
to provide general guidance for the protection of the population
against acute exposure resulting from the accidental release of
radioactive materials into the environment.

Subsequently, in June, 1965, the Joint Committee on Atomic Energy held extensive hearings on the RPG's. At that time Dr. Paul Tompkins, the Executive Director, said:

"The numerical values for these Guides were placed as close to the annual dose from natural background radiation as technical, economic, and operational considerations in the nuclear industry allowed." (39)

Four years later, in November, 1969, Dr. Tompkins expressed his opinion that

"...increasing knowledge over the past 15 years indicates that the radiation dose prescribed by the FRC is probably less rather than more hazardous to health and well-being than was thought at the time." (40)

However (in December 1972), the NAS-NRC BEIR Committee suggested that this opinion might not reflect the actual case, and that the estimated risks associated with the RPG's might be in fact too low.

In developing the RPG's, both technical and policy considerations were necessary. The FRC attempted to strike a balance between maximum unregulated use of nuclear technology and zero risk; it has never been clear how this was accomplished, however. Nevertheless, as a consequence, the concept of "acceptable risk" has come to mean a risk that is presumed to be present but cannot be quantified by available scientific studies. This demonstrates the tenuous control that science has over the determination of radiation risk. In other words, science has not yet produced sufficient information to advance the present subjective judgments involved in establishing radiation standards to a point where quantitative benefit-cost analyses can be performed.

Then, in November, 1969, during hearings before the Senate Public Works' Subcommittee on Air and Water Pollution on the environmental effects of the underground uses of nuclear energy (41), testimony was received by Sen. Edmund S. Muskie (D.-Me.), Chairman, from Drs. John W. Gofman and Arthur R. Tamplin, who urgently recommended that the RPG's be revised downward at least ten-fold. Their proposal had been initially presented, one month earlier in San Francisco, at a symposium on nuclear sciences sponsored by the Institute of Electrical and Electronic Engineers.

The significance of this proposal was immediately obvious. Since the AEC standards for nuclear power plants were based

upon the RPG's, they would have had to be lowered concurrently.
Fortunately, nuclear power plants were then operating at
one-tenth to one-twentieth the AEC's standards. Consequently,
the technically and economically feasible had already been
demonstrated. Nevertheless, such a revision of the RPG's was
viewed as not providing any allowance for exposures from other
than nuclear industry sources.

Following the hearings Sen. Muskie transmitted the testimony
to DHEW Secretary Robert H. Finch, as Chairman of the FRC, for
comment. Secretary Finch responded on January 29, 1970,
commenting on the adequacy of the then current RPG's:

"In the past ten years, since the formulation of the FRC
basic guides, sufficient additional information has developed
from epidemiologic studies and animal experiments so that a
reevaluation of such guidelines is believed to be warranted.

In view of our concern with the potential hazard of ionizing
radiation in the environment, and as Chairman of the FRC, I am
recommending that the Council institute a careful review and
evaluation of the relevant scientific information that has
become available in the past decade. I am recommending that
this reevaluation provide, as definitively as possible,
estimates of the risks associated with low levels of
environmental radiation as a basis for review of the adequacy
of current FRC guidelines as applicable to projected radiation
levels. Based on projected exposure classes of radiation
sources, such as nuclear power reactors, other peaceful uses
of nuclear energy, and radiation from consumer products would
also be considered." (42)

Seven months later, the FRC initiated a review of current
guidelines and standards for ionizing radiation under contracts
to the NAS and the NCRPM. (Responsibility for this contract was
subsequently assumed by the Environmental Protection Agency.)

In November 1972 the NAS's BEIR Committee completed for the
EPA the task contracted by the now defunct FRC. The BEIR
Committee concluded that

"...over the next few decades, the dose commitments for all
manmade sources of radiation except medical should not exceed
more than a few millirems average annual dose to the entire
U.S. population. The present guides of 170 mrem/yr grew out of
an effort to balance societal needs against genetic risks. It
appears that these needs can be met with far lower average
exposures and lower genetic and somatic risk than permitted

by the current Radiation Protection Guide. To this extent, the
current Guide is unnecessarily high.

The exposures for medical and dental uses should be subject
to the same rationale. To the extent that such exposures can
be reduced without impairing benefits, they are also
unnecessarily high." (43)

The BEIR Committee did not suggest a revision in the FRC
guides, however; rather, it strongly urged that the government
use their risk estimates, as uncertain as they are, to form
numerical cost-benefit judgments in setting future radiation
standards. The BEIR Committee commented that no ionizing
radiation exposure should be permitted without the expectation
of a "commensurate" benefit.

Recognizing that sound radiation protection decisions
require complex economic, societal, and scientific
considerations, the BEIR Committee stated a number of general
principles: First, although the public must be protected from
radiation, it should not be to the extent that the degree of
protection provided results in the substitution of a hazard
worse than the radiation avoided. In addition, where small
reductions of risk involve large expenditures which could
clearly produce greater benefits elsewhere the reductions
should not be attempted. Second, an upper limit should be
established for manmade nonmedical ionizing radiation
exposures to an individual in the general population such that
the risks of serious somatic injury in such individuals is
very small relative to risks that are normally accepted. Third,
a similar limit should be established for the general
population such that the average exposure permitted is
considerably lower than that permitted for an individual.
Fourth, medical radiation exposure can and should be
considerably reduced. This should be accomplished by limiting
its use to clinically indicated procedures utilizing efficient
exposure techniques and optimal operation of radiation
equipment. It also was recommended that consideration be given
to restricting the use of ionizing radiation for public health
surveys, to the inspection and licensing of radiation and
ancillary equipment, and to appropriate training and
certification of all involved personnel. Fifth, with respect
to nuclear power, the Committee recommended the establishment
of guidelines based on cost-benefit analysis, taking into
account the total biological and environmental risks of the
various options available and the cost-effectiveness of
reducing these risks. In quantifying "as low as practicable"

the Committee further stated that consideration be given to
the net effect on the "welfare of society."

The remaining question is that of EPA's future actions as
the repository of the FRC's former authority. This is of
particular interest since the existing RPG's and standards
which were established by the FRC do not apply to medical
sources of ionizing radiation. About all the RPG's apply to is
the nuclear power industry -- uranium mines and mills, the
power reactors themselves, and waste depositories.

Apportionment of RPG's  The RPG's do not reflect the combined
effect of the various sources of ionizing radiation.
Consequently, any single source might well contribute exposures
approaching the full value of an RPG, creating no allowance
for potential exposures from other sources.

In recognition of this, some have suggested that the RPG's
be apportioned among the various sources of ionizing radiation.
For example, fractions of the RPG's could be assigned to the
nuclear power industry, electronic products, and the medical
profession, recognizing that medical and dental exposures are
specifically exempted from the RPG's.

The possibility for apportionment of voluntary radiation
standards was first proposed in 1959 by the ICRP (44). In
1966, the ICRP recommended that the responsible authorities
should base their apportionment of the RPG's on "...national,
economic, and social considerations." (6)

The desirability of further apportionment follows upon the
advent of increased numbers and types of consumer products
which contain radioactive materials or emit both ionizing and
nonionizing radiation. A logical framework could easily be
provided for assigning fractions of a RPG to specific consumer
products, or classes of products, by balancing established
benefits versus risks (45). This possibility has been discussed
at length in the literature (46, 47). Approaches have been
suggested such that the total risk from individual commercial
and consumer uses of radioactive materials and radiation-
emitting devices will never exceed the RPG's or other standards
recommended by independent professional committees (46). For
example, the annual maximum exposure limit for all consumer
items could be averaged over the population at risk (46). One
possibility is shown in Table 5. A distinction is provided
between allocations of "permissible" exposures and those that
might be "attainable" by the application of proper technology
and practice. Additional sources not mentioned in the table
include exposures during commercial round-trip flights across
the United States (2 to 4 mrem), local exposures from Plowshare
operations, or from nuclear rocket tests.

Table 5   Federal Radiation Council RPG For Ionizing Radiation (47)

| Sources | Radiation Level (mrem/yr) | |
| --- | --- | --- |
| | Permissible | Attainable |
| Total | 170 | 22 |
| Nuclear power | | |
| Internal exposure | 50 | 5 |
| External exposure | 17 | 2 |
| Other industrial operations | | |
| Internal exposure | 30 | 3 |
| External exposure | 15 | 2 |
| Medical exposures | | |
| Diagnostic | 40 | 5 |
| Therapeutic | 10 | 5 |
| Other occupational contributions | 4 | 0.1 |
| Weapons fallout | 2 | |
| Miscellaneous (Watches, television, high voltage switches, etc.) | 2 | 0.1 |

In the end, however, someone ultimately must make a subjective decision, on the basis of available knowledge, regarding the benefits to be derived from the use of a given consumer product. The limitations of this approach are somewhat the same as those inherent in the establishment of "maximum permissible concentrations" for radioactive materials in the environment.

Criteria And Standards For Nonionizing Radiation   The nonionizing portion of the electromagnetic spectrum has been arbitrarily divided into categories based upon the frequency or wavelength of the radiation (see Figure 1). Many questions remain unanswered regarding the hazards of nonionizing (low energy) radiation. What is obvious, however, is that consumers and the general public are being subjected to a wide range of radiation exposures often without their knowledge or a full appreciation of the possible or actual risks attendant to such exposure. For example, one small but growing consumer group

particularly susceptible to environmental radiation pollution
is that composed of individuals with implanted cardiac
pacemakers. For these devices have been observed to dysfunction
when near diathermy and electrocautery apparatus, radar and
communication systems, electric shavers, spark coils, and
gasoline-engine ignition systems. Such general environmental
radiation pollution may create some unpleasant surprises.

The dangers of nonionizing radiation are particularly
subtle; biological effects are, to a greater degree than for
ionizing radiation, less easy to pinpoint. Often the effects
do not manifest themselves until after the passage of latent
periods of years (for somatic mutations) or generations (for
genetic mutations). Consequently, from the standpoint of
prudent public health policies, it is essential that the same
general radiation-protection principles that operate for
ionizing radiation standards also operate in the case of
nonionizing radiation standards.

Microwaves  A form of electromagnetic radiation, microwaves
encompass a wide frequency range from 100 to 100,000 megahertz
(mHz) (see Figure 1), where one hertz equals one cycle per
second. Although microwaves do not possess sufficient energy
to ionize matter, they can excite atoms, and thus produce
heating and electrical and magnetic forces -- situations which
have been shown to lead to adverse biological effects. (The
energy and hence the potential biological effects of
electromagnetic radiation varies inversely with wavelength.
Thus the energy per amount of microwave exposure is much less
than for X rays.)

About one-half of U.S. population is at risk of being
exposed at home, in commercial establishments, in schools, and
in hospitals to radiation from microwave ovens alone. An
additional 2 million people are treated annually with microwave
or radiofrequency diathermy, and some 60,000 individuals may
be occupationally exposed in medical offices and clinics (4).

Still another source of public exposure to microwaves in
varying degrees is broadcasting and communication services and
radar. In addition to a public health concern for individuals
in the immediate locale of individual communication
transmitters, there also is general environmental pollution
resulting from the myriad of broadcast towers, communication
links, radar installations, and other sources of microwave as
well as radiofrequency radiation that are typical of a large
city. The public health implications of such chronic general
population exposures is virtually unknown but cannot be
discounted.

Acute biological effects following high microwave exposures
include cataract formation where the eye is directly exposed,
death following hyperthermia after excessive whole-body
radiation, and testicular damage resulting from both whole-body
and testicular exposure (4). In general, these effects have
occurred at exposures greater than 50 milliwats per square
centimeter (mW/cm$^2$) (4).

Similar to ionizing radiation, for microwave exposures
there are apparent segments of the population at high risk of
adverse effects (4): First, persons being treated about the
head and neck with diathermy may experience a higher risk for
the development of microwave cataracts; and, second, the fetus
is possibly the most sensitive segment of the population to
microwave radiation effects.

Animal studies have shown congenital anomalies following
microwave exposure of the developing fetus (4). Preliminary
studies at Johns Hopkins University (supported by the DHEW)
also indicate possible relationships between paternal radar
exposure and Down's Syndrome (mongolism) among offspring (48).
Efforts are being undertaken to confirm these initial
observations by enlargement of the study group and collection
of detailed exposure histories of the fathers of the children
in the study.

The susceptibility of the eye to microwave-induced cataracts
is demonstrated by a case of a 38-year-old man, who, following
microwave diathermy treatment for strained neck muscles,
developed bilateral posterior subcapsular cataracts (3). This
experience highlights the fact that medical practitioners who
employ microwave diathermy are often unaware of the potential
hazards and, therefore, are not alert to possible adverse
radiation-related sequelae.

Nevertheless, there has emerged the situation of widespread
use of diathermy in medical and dental practices (3). In 1972,
there were an estimated 15,000 microwave and 15,000 shortwave
units in civilial operation (4). A major factor in contributing
potential public exposures is the lack of qualifications of
the operators of this equipment. A survey (3) of all diathermy
apparatus in use at 118 locations in Pinellas County, Florida,
by physicians, osteopaths, chiropractors, physical therapists,
hospitals, nursing homes, and health spas revealed 256
individual diathermy units: 45 percent were ultrasonic; 26
percent, shortwave; and 29 percent, microwave. Ninety percent
of the actual operators of the diathermy machines had received
only on-the-job training. In any one month, approximately 3
percent of the population of Pinellas County is treated with
diathermy an average of seven times (3).

The human body must dissipate heat by radiation, conduction, or the evaporation of perspiration. At frequencies of about 3,000 mHz superficial penetration of the body occurs, and the body tissues are heated. When the body cannot dissipate this heat fast enough, the body's temperature rises. However, the ability of the whole body to tolerate such temperature increases is limited. Under normal circumstances the human body can transfer 10 mW/cm$^2$ of heat of body surface. When the microwave exposure is greater than this, tissue damage which occurs is indistinguisable from that due to a fever caused by illness. A warming sensation, similar to that from sunlight, may be felt. Such a sensation serves as an indication that whole body damage is imminent. However, there is no warning sign for damage of the eyes which are particularly sensitive to heat damage.

Other significant bioeffects include microwave-induced chromosome abnormalities and alterations of protein synthesis (49). Some observers, mainly in the Soviet Union, claim microwave exposures can cause behavioral changes, associated with central nervous system damage (4). However, these effects have yet to be confirmed in the United States for exposures which are less than the levels for heat-induced effects. Nevertheless, these reports suggest the need for extreme prudence in our approach to microwave radiation. The long-term bioeffects of chronic, low-level microwave exposures have not been investigated in this country.

On the basis of available evidence, a voluntary occupational health standard of 10 mW/cm$^2$ was adopted by the American Conference of Governmental Industrial Hygienists (50). At the time, it was intended to be used as a guide for evaluating the work environment -- not general population or consumer exposures. Concern also was for thermal bioeffects resulting from whole-body exposure to microwaves; consideration was not given to sensitive segments of the population or to particularly sensitive parts of the body.

This standard also was adopted by the Department of Defense (DOD) as an occupational health standard for radar and other technicians. However, the DOD also had available the results of animal studies indicating testicular injury at power densities of only 5 mW/cm$^2$ (51, 52). This experimental evidence suggests that the standard is in need of revision.

Also, the standard was established when microwave exposures were fairly uncommon except on warships and at airports, and when the general population was unlikely to be exposed. Consequently, this standard may be inappropriate for microwaves emitted from sources in the home, in some cars, traffic lights,

and utility poles. For example, proposed collision-avoidance
systems for cars produce a microwave beam angle of two degrees
with anticipated power densities of 0.1 mW/cm$^2$ at a distance
of 5 meters. Although these power levels are small compared to
the American National Standards Institute (ANSI) voluntary
occupational standards for electromagnetic radiation, we shall
see that they exceed the standards proposed by the U.S.S.R.

In 1967, Dr. Sol M. Michaelson, now a consultant to the
Association of Home Appliance Manufacturers, expressed (53)
the view that sufficient factual data was not available to
establish a comprehensive safe level for microwave exposure
and, further knowledge of microwave hazards, especially those
of a subacute nature, was required to establish safety
regulations.

Although the research Dr. Michaelson mentioned in 1967 had
not been completed six years later (March 1973), when he again
appeared before the Senate Commerce Committee -- during
oversight hearings on P.L. 90-602, as the Home Appliance
Manufacturers' expert witness -- he advised the Committee that

"There is no evidence in the scientific literature of the
Western world that the present U.S. standard of 10 mW/cm$^2$
represents a hazardous exposure level or to suggest that this
limit should be lowered.

There is no reason to believe that current standards are
inadequate for the protection of the public. Confusion has
been created by reports which have alleged microwave injury
without substantiated proof. No new data from the literature
and no new valid arguments have been presented to change the
situation from what it was last year, 4 years ago, or 15 years
ago." (54)

The controversy over the adequacy of the present U.S.
microwave standard led the Federal Government to launch a
major research effort on the biological effects of microwave
radiation, which will be discussed on the following pages.
Thus the cost and burden of proof for revision of this
electromagnetic radiation standard now rests almost solely on
the government and the taxpayer. Meanwhile, the electronic-
product industry is in the position of continuing to supply an
expanding market on the basis of a microwave exposure standard
which is questionable as well as an occupational standard not
originally developed for application to consumer exposures.

The logical question is: What if anything is industry doing
in the area of bioeffects studies?

The appropriateness of this question is highlighted by the
fact that the Institute of Labor Hygiene and Occupational
Disease of the U.S.S.R. Academy of Medical Sciences in 1960
set a maximum occupational level for microwave exposure at
0.01 mW/cm$^2$, based, they say, upon actual case histories of
humans exposed to microwave energy (55). A large number of
general effects have been linked to chronic low-level microwave
exposures in the U.S.S.R., including bradycardia (slowing of
heart rate), hypertension, hyperthyroidism, exhaustion,
decrease in sense of smell, and changes in the intraocular
pressure (55). The Soviet permissible exposure is thus 1,000
times lower than that acceptable in the United States, which
has been in effect for 15 years. The Soviet Union's maximum
permissible occupational exposure standard, however, is an
average for a work day and can be raised to 1 mW/cm$^2$ for a
15 to 20 minute exposure during the work day (55).

The foregoing disparity was noted in 1968 by the Senate
Commerce Committee and has led to considerable controversy,
particularly regarding the Soviet announcements of effects
on the central nervous system.

For example, Dr. Michaelson questions whether presently
available experimental data can be validly applied to humans
and used as the reason to lower the present United States
microwave exposure standard (55). The dilemma is how to
establish responsible exposure standards given the inadequate
scientific information on somatic and genetic effects of
microwaves. Moreover, there is at issue what level of
commercial, industrial, and consumer usage of microwave
technologies should be permitted, while reasonably protecting
the public health, until research can provide sufficient
information to establish consumer exposure standards for
microwaves which reflect known risks.

Meanwhile, some of the effects of acute, high-dose-rate
exposure of the tissues of experimental animals are known.
The degree to which this information can be extrapolated to
the human situation is limited because of inadequate dosimetry
and peculiarities of the experimental situations. The
biological effects of chronic, low-level microwave exposure
are unknown (4).

In 1973, the Federal Government (the largest single user of
electromagnetic devices in the United States) launched a five-
year, $63 million program to evaluate the biological hazards
of electromagnetic radiations arising from communication
activities (56). This research program is under the direction
of the White House's Office of Telecommunications Policy. The

nongovernmental Electromagnetic Radiation Management Advisory
Council (ERMAC) played a key role in the design of the study.

Under this program, DOD is responsible for 31 out of the
54 projects in the study. In 1973 the Department of the Navy
was also conducting studies of microwave effects at Pensacola,
Florida, using human volunteers (51). Similar irradiation
studies on monkeys had been begun earlier but were cancelled
before results could be obtained (51).

The federal radiation protection posture for nonionizing
radiation was described by Clay T. Whitehead, Director of the
Office of Telecommunications Policy, at March 5, 1973 oversight
hearings of the Senate Commerce Committee, as follows:

"With the proliferation in the use of radio and other
electronic devices in responding to society's demands, we must
be more aware of the potential impact of electromagnetic
radiations upon people and things and must better understand
the mechanisms involved so that corrective actions may be taken
as needed. In these endeavors, we must ensure that a sound
scientific foundation is established for protecting man and
his environment, while at the same time permitting continued
effective use of communication equipment with its great social
and economic benefits. I am pleased to be able to report to
you that the Government has anticipated these needs and is
moving to be sure that the scientific information needed will
be available to protect man within his growing electromagnetic
environment." (56)

In short, "more research" is contemplated pending future
policy guidance on exposure standards. In other words, the
radiation protection policy that has so significantly
characterized the control of ionizing radiation is almost
nonexistent in policies governing nonionizing electromagnetic
radiation. Perhaps this is because of the obvious vested
interests which already exist. More likely this situation
obtains because no epidemics of microwave injuries have been
reported as yet.

Nevertheless, considering the projected proliferations of
microwave systems, it is imperative that some assessment be
made in advance. Since large numbers of these microwave sources
actually will be in the hands of the consumer, it is imperative
that their biological implications be fully understood in
advance.

Radiofrequency Sources   When mention is made of electronic
devices emitting radiofrequencies, attention usually is directed

to AM, FM, TV, and radar transmitters. However, radiofrequencies also are used extensively in diathermy units in hospitals, physicians' offices and clinics, and in the athletic departments of secondary schools, colleges, and universities. Moreover, the equipment is operated by personnel with all types of training (or the lack thereof), not just those specialists identified with medicine (57).

The radiofrequency portion of the electromagnetic spectrum that has received the most intensive attention regarding bioeffects is from 100 to 3,000 mHz (57). The available information precludes the drawing of any specific conclusions about the relationship between general population exposures to radiofrequency energy and any possible adverse effects. Nonetheless, general guidelines can be established. The current American National Standards Institute (ANSI) radiation protection guideline for occupational exposure (58) to electromagnetic radiation is 10 mW/cm$^2$ over any average 0.1 hour period; under no circumstances should the total energy delivered be greater than 1 mW-hour/cm$^2$ (in the range of 10 megahertz to 100 gigahertz). However, more research is needed to determine whether this value should be extended to frequencies below 10 megahertz (59) or to general population exposures.

A major source of concern is the exposure of the population resulting from the myriad of radiofrequency and microwave broadcast towers, communication links, radar installations, and other similar sources typical of any large city. Such sources represent the greatest single class of contributors of ambient radiation levels in the radiofrequency range. A study in the Washington, D.C., area recorded a maximum ambient radiofrequency radiation level of 0.01 mW/cm$^2$, only three orders of magnitude less than the ANSI recommended occupational exposure standard (60).

Such AM, FM, and TV broadcast stations are regulated by the FCC; but the Commission's concern is mainly to prevent mutual interference of activities. Various FCC regulations reflect this philosophy.

Although the FCC's authority is sufficient to regulate power densities on the basis of potential physiological effects, no such regulations have as yet been issued. For instance, while both maximum antenna-tower height and radiated power are specified to limit transmission area, no minimum antenna height is specified for TV transmitters to limit public exposures. Permissible designs for UHF TV broadcast antennas (Channels 14 through 83) could lead to ground level radiation near the antenna in excess of 2 mW/cm$^2$ (57).

It is possible that radiation levels in tall buildings, or in the vicinity of buildings supporting transmitter towers, may be considerably higher than 2 mW/cm$^2$, particularly where one antenna broadcasts several signal frequencies (57). Although radiofrequency radiation is generally considered less of a biological hazard than microwave radiation (59, 61), Russian workers have reported bioeffects near broadcast transmitters (62). These effects have yet to be corroborated by research in the United States.

The formulation of general population exposure standards for radiofrequency radiation will have to incorporate many biological and physical variables. Within the high radiofrequency range, thermal effects appear to predominate, although nonthermal effects also may be induced. At very high frequencies resonant heating of some organs can occur: primarily effected are the eyes and testes. At frequencies below 30 mHz resonant heating does not occur, although the radiation penetrates the body, exposing all organs (63).

"Ultra-short wave" therapy utilizes ultra-high radiofrequency electrical currents; the commonly used frequency is 27 megahertz (64). The application of these currents to diathermy stems from their ability to simulate the effect of electromagnetic waves in tissue.

Functional nervous system and cardiovascular system changes from exposure to radiofrequency and low-frequency electromagnetic radiation have been alleged by Soviet scientists. Some of the observed effects which have been categorized as nonthermal must be viewed critically (64, 65). Along with the more common symptoms of headaches, insomnia, irritability and fatigue, Russian observers have found: changes in the EEG, sugar tolerance responses, increase in gamma globulin (66), pyramidal symptoms (67), slight enlargement of the thyroid gland, increases in leukocyte count, and slight shifts in the protein composition of the blood (68). These biological effects of radiofrequency electromagnetic radiation described have been termed nonthermal since no appreciable change in temperature of the system can be detected. However, the distinction between thermal and nonthermal effects in biological systems might very well rest in our inability to detect highly localized or microthermal centers (69).

Infrared Radiation  Infrared radiation (see Figure 1) can produce burns of the skin, cataracts, or retinal burns. The more common industrial exposures are found in hot-metal operations, glassmaking, photoengraving, paint and enamel drying, and welding (57). Infrared is also used in homes and eating establishments for both heating and cooking, there being

an estimated 13,400 infrared ovens in food service
establishments in the United States (57).

The infrared portion of the spectrum should be divided into
two regions: that which penetrates the eye to the retina
(designated near infrared) and that which does not. Very little
is known regarding the bioeffects of exposure to either portion
of the spectrum; however, eye and genetic damage can occur
(57). There is some concern regarding the possible
psychophysiological effects (neuroendocrine mediated) (57).

Chronic exposure to artificial infrared radiation (as well
as to visible and ultraviolet light) may have subtle but very
important bioeffects; for example, changes in the natural
rhythms in certain species (57).

Visible Light    There are numerous sources of visible light,
most of which are relatively innocuous. Certain high-intensity
noncoherent light sources emitting energy fluxes greater than
50 cal/cm$^2$ min, may cause eye injury (70). Estimates are not
available on the total number of devices capable of delivering
this amount of energy to the eye. Items which would fall in
this category include high-intensity reading lamps, movie and
slide projector bulbs, spotlights, floodlights, and so forth.
These items, like ultraviolet lamps, probably number in the
tens of thousands, or even millions (57).

The entire population, in effect, is at risk from exposure
to noncoherent light devices. Certain groups are at greater
risk from certain sources; e.g., actors and models with intense
studio lights, welders to arc lights, etc. (Noncoherent sources
exist that emit in other parts of the spectrum. Examples of
population at risk from "invisible light" are students with
their blacklights, and doctors, nurses, and health-spa devotees
with their germicidal ultraviolet and heat (infrared) lamps.)

The only coherent light sources of importance here is the
laser. Lasers are expected to number 260,000 by 1980 (4). Most
of the general population could be exposed to lasers employed
in information processing and surveying. High-risk groups are
construction workers, science students, and scientists.

Ultraviolet Radiation    Ultraviolet light encompasses that
region of the electromagnetic spectrum between visible light
and X rays (see Figure 1). Ultraviolet radiation results from
a variety of industrial processes, including some hot metal
operations, and the operation of various lamps specifically
designed for ultraviolet emission. A prominent natural source
of ultraviolet light is the sun.

The ultraviolet portion of the electromagnetic spectrum
extends into the short-wave region where atoms and molecules
can be ionized. Specific ultraviolet-induced molecular

breakdowns have been circumstantially implicated in mutational
and biological events, which lead to altered metabolism, death,
or genetically transmitted damage in cells (71).

Since ultraviolet light does not penetrate deeply into body
tissue, most effects occur in the skin. The occurrence of
erythema (reddening of the skin) is useful as an index of
exposure and in the establishment of standards. Little is
known, however, about the relationship of erythema to real
hazards. Particular consideration must be given to the role of
photosensitizing compounds, many of which may be unwittingly
used by consumers.

"Whole body" exposure of large numbers of humans to
ultraviolet radiation is unlikely, since common articles of
clothing effectively screen out this portion of the spectrum.
Viewed from the standpoint of critical organs of exposure (72),
the skin is the main absorber of ultraviolet radiation and
reacts by erythema, tanning, and pigment darkening (73).
Exposure of the eye also may result in painful corneal burns
and blindness. Such a hazard exists for persons in the presence
of welding arcs and germicidal lamps (71).

The major possible result of chronic exposures to
ultraviolet radiation is the production of skin cancer.
Repeated exposures are necessary to induce malignancy (74).
Production of skin cancer also is associated with prolonged
exposure to the trace amounts of ultraviolet light in natural
sunlight.

In 1943, AMA's Council on Physical Therapy recommended
exposure standards for germicidal ultraviolet lamps (75) which
were updated in 1948 (76). The recommendation is based upon
the observation that 15 minute exposures to 36 microwatts per
square centimeter (36 $\mu W/cm^2$) of short-wave-ultraviolet
radiation produces erythema. On the assumption of reciprocity
for low intensities and long exposures, a maximum of 0.5
$\mu W/cm^2$ was recommended for persons exposed for 7 hours or less.
For general population exposures (24 hours per day) the AMA's
recommended exposure standard is 0.10 $\mu W/cm^2$ (76).

Electronic product sources of ultraviolet radiation have
been principally arcs and incandescent sources operating at
high temperatures. In recent years high-intensity ultraviolet
lamps have also become available for consumer use. Overall
estimates are not available for the total number of ultraviolet
devices; however, they easily number in the tens or hundreds of
thousands. For example, ultraviolet sources are used in
cosmetic and therapeutic sun lamps, disinfection, sterilization,
and analytical instruments. They are widely used in homes,
industries, and scientific and medical environments. These

lamps produce electromagnetic radiation near the peak lethal
range for biological systems. Although used primarily for
germicidal purposes, newer lamps reproduce the light spectrum
of natural sunlight and are being widely used for indoor
greenhouses.

Ultrasound  Ultrasound is not a species of electromagnetic
energy; instead, it is mechanical vibration at frequencies
above the limit of human audibility, greater than 16 kilohertz
(kHz). The interactions of ultrasound in tissue are highly
complex and poorly understood. While some of the reported
cause-effect relationships for ultrasound are consistent with
existing theory, certain cases cannot be explained (4).
Considering the potential consequences of the widespread
application of ultrasound, e.g., in medicine, there is ample
justification to proceed with caution. In fact, it is
imperative that the health risks of ultrasound be adequately
evaluated and standards for human exposure established, where
they do not now exist.

Although ultrasound is a relatively new energy source, its
versatility has led to widespread employment in various
industrial, medical, scientific, and consumer products. The
most important and successful industrial applications for
ultrasonics can be divided into two distinct categories:
First, low-power applications for measurement and control; and,
second, high-power applications to modify materials by the
dissipation of energy. Low-power nondestructive testing is
accomplished by means of the higher ultrasonic frequencies.
Procedures requiring high power, with significant energy
dissipation, operate best at lower frequencies. The following
warning was issued by E. B. Steinberg (77):

"It must be kept in mind that the energy used in most
industrial applications is several million times greater than
that radiated by an average radio loudspeaker. Hence, for
convenience, comfort, and safety, the majority of industrial
applications make use of 'ultra'-sonic frequencies."

Although an accurate inventory is not available of various
ultrasonic devices, the rapidly expanding use of ultrasonic
power puts some urgency on the need to determine the
biological effects of ultrasonic radiation.

Present ultrasonic cleaners range from small consumer units
designed to clean dentures and jewelry, to large industrial
units, used to degrease instruments, tools, or materials prior
to other processing such as electroplating (4). In 1972, there
were 100,000 commercial-industrial cleaning applications alone.

The associated occupational population at risk about 125,000
persons (4). Moreover, the number of cleaning and commercial-
industrial applications is expected to increase to 380,000
units by 1980 (4).

Commercial-industrial uses of ultrasound also include
mixers, milling machines, sewing machines, nebulizers,
grinders, welders, sonars, burglar alarms, rodent-control
devices, and bird-repelling units (4).

The use of ultrasonic radiation in medical diagnosis and
physiotherapy are two of the most rapidly growing examples of
medical ultrasonics. In the future, the extent of this use
alone is expected to be comparable to that for X rays (4). As a
result, this is a significant area of public health concern.
In 1970, there were some 3,000 installations (57), and growth
patterns suggest there were 10,000 installations in 1972 (78),
and that there will be some 175,000 medical diagnostic
installations by 1976 (4). Although the anticipated population
at risk is not known, the number of people treated annually
with ultrasonic diathermy could easily increase from the 1970
figure of 2 million to more than 110 million  by 1976 (47).

A review of the evidence on ultrasound bioeffects indicates
that the intensities used in diagnostic procedures, in the
hands of a trained operator, do not seem hazardous (79).
However, this conclusion is not based upon long-term
epidemiologic evidence. Nevertheless, ultrasound of therapeutic
intensities can be hazardous even in the hands of trained
operators. At still higher intensities ultrasound is
destructive.

The safety of ultrasound cannot be guaranteed simply because
there are minimal short-term detectable effects. However, the
unknown risks can be viewed as justified where the lack of
treatment presents a high risk to a patient; e.g., when
ultrasound is used in the treatment of brain tumors. Yet even
when used in surgical procedures ultrasound should be used
with extreme caution.

Present knowledge of the bioeffects of ultrasound emphasizes
the biophysical aspects of the associated cause-effect
relationships rather than the biological consequences of
exposure. These effects include heating, destruction of cells
and molecules, induction of cataracts, and interference with
the hearbeat and with the transmission of nerve impulses.
Ultrasound also may induce chromosomal abnormalities.

Although the value of the use of ultrasound in clinical
medicine as a diagnostic tool is apparent, the attendant risks
are poorly understood. This is in part due to the inability to
quantify tissue exposures or to measure the energy actually

imparted to tissue. Nevertheless, the widespread use of ultrasound for in utero diagnostic procedures suggests that fetuses comprise the segment of the population at greatest risk. Unfortunately, these risks cannot be settled by casual observation by practicing physicians. One is impressed with the almost total lack of the long-term effects of ultrasound on the fetus exposed in utero (80). Even if one were to accept the view that the benefits of diagnostic ultrasound as used in obstetrics outweighs the risks, which is in itself debatable, there still remains the question of whether the procedure itself is being performed with minimum risk to the patient, or if the operator is even qualified to make this judgment.

Ultrasound can cause general heating. A particularly important form of ultrasonic energy absorption is called "mode conversion"; this results in strong local deposition of energy. This may occur at any acoustic impedance boundary of fluid, or soft tissue, where ultrasound can be refracted. Mode conversion at soft tissue/bone interfaces is probably responsible for some of the cases of bone and periosteal damage that have been reported following the therapeutic use of ultrasound (81).

Another effect, called "cavitation," occurs when ultrasonic vibrations are transmitted in liquids. It is an acoustical phenomenon producing the enormous shearing forces employed in cleaning devices, homogenizers, nebulizers, and devices which degrade cellular and microbial structures. Cavitation can be explained as follows:

"Most ordinary liquids contain stable micro-bubbles, or other minute nuclei, around which bubbles of dissolved gas are able to grow under the influence of moderate ultrasonic fields. Upon reaching a certain size which is characteristic of the sound frequency, such bubbles exhibit mechanical resonance, with vibration amplitude that may be several orders of magnitude greater than that of the particles of the liquid in the absence of the sound frequency. This enhancement of vibration amplitude, together with the small-scale patterns of fluid movement or 'microstreaming' that it induces, can lead to high shear and tensile stresses being set up in the liquid, sufficient to break structures such as macromolecules and cell membranes." (82)

Cavitation can thus lead to rapid tissue damage. The complex question of whether cavitation occurs in tissue from the use of diagnostic and/or therapeutic ultrasonic energy has not been resolved.

The possibility of health effects where ultrasound emanates into air is lower than for direct contact or contact mediated by liquids. However, care is warranted to prevent hearing damage or systemic and psychological effects (79).

It is clear that the higher-intensity exposures are of significance in relation to both acute and long-term effects. Experimental, as opposed to clinical, studies at low ultrasound exposure intensities suggest strongly that there is biological damage associated with diagnostic ultrasonic exposures. There is a high probability of subtle long-term effects or irreparable acute changes following exposure to diagnostic intensities of ultrasonic energy (83, 84).

Exposure standards are not available for ultrasonic equipment for cleaning, medical diagnostic, or diathermy uses. Biomedical and biophysical research efforts analogous to past radiobiological investigations are clearly necessary to investigate and to identify levels of ultrasonic radiation exposure that cause overt biological damage (79).

While performance standards for continuous ultrasound devices are difficult enough to develop, the measurement of pulsed ultrasound presents yet more technical problems. The FDA is currently evaluating medical ultrasound diathermy equipment for purposes of determining whether appropriate performance standards can be established (4).

Sonic Vibration  Vibrations perceivable by the auditory system (16 Hz to 16 kHz), in contrast to those vibrations in excess of 16 kHz (ultrasound) and those less than 16 Hz (infrasound), can cause a wide range of physical and emotional effects in humans including deafness, fatigue, and decreased concentration. The tolerable noise level for the human ear is about 90 decibels (db). Surveys indicate that the sound intensity in the average residence was five times greater in 1968 than it was in 1938, climbing from 30 to 45 db in 30 years (85).

The sources of this noise typically include radios, televisions, phonographs, power mowers, power saws, electronic music instruments, automobiles, trains, aircraft, industrial equipment, construction equipment, air conditioners, and boats. Obviously, many of the sources of noise are not electronic products.

Infrasonic Vibration (85)  Infrasonic vibrations, of the low-frequency (less than 16 Hz) vibration of a number of mechanical devices and structures, can cause physical discomfort. The majority of these sources probably cannot be

considered electronic products in the context of P.L. 90-602.
Some natural sources of infrasound are earthquakes, erupting
volcanoes, thunder, and wind.

Magnetic Fields   Magnetic fields are associated with the
movement of electric charges (86). Exposure to extremely
intense magnetic fields will produce subtle biological effects.
From a public health standpoint, the risk of large population
groups being exposed to harmful magnetic fields appears
relatively small. Only a few sources are considered capable of
producing field strengths, under conditions for potential human
exposure, of sufficient magnitude to present biological hazards.
These sources include accelerators, plasma-physics experiments,
and high-capacity electric power generating apparatus. However,
the use of superconducting magnets and motors in industry,
and proposals to store electrical energy in superconducting
magnets, may well cause more occupational exposure to magnetic
fields in the near future.

## Electronic-Product Performance Standards Of The Radiation Control For Health And Safety Act Of 1968

In the application of radiation protection principles and
exposure standards to electronic products several forms of
radiation emission standards and regulations have emerged.
First, there are design standards which are intended for
application by the manufacturer of radiation-emitting
equipment. Second, there are performance standards which apply
after an electronic product is placed in operation. Obviously,
such performance standards are closely linked to design
standards. Third, there are those guidelines and recommendations
which represent standards of good practice. These latter
standards are intended primarily to judge the actions of
individuals actually using electronic devices. Such operators
are particularly difficult to regulate, for good practice
entails issues of personal judgment.

Whatever their form, the purpose of performance standards
is to reduce unnecessary public radiation exposure as well as
to protect the individual users of electronic products.

Regulatory, as distinguished from advisory, standards are
the tools for the government's enforcement of public policy
where voluntary compliance proves ineffective or unsuccessful.
To this end, the Radiation Control for Health and Safety Act
of 1968 provides for the establishment and the administration
of performance standards governing radiation emissions from
electronic products. As defined by statute, "electronic
products" cover sources of radiation encompassing the whole
electromagnetic spectrum as well as the sonic spectrum.

The critical standards are those performance standards which
set the emission limits with which a manufacturer's products
are expected to comply. The purpose of performance standards
are:

- to assure that all products or equipment meet minimum
standards of quality regarding radiation emissions; and

- to establish a market environment within which suppliers may
compete without endangering the health of the consumer.

In this regard, there are two types of safety standards:
first, mandatory standards which are established and
administered by a federal, State, or local governmental agency;
and, second, recommended or voluntary standards, which may be
prescribed by private standards associations such as the ANSI,
or by manufacturers themselves.

In the past, completely different issues were associated
with each of these standard types. The mandatory standards,
of course, are enforceable, carrying various degrees of penalty
for noncompliance. On the other hand, voluntary standards or
recommended standards all too often have been interpreted
loosely, or even ignored.

Performance standards are concerned not only with permissible
radiation levels but also with adequate labels, warnings, and
identification. They also can include provisions for
installation, operation, and use of an electronic product.
However, while it is possible to require the manufacturer to
provide instructions for use, such standard provisions are
difficult to enforce, even under conditions where operators
must be licensed.

The application of performance standards is of necessity on
a product-by-product basis. The criteria for inclusion of an
electronic product under performance-standard provisions is
that control of the product's radiation emissions is necessary
to protect the public health and safety. Under the Radiation
Control for Health and Safety Act of 1968 a performance
standard also must be tested for reasonableness and technical
feasibility. As will be discussed, this has presented a problem
for the initial draft standards for color TV's and for medical
X-ray equipment standards.

The Act also created the Technical Electronic Product
Radiation Safety Standards Committee to advise the Secretary
on the issues as technical feasibility and reasonableness. This
expert fifteen-member Committee is made up of five
representatives from industry, five from government, and five
from the private sector.

Since enactment of the Radiation Control for Health and Safety Act of 1968, the Food and Drug Administration (FDA), which administers the Act through its Bureau of Radiological Health, as of September 1973 had established performance standards for television receivers, microwave ovens, certain electron tubes used in high school and college science instruction, and diagnostic X-ray equipment systems. These products also are required to have compliance certification labels or tags. But, the progress has been slow because of the constraint of inadequate funds.

The first regulations, promulgated on June 4, 1969, and subsequently revised, set forth the corrective action to be taken by manufacturers when their products are found to have a radiation safety defect or fail to comply with a federal radiation control standard (87, 88). The regulations establish procedures for a manufacturer's notification of the FDA when he finds defects in his electronic products and spell out the steps that the manufacturer also must take to warn distributors and users of such defects and to offer repair, replacement, or cost refunds.

Two classes of electronic products are covered by the definition of safety-related radiation defects:

- products emitting radiation as part of their function (such as X-ray machines), but which fail to conform to radiation-emission design specifications or which emit radiation beyond levels necessary for their performance; and

- products not utilizing radiation as part of their function (such as television sets), but which emit unintended radiation at levels creating a risk to health or which do not conform to design specification.

Proposed regulations relating to record-keeping and reporting requirements for manufacturers and distributors of certain electronic products were published and subsequently revised (88, 89, 90). These requirements apply to manufacturers of television receivers, television projection devices, shunt regulator tubes, high-voltage rectifier tubes, high-voltage vacuum switches, all types of X-ray producing devices, microwave ovens, microwave diathermy units, all types of lasers, and ultrasonic devices. Under the FDA's regulations a manufacturer is required to maintain records for 5 years, beginning with the first date on which the product is offered for public sale. These records are to include: (1) radiation test results and methods, (2) product durability and stability tests, (3) quality control procedures, and (4) product use, maintenance, and testing instructions that have radiation control

significance. Additional reporting procedures and required
records also are described in the regulations.

The FDA, as of July 1973, also had under development (4):

- laser product standards;
- nonmedical cabinet X-ray system standards;
- microwave oven standard amendments;
- ultrasonic therapy standards;
- microwave therapy standards; and
- diagnostic X-ray standard amendments.

The status of the various standards promulgated by the FDA
under P.L. 90-602 is summarized in Table 6 (4).

<u>Television Receivers</u> In the 1950's, black-and-white TV's, using
cathode ray tubes, were recognized as a potential source of
consumer exposure to ionizing radiation (91). The first
voluntary standards were recommended in 1960 by the NCRPM (92).
With the advent of color television receivers, the NCRPM in
1965 reaffirmed their earlier recommendation, that X-ray
exposure at any accessible point 5 centimeters from the surface
of any home television should not exceed 0.5 milliroentgens per
hour under normal operating conditions (13). The standard was
based on an arbitrary assumption that emissions from television
receivers should be about 5 percent of natural background (12).
This standard was reaffirmed in February 1968 when the NCRPM
stated:

"The judgment of the NCRP is that the use of television
receivers in the home should not contribute to the annual
genetically significant dose to the population in excess of
about 5 percent of the average dose from natural background
radiation (about 120 mrem)." (93)

No reason was seen for modifying the numerical values given
in its 1959 recommendation in that, although higher operating
voltages create a larger absorbed radiation exposure, "...this
increase is not significant to the viewer, who is normally two,
or more, meters from the set." (93). This voluntary emission
standard, however, was not adopted by the U.L. until September
1, 1967 (13). Since 1948, the U.L. had been testing televisions
against a standard of 2.5 milliroentgens per hour (13).

Following the discussed experience with G.E. color
televisions, in early 1968, an extensive survey (94) in the
Washington, D.C. area revealed that six percent of the sets
(66 out of 1,124) examined emitted X radiation in excess of
0.5 mr/hr; forty of these were in excess of 1.0 mr/hr and two
exceeded 12 mr/hr.

Table 6  Summary of Performance Standards Promulgated or Anticipated Pursuant to the
Radiation Control for Health and Safety Act of 1968 (P.L. 90-602)

| Equipment Type | Standard Proposed | Standard Promulgated | Effective Date (a) |
|---|---|---|---|
| Television receivers | | Dec. 25, 1969 | Jan. 15, 1970 |
| Cold-cathode gas discharge tubes | | May 19, 1970 | May 19, 1970 |
| Microwave ovens | | Oct. 6, 1970 | Oct. 6, 1971 |
| Diagnostic X-ray systems and other major components | | Aug. 15, 1972 | Aug. 15, 1974 |
| Draft standards, with anticipated dates (as of March 1973) (57) | | | |
| Laser products | July 1973 | Nov. 1973 | Nov. 1974 |
| Nonmedical cabinet radiography systems | July 1973 | Nov. 1973 | Nov. 1974 |
| Amendment to microwave oven standard | April 1973 | Aug. 1973 | Aug. 1974 |
| Amendment to diagnostic X-ray standard relative to dental X-ray equipment | Oct. 1973 | Feb. 1974 | Feb. 1975 |

Table 6 (cont.)

| Equipment Type | Standard Proposed | Standard Promulgated | Effective Date (a) |
|---|---|---|---|
| Other Possibilities (57) | | | |
| Microwave diathermy (b) | | | |
| Microwave communication devices (c) | | | |
| Ultrasonic cleaning equipment (c) | | | |
| Medical diagnostic ultrasonic equipment (c) | | | |
| Ultrasonic diathermy (d) | | | |
| Industrial-commercial ultrasonic equipment (c) | | | |

(a) Section 358 (c) of the Act provides that the effective date of a standard shall be between one and two years following final publication of the standard in the Federal Register unless the Secretary of HEW finds out that an earlier date is in the public interest.
(b) Voluntary standard unknown.
(c) Industry concensus on standard unknown.
(d) International Electrotechnical Commission voluntary standard.

These numbers appear small; however, when extrapolated nationally the population at risk was some 140,000 children and 310,000 older viewers. While a small population at risk, this exposure could have been prevented, thus reinforcing the justification for federal regulation.

The initial performance standard for X-ray emissions from color television (95) became effective on January 15, 1970, some 14 months after enactment of the Radiation Control for Health and Safety Act of 1968, for all units manufactured after June 1, 1971. The 1965 NCRPM recommended standard was adopted restricting the leakage of radiation from color television receivers to less than 0.5 mr/hr at 5 cm (about 2 inches) from any surface of the set operating at a maximum of 130 line volts.

There also is a requirement that the manufacturer must label all the critical components in the set and identify their operating characteristics. Another provision of the regulation, effective July, 1971, was that should certain components fail, the standard had to be met anyway. For example, certain circuits can fail without loss of a viewable picture. However, due to the circuit failure, voltages or other components may be increased, thereby increasing the leakage radiation.

When the color television standard was being drafted, a leakage radiation limit of 0.1 mr/hr was proposed. However, when the test of "reasonableness and technical feasibility" was applied, the final standard of 0.5 mr/hr was adopted (94). In order to meet the lower proposed standard, the manufacturer's quality control programs would have had to produce sets with emissions well below this value and the necessary instrumentation was not available at the time.

A survey of color television sets manufactured after the effective date of the federal standard shows improvement in the reduction of X radiation (96). The EIA's Ad Hoc Committee on X-Radiation from Television, when expressing viewpoints on testing of the television receiver standard, indicated that (49):

- Replacing older small components with better designed tubes, such as shunt and rectifier tubes, is possible and is being carried out.

- The cathode-ray picture tube is much more difficult to control because of the prevalence of rebuilt tubes and because of the economic problems of deliberate obsolescence.

- At the present time, there are no plans for recircuiting, "modernizing," or adding new shielding to older television receivers. The emphasis will be on correct service adjustments and proper installation of replacement parts.

The elimination of any remaining hazard associated with color television sets manufactured before the effective date of the FDA's standard, of necessity, will require the cooperation of their owners as well as individual television servicemen.

Cold Cathode Gas Discharge Tubes   A 1970 Federal-State survey brought to light that demonstration-type cold cathode gas discharge tubes used in science, biology, and chemistry classes in high school and college represented potentially harmful sources of radiation exposure (97). The electronic tubes were designed to demonstrate properties of cathode-ray (electron) beams. Three types of electronic tubes, not intended to emit radiation, were found to leak X rays at rates in excess of the NCRPM's recommended standard (98). Under an FDA directive the sole domestic manufacturer ceased production and recalled distributor stocks. Some 37 States took actions to locate cold cathode tubes being used in secondary schools. Several States also undertook a survey of radiation sources in schools and initiated educational programs on the control of radiation exposure.

On January 30, 1970, performance standards were proposed by the FDA (99) and, later, finalized for demonstration-type cold-cathode gas discharge tubes (100, 101). The USPHS based its standard on a 1966 NCRPM recommendation that students under 18 years of age, while participating in educational activities, should not receive an ionizing radiation dose which exceeds 100 millirem per year, nor should they receive a radiation dose which exceeds 10 millirem during any one experiment (98).

The final standard (99) promulgated by the FDA's Bureau of Radiological Health, was 10 milliroentgens per hour at a distance of 30 centimeters (99, 100, 101). Taking effect on the date of final promulgation, May 19, 1970, manufacturers also are required to provide appropriate safety instructions and warning labels or tags.

Microwave Equipment   A variety of electronic devices emit microwave radiation: ovens; diathermy units; heating devices; and television, communication, navigation, and radar units. Although microwave electronic products are currently expensive, anticipated developments in solid-state circuits, when mass produced, may ultimately reduce their costs to a few dollars

compared to current microwave tubes which now typically cost
hundreds of dollars (102). At these reduced prices it is
expected that there will be massive introduction of microwave
devices into homes, in automobiles, and in boats as well as in
commercial and industrial applications (103).

Industrial application of microwave energy has developed
to a point where it can economically compete with, and
complement, conventional heating systems. Although, in 1969,
there were only about 270 units in use, in 1974 there will be
approximately 600 to 800 units in use (4).

Other applications include finish drying of potato chips,
precooking chicken parts, donut cooking, thawing frozen food,
veneer drying, paper drying, and match head drying, as well as
numerous other experimental drying and heating applications
(104).

There are no federal emission standards governing the
performance of industrial microwave heating equipment. However,
the American Conference of Government-Industrial Hygienists
has proposed a Threshold Limit Value (48), which has been
adopted by manufacturers, in cooperation with the International
Microwave Power Institute (IMPI). As an added precaution the
IMPI recommended (105) that the microwave manufacturers
routinely examine their customers' installations to assure
that all safety features are functional.

In recent years, microwave diathermy also has achieved
widespread application. In all, there are an estimated 10 to
15 thousand units in use in this country, with an annual growth
rate of about 3 percent (57).

Other new and novel medical devices are being developed;
for example, a microwave blood warmer (106). While, in 1969,
there were only five units undergoing a testing period in
hospitals, eventually most hospitals may utilize them (106).

The availability of solid state microwave circuitry is
expected to greatly increase other use of microwave; for
example, for various guidance and control functions. Radar
units, which come in a wide range of power levels, are already
utilized in both fixed ground installations (e.g., airports)
and in mobile stations (e.g., marine or air transportation
units). However, a complete inventory is not available.

Automobile radars are anticipated for automatic highway
control, clear-land indication, backup obstacle warning, and
triggering of passive restraint devices. Police radar and
burglar alarms also offer other potentially significant
applications. In addition, various remote control devices
exist, including TV controls, garage door openers, and burglar

alarms; however, no inventory information is available on these devices, either.

An area of potential public health concern is emissions from communication devices. Presently there are some 120,000 microwave communication towers (4), each with several separate sources; altogether greater than 386,054 different sources are involved, not including certain military radar or commercial mobil radar units on planes and ships (57). In addition, there are land-mobile radio services which increased by some 300,000 units annually between 1968 and 1971 (4).

The policy issue is whether these sources will come to represent a form of environmental pollution capable of producing undesirable public health effects. The benefits from anticipated new microwave applications are numerous, including economical communication systems; improved safety and convenience for transportation systems; reduction of fire damage; easier detection and prevention of crime; and possibly, improved health care. Nevertheless, prior to this proliferation, it is essential that there be an assessment of the potential consequences of anticipated growth in microwave usage.

Microwave Ovens  Microwave ovens, first introduced in the late 1940's for use in food service establishments, now represent perhaps the single most significant consumer source of microwave exposure being employed in homes, commercial and vending establishments, and restaurants.

While in 1966 there were about 7,700 microwave ovens (107), by 1972 their number has increased to about 425,000 units in the United States (57) with estimated 1973 annual sales of 500,000 to 600,000 units (108). Their number is expected to increase to some 5 million units by 1980 (57).

Following passage of P.L. 90-602, the manufacturers of microwave cooking immediately began to improve their products. Nevertheless, a 1969 survey of units in New York, New Jersey, Massachusetts, and Mississippi found that one-third of the units exceeded the industry's voluntary standard of 10 mW/cm$^2$ (109). Similar results were found in Florida (110).

These findings, and others, prompted, in early 1970, a nationwide Government-industry survey of microwave ovens. An Ad Hoc Task Force on Microwave Ovens also was convened by the Surgeon General to identify those makes and models which leaked excessively as the basis for corrective action by the manufacturers. Some 10 percent of the ovens in use were found to leak radiation in excess of the industry's voluntary standard (109, 111).

The 1970 survey also found that the principal factors affecting radiation leakage were oven design, user maintenance, and frequency of service (111). The most frequent cause of excess leakage was interlock maladjustment, although improper servicing and maintenance also played an important role.

While the survey was in progress, the following precautions were recommended: (a) keep at least an arm's length away from the front of an oven while it is on; (b) switch the oven off before opening the door; and (c) do not allow children to use the viewport to watch food while cooking.

In May 1970 standards were proposed by the FDA for microwave ovens (112). The final standard was promulgated for microwave ovens limiting the power density of the microwave radiation at a distance of 5 centimeters from the oven to 1 mW/cm$^2$ before sale and 5 mW/cm$^2$ thereafter (113, 114). This standard was applicable to all ovens manufactured after October 6, 1971. Ovens manufactured between October 16, 1968, the effective date of P.L. 90-602, and the above date also are covered by the defect provisions.

In addition, the standards prescribe requirements for the door interlocks, including the requirement that one of the interlocks must be concealed. Nevertheless, operational problems remained because of the difficulty in adjusting safety interlocks, which operate from the motion of the door (60). The potential for leakage of microwave radiation due to misadjusted safety interlocks was considered of sufficient concern that the FDA, on April 9, 1973, proposed amended performance standards for microwave ovens (115).

The existing standards (113) required each oven to have two safety interlocks, either of which can terminate the generation of microwaves upon opening the oven door. The amended standard would require two safety interlocks, one of which must be concealed so that it cannot be operated by any part of the body.

In April 1973, however, the Consumer's Union (C.U.) brought the issue of the safety of microwave ovens into sharp focus by advising against the purchase of microwave ovens (108), stating that, "After thoroughly testing fifteen popular models of counter-top microwave ovens, and examining available literature, we are not convinced that they are completely safe to use. We've therefore designated them all Not Recommended."

This position was taken although all of the ovens tested met the FDA's Bureau of Radiological Health's emission standards. C.U. argued (108) that, "Until much more evidence is available regarding the safety of low-level microwave radiation,

we do not feel we could consider a microwave oven Acceptable
unless there is no radiation leakage detectable."

An additional aspect of their recommendation was a specific
point of caution to the wearers of pacemakers to stay away
from microwave ovens and a demand of the manufacturers to
inform consumers of the possibility of intereference with
pacemakers by microwave radiation (108).

Thus, despite accomplishments to date, there is a need for
the continued surveillance of microwave ovens to monitor (a)
the thoroughness of the manufacturers' corrective action
program, (b) the manufacturers' efforts to improve their
customer service capability in the area of owner and operator
education and microwave emission control, and (c) compliance
with the microwave oven performance standard (111).

<u>Diagnostic X-ray Equipment</u> As the practice of medicine is very
dependent on the science of radiology including the diagnostic
use of X rays, radio-therapy, particle-accelerators, and
radioisotopes, consequently medical and dental X-ray usage is
now the largest single source of manmade radiation exposure.
However, then FDA Commissioner Charles C. Edwards has commented
that

"While the beneficial applications of X radiation in the
healing arts are well recognized, exposures from diagnostic
X-ray procedures have far more public health significance than
exposures from all other manmade radiation sources. More than
90 percent of all human exposure to manmade radiation comes
from the diagnostic use of X-ray in contrast with about one
percent from radioactive discharges from nuclear power plants
about which there has been so much public concern." (116)

Potentially the whole United States population are at risk;
for example, in 1970, alone, some 130 million people had 179
million X-ray examinations (4). Selected groups such as older
people experienced an even greater incidence of examinations.
The attendant risk of unnecessary radiation exposure can be
reduced by three complementary regulatory approaches:

- the setting of performance standards for the manufacture of
electronic devices, such as X-ray equipment and their
accessories.

- licensing of the possession and use of radiation devices.

- licensing or certifying operators of X-ray equipment.

This discussion centers on equipment performance standards
for the equipment  itself. Licensing the possession of
radiation devices and their operators is discussed in
Chapter 5.

The number of diagnostic X-ray units in the United States
have grown from about 125,000 in 1959 (117) to about 200,000
units in 1969 (118), with an anticipated 250,000 units by 1980
and 300,000 units by 1990 (119).

This equipment generally is sold on an installed basis.
Medical X-ray equipment usually is owned and operated by
non-radiologist physicians, who often have no training in the
operation of the equipment nor in radiation protection.

The medical profession, generally, depends upon the
equipment manufacturer for installation of a variety of
radiographic and therapeutic equipment (see Table 7), as well
as for training in the equipment's operation. The manufacturer
also is depended upon for preventative maintenance, overhaul,
and upgrading through the useable life of the equipment,
although this service is not rendered automatically (Table 7).

Nevertheless, current federal radiation control programs
emphasize establishment of equipment performance standard under
P.L. 90-602. However, existing national and international

Table 7  Medical and Dental Equipment Types and Functions (4)

| Function | Use | Type |
| --- | --- | --- |
| Medical | General purpose | Radiographic - stationary<br>Radiographic - mobile<br>Radiographic - portable<br><br>Fluoroscopic - stationary<br>Fluoroscopic - mobile |
|  | Special purpose | Mammographic<br>Urological<br>Chest<br>Podiatric<br>Tomographic<br>Head and neck<br>Hip-pinning<br>Stereotaxic |
| Dental | General purpose | Intraoral<br>Cephalometric<br>Panoramic |

exposure standards are not directly transferrable into equipment
performance standards, as required under the 1968 Act.

Although the FDA proposed standards for diagnostic X-ray
equipment in October 1971 (120), the final standards did not
take effect until April 15, 1973, requiring (121) that

- stationary general purpose X-ray machines to be designed to
insure limitation of the beam to approximately the size of
the body area to be examined; and

- radiographic (film using) equipment to be able consistently
to reproduce exposure, and, therefore, image quality for given
settings for voltage, current, and time.

The standards also limit radiation leakage from diagnostic
radiation equipment to 100 milliroentgens per hour at a distance
of one meter. This limitation was considered appropriate "...in
view of the small exposures from leakage radiation relative to
other sources of X radiation to which the patient is exposed
during a diagnostic examination." (116)

Although the performance standard for diagnostic X-ray
equipment was characterized as reflecting consideration for
both the patient and operator, a single performance standard
was adopted for what is a great diversity of equipment types
(see Table 7). In other words, the Act's criteria for
"reasonableness and technical feasibility" overrode any
distinction between intended equipment uses, for example,
dental and medical purposes; there exists entirely different
issues of benefit and risk.

Specific provision also was made for variances for special
purpose new equipment or techniques based upon three criteria
(121):

- the equipment designed to have identifiable technical
advantages as compared to conventional equipment, which is to
be used as a prototype;or experimental units for clinical
evaluation;

- the equipment required to obtain diagnostic information not
obtainable with equipment meeting all requirements of the
standard; or

- equipment utilizes alternative means for providing protection
at least equivalent to that provided by equipment which
conforms to the standard.

Another feature of the diagnostic X-ray equipment standard is
the requirement for positive beam limitation. Thus, stationary
general-purpose radiographic equipment -- the largest single

source of consumer exposure to ionizing radiation -- must be
equipped with the means for automatically adjusting the X-ray
beam to the size of the image receptor (e.g., film). This
requirement can be met in two ways: automatic adjustment of
the X-ray field to the size of the image receptor, or an
interlock, which would prevent operation until the equipment
had been manually adjusted to restrict the X-ray beam size.
Extension Of Effective Date; Used Equipment   On June 23, 1973,
two months before the August 15, 1973 effective date for
diagnostic X-ray equipment (121), the FDA granted an extension
(122) of one year to August 15, 1974 -- almost six years after
enactment of the statutory authority to deal with this source.
This effective date also is almost three years after the
standards were originally proposed (120). The validity for
granting this extension is debatable. The request from the
manufacturers and the National Electrical Manufacturers
Association was predicated on "...a need for more time to:
Redevelop and redesign X-ray equipment to comply with the
standard; obtain components and parts from suppliers; develop
instruction and manuals and assemblers; train assemblers; and
develop testing programs to document quality control." (122)

The FDA Commissioner concluded that the one-year extension
was due, in part, to late recognition by the manufacturers of
the extensive redesign and development of new equipment that
would be required to meet the standard (122). The Act's
criteria for "reasonableness and technical feasibility" again
was the overriding concern!

The extension was resisted by two State agencies and the
American Dental Association (122). The American College of
Radiology also expressed concern should the extension result
in the "unloading" of non-conforming equipment (122).

All diagnostic X-ray equipment systems in existence prior to
the August 15, 1973 effective date (about 126,000 dental and
about 118,000 medical units) are exempt from coverage.

In an attempt to extend coverage of the federal standard to
existing equipment, legislation was introduced on August 17,
1972, by Rep. Edward I. Koch (D.-N.Y.) (123). He reintroduced
a similar measure, H.R. 672, the X-Ray System Radiation
Control Act of 1973, in the 93rd Congress (124).

This amendment to P.L. 90-602 directs the Secretary of
Health, Education and Welfare to prescribe radiation
performance standards for existing X-ray systems and to conduct
annual inspections to ensure compliance with applicable
standards. The bill also would require patients be covered
with protective shielding to avoid unnecessary radiation
exposures. It is Representative Koch's premise that

"If performance standards currently exist for new diagnostic X-ray equipment because they are necessary to protect the public from dangerous X-ray exposure, there seems to be no valid reason why the great percentage of machines currently in use should not be subject to the same controls in the public interest, wherever this is feasible." (124)

On September 10, 1971, the administrator of the federal program, Mr. Villforth, expressed the noteworthy point that

"It will be many years before the X-ray machines that are currently being used today will be replaced by new machines that meet the performance standards, unless the present federal law is amended accordingly." (125)

Consequently, the only mechanism to deal with existing equipment is where a component is replaced; the new component must meet applicable performance standards. To illustrate, all performance standards are directed at the manufacturing process, which is a multistage operation: first, the production of individual components; second, the assembly of major components; and, third, assembly of the major components at the user's site. The current federal regulatory effort is directed at component manufacturers, alone.

Complicating regulation, site assembly may involve the components of different manufacturers. Regulation of site assembly is left to the States, where there is considerable room for improvement.

Presently, there also is no control over second-hand X-ray equipment sold by dealers or by members of physician groups or widows of physicians or radiologists (51). Where they exist, State requirements for notification, by vendors, to State agencies of the sale or transfer of X-ray machines are ineffective.

Lasers   Lasers, a significant source of possible consumer radiation exposure, eventually will be subject to control.

The basic principles of microwave amplification (maser) were clearly stated in 1917 by Albert Einstein. However, the first successful demonstration was not achieved until 1953, by Dr. Charles H. Townes, at Columbia University (126).

Seven years passed before T. H. Maiman announced the first laser, or light amplification system, operating in the visible and near visible range of the electromagnetic spectrum (127). Lasers now operate over a frequency range from audio to ultraviolet, representing perhaps the most widely applicable device available for the generation, amplification, transmission, or detection of electromagnetic radiation (128).

Functional laser applications now include range-finding alignment, leveling, pollution detection, aid to navigation, spectrometry, holographic illumination, teaching, surgery, cell microprobes, photo-coagulation, welding, drilling, scribing, cleaning, credit card validation, tape reading, label reading, communication, holography, diamond drilling, the adhesion of detached retinas, and even salmon tagging. Easily built from readily available components, lasers also are widely used in classrooms to demonstrate the physical properties of light (129).

Although there now are over 150 different laser systems (130), only about a dozen are commercially available (57). Between 1963 and 1968 an estimated 18,000 units were sold in the United States; the majority, 62 percent, were "Helium-Neon" systems; ruby lasers amounted to 12 percent; and the remainder were principally Nd Glass, Carbon Dioxide, Argon, or YAG systems (57). Sales have grown exponentially, 70 percent annually, since 1963 approaching some 50,000 systems in 1970 (57, 131).

The hazards of laser radiation are difficult to quantify because of variations in laser types and in biological factors. The degree of damage is directly influenced by wave-length, intensity levels, pulse duration, and pulse repetition rates, as well as tissue pigmentation, vascularity, and spectral absorption.

Current radiation guides are based on the eye as the critical organ; but more importantly, they are based on the exposure required to produce a visible lesion. Surveys conducted in California on the basis of manufacturers' "codes of good practice," observed that 4 percent of users of lasers exhibited some retinal injury (132). A Massachusetts survey reported 2 percent incidence of similar damage, and New Jersey reported a 2 percent incidence (132).

Macroscopic damage, burn, lesions on the eye's retina have been observed from continuous laser exposures at energy intensities of about 6 $W/cm^2$ and from pulsed exposures at intensities of 0.85 Joules/$cm^2$ (133). Damage also has been observed at about one-tenth these levels with more sophisticated techniques, electrocephalography or electro-retinography (133).

Because the human eye optically concentrates incident light (or energy) about 100,000 times onto the retina (133), a macroscopically visible retina lesion could possibly be produced at a corneal power density of only 0.06 $mW/cm^2$ (134).

Without question, many laser devices constitute a health
hazard when used improperly or by unskilled personnel. Thus,
on October 8, 1971, draft laser equipment performance standards
were presented by the FDA to their Technical Electronic
Products Radiation Safety Standards Committee, and in August
1973 Laser Safety Performance Standards were proposed by the
FDA's Bureau of Radiological Health (135).

Four classes of lasers were designated based on their
potential hazards to the user. Class I lasers would be used in
any environment and allow human access to no more than 0.39
μW of continuous visible radiation and no more than 0.79 μW in
the far infrared spectrum. These lasers would not require
warning labels but would require special housings equipped
with safety interlocking devices to shut down excessive
radiation.

Class II includes any laser with visible light emissions
which cannot exceed 1 mW for continuous human exposure. Such
lasers would be classified as unsafe for continuous viewing
and to have a low probability of injury for single short
exposures. A label carrying the warning, "Do Not Stare Into
Beam," would be mandatory.

Class III includes any laser with continuous wave power up
to 5 mW with the laser beam sufficiently wide to prevent more
than 1 mW (or a power density no greater than 2.5 mW/cm$^2$) from
entering the bare eye of the user. Other continuous wave lasers
in this category cannot emit greater than 0.5 Watts in either
the visible or infrared frequency range. Class III lasers are
considered to present a high probability of eye injury even
during a single short exposure, and a low-power device could
carry warnings against staring into the beam. High-power
devices would have to display a warning against direct beam
exposure.

Class IV electronic products would include any device
emitting radiation in excess of the upper limits of Class IV.
Since these lasers present a hazard to both skin and the eye
the admonition "Avoid Eye or Skin Exposure to Direct or
Scattered Radiation" would have to be posted.

Other labeling requirements would include maximum output
ratings, disclosure of open apertures, and various cautionary
and danger warnings. In addition, the FDA's regulations would
require the use of interlocking and anti-interlock-defeating
techniques. Thus the main responsibility for complying with
the standards will be left for the most part to the actual
designer of a final laser system.

However, an effective control program also must extend to
the "safe use" of lasers, performance standards alone being

insufficient (129). A vigorous federal program directed toward laser safety and hazards evaluation also has been suggested now, while the industry is still in its infancy, rather than after-the-fact.

## Epilogue And Concluding Comments

From the available evidence on adverse effects of ionizing and nonionizing radiation, there is good reason for attempting to insure that man's radiation exposure be kept at the lowest levels possible. However, there is unprecedented growth in the number and variety of new electronic products being offered to the consumer and used in industry; and many of these devices emit unwanted and dangerous radiation.

While the benefits of many of these electronic devices are obvious, it also is apparent that many consumers are using them, or receiving services from their use, without an awareness that they often also present radiation hazards.

In 1968, in an attempt to minimize the potential consumer radiation hazards from electronic products, the Congress enacted the Radiation Control for Health and Safety Act (P.L. 90-602). Examination of this statute and of its implementation by the FDA in summary, indicates that:

- While the FDA's Bureau of Radiological Health has had authority, since 1968, to regulate radiation emissions from electronic products, it has no statutory authority for the promulgation of exposure standards or to regulate consumer radiation exposures; the only mechanism available to the Bureau is that of State assistance in implementing an overall national response to radiation protection.

- Although the Act of 1968 provides for the control of radiation emissions from a variety of new electronic products, federal statutory authority, including responsibility for the control of consumer electronic product radiation and certain types of radioactive material, is limited to product approval at the manufacturing stage, to specified occupational situations, radiation uses, and locations and to certain types of radiation (48).

- There is a general lack of adequate guidelines covering the commercial and industrial uses of electronic products; for example, industrial radiographic and fluoroscopic X-ray units, particle accelerators, and analytical X-ray equipment. Such equipment is designed to produce radiation and the hazard relates largely to conditions of use. Such guidelines must extend to those conditions of use which affect radiation safety

including location, facility design and shielding, safety
interlocks, warning devices, and proper radiation safety
procedures (48).

- Although the Federal Government is a major user of electronic
products and certain radioactive materials that may be
potentially hazardous to employees and the general public,
radiation control programs within the various agencies vary
considerably, and range from inadequate to comprehensive and
effective. Uniform standards, procedures, and guides are
needed for use by the agencies (48).

- Federal specifications for purchase of equipment and
requirements for disposal of equipment which contains
radioactive materials or which may produce radiation do not
always include considerations of safety to users or the public
(48).

- There is a general lack of adequate data on the biological
effects of low-level exposures to ionizing and nonionizing
radiation needed to support the development of performance
standards and the numerical emission values that are a part
of these standards.

- Although the promulgation and enforcement of the microwave
oven safety performance standard will reduce the potential for
adverse effects from microwave radiation from this particular
consumer product, there still remains the issue of what is the
responsible radiation protection policy in light of the
1,000-fold difference between American and Russian permissible
occupational microwave exposure standards.

- There is a lack of availability of appropriate measurement
techniques and instrumentation, for example, in ultrasonics,
microwaves, or lasers, which acts as a constraint on the
development of quantitative exposure and performance standards.

- In the six-year period following enactment of P.L. 90-602,
there has been an actual decrease in federal support for FDA
activities related to consumer radiation hazards, decreasing
from about $16.2 million in Fiscal Year 1969 to $12.4 million
for Fiscal Year 1974 (57).

    The industry being regulated represents annual sales of
$25 billion. However, following enactment of a statutory policy
for control of the radiation hazards of electronic products,
there has been an actual decrease in federal support for the
associated programs of the FDA's Bureau of Radiological Health.
    Because of budgetary constraints and lack of adequate
authority to control electronic products in use, it is the

general policy of the FDA to rely on the States to control electronic products after sale. However, most states, also suffering from budgetary constraints, have insufficient personnel to conduct comprehensive environmental ionizing-radiation control programs, let alone taking on additional programs directed at control of ionizing and nonionizing radiation hazards from electronic products.

Since 1951, among the 50 States, Puerto Rico, the Virgin Islands, and the District of Columbia (53 jurisdictions), some 47 have enacted legislation (as of March 1969) to control all sources of ionizing radiation not subject to the Atomic Energy Act of 1954. However, only about 50 percent of these State programs are consistent with the Council of State Governments' model legislation (48). The major inadequacies include:

- lack of regulations or failure to update regulations to implement radiation control authority;

- insufficient funds and personnel to conduct comprehensive control programs in the areas of ionizing and nonionizing radiation;

- no provision to license, certify, or set qualifications for operators of X-ray machines used in the healing arts; and

- lack of uniformity in the control of health hazards from the use of radium and accelerator-produced radionuclides including safety standards, inspection requirements, regulations, and enforcement.

Recognizing the full public health implications of this situation, the 1972 Conference of Radiation Control Program Directors recommended (136) that:

- Equipment users should be motivated to minimize human exposure from diagnostic X rays through persuasion, education, and training, "including material on radiation protection in the long-term or formal education of users";

- In addition to carrying out programs to assess healing arts and industrial uses of X rays, the (FDA) Bureau of Radiological Health should initiate studies of the efficacy of specific X-ray examinations;

- The Food and Drug Administration should bring all non-agreement radioactive materials (naturally occurring and accelerator-produced materials) under the Federal Hazardous Substances Act and a standard procedure developed for evaluation of radioactive material hazards; and

- Regarding Radiopharmaceutical Controls, a joint task force of State and federal agencies should be established as soon as possible to develop an interagency communications program to review and evaluate regulatory controls, to plan regional training sessions, and to investigate the possibility of joint compliance activities.

The workshop's concern was the right of the consumer to expect and receive efficacious radiologic services. While initial statutory controls have dealt with electronic equipment and accessories, there still remains the issue of assuring competent operation.

Besides the FDA's program under P.L. 90-602, there are five other federal programs which exercise some control to limit public radiation exposure from the use of non-AEC-controlled radioactive materials: the Environmental Protection Agency (EPA), through its standard-setting authority for environmental problems, including radiation, transferred from the Federal Radiation Council (FRC) and the Atomic Energy Commission in Reorganization Plan No. 3 of 1970; the Department of Labor, through the Walsh-Healey Public Contracts Act, and the Occupational Health and Safety Act of 1970 (P.L. 91-596); the Department of Transportation, through its transportation regulations; the FDA through its responsibility for approval of drugs containing any radioactive material and the Federal Hazardous Substances Act; and the National Institutes of Health, through their responsibility for assuring the quality and safety of biological products under its jurisdiction.

Based upon a review of the various federal activities for the control of consumer radiation exposure, the following general observations can be made regarding the adequacy of this combined, but fragmented, program:

- Perhaps the most significant federal radiation policy to date is the Atomic Energy Act of 1954, as amended, which is directed toward protecting the public from radioactive materials used in or derived from the production and use of nuclear energy. The emphasis of current regulatory standards is the licensing of the users of fissionable and radioactive materials and individual reactors. Not covered under this Act are, notably, radium and radioactive materials produced in accelerators (48).

- Radium, the longest and most widely used radioactive material, has little if any control. This has presented difficulties in locating all radium and radium users and in securing user compliance with appropriate regulations (48).

- While the safety and efficacy of radiopharmaceutical and radiobiological products are subject to federal control, no other products or devices, either domestic or imported, containing radium or accelerator-produced radionuclides and sold in interstate commerce are required to meet federal safety standards (48).

- With the formation of the Environmental Protection Agency in December, 1970, the President transferred the functions of the Federal Radiation Council and the standard setting responsibilities of the Atomic Energy Commission to an independent agency; however, since that time no radiation guidelines or standards have been issued by the EPA and the AEC has revised its regulations concerning radioactive effluents in spite of EPA.

- Although the Department of Labor administers the Occupational Health and Safety Act of 1970, all radiation exposures of workers are not covered -- individuals operating under an AEC license are excluded. More significant, however, is the limited expertise in radiation protection the Department of Labor now posseses.

In addition, the National Environmental Policy Act of 1969 (P.L. 90-1901) requires all federal agencies to file environmental impact statements prior to taking actions which may affect the environment. To date, however, the FDA has not filed such statements in connection with the promulgation of electronic product performance standards.

The task of minimizing the consumer's exposure to ionizing and nonionizing radiation is difficult and complex, to say the least. In addition, there is the added concern that there are apparently high-risk groups within the population. Moreover, there is the lack of awareness, on the part of the consumer, of the potential radiation hazards of some electronic products. One needed alternative might very well be to require that the manufacturers of such consumer products label them to the effect that they may be hazardous to the user or the general public if improperly used.

## Acknowledgments
This author, faced with a myriad of recent information on the biological effects of radiation, was deftly guided through the maze by the able and deeply appreciated assistance of Dr. Emanuel Landau and Dr. Robert Albrecht with the Epidemiological Studies Branch, Division of Biological Effects, Bureau of Radiological Health, FDA. The author also would like to express

his appreciation to Dr. Warren H. Donnelly, Senior Specialist, Environmental Policy Division, Congressional Research Service, Library of Congress, and Dr. Richard C. Riley, Head, Division of Radiological Sciences, The University of Kansas Medical Center. However, the view and opinions expressed in this chapter are those of the author alone.

## References

1.   Public Health 2:25 (March) 1897.

2.   Morgan, Karl Z. "Why the 1968 Act for Radiation Control for Health and Safety is Required." Symposium on Radiation Legislation: Its Meaning to the Radiologist, Radiological Society of North America, Chicago, Illinois, December 1, 1969.

3.   Department of Health, Education and Welfare. "Annual Report on the Administration of the Radiation Control for Health and Safety Act of 1968," May 20, 1971 (H. Doc. 92-113).

4.   Villforth, John C. Response to letter from Senator Warren G. Magnuson, December 18, 1972, reprinted in hearings before the Committee on Commerce, U.S. Senate, on P.L. 90-602, Radiation Control for Health and Safety Act of 1969, 93rd Congress, 1st Session. March 8, 9, and 12, 1973.

5.   Department of Health, Education and Welfare, "Radiation Incidents Registry Report, 1970," BRH/DBE 70-6 (December, 1970).

6.   ICRP, Recommendations of the International Commission on Radiological Protection (Adopted September 17, 1965) (ICRP Publication No. 9), Pergamon Press, London (1966).

7.   Mills, Loren F., and Segal, Phyllis. "Radiation Incidents Registry" (Radiation Bio-Effects Summary Report, January - December, 1970), U.S. Department of Health, Education and Welfare, Public Health Service, Bureau of Radiological Health Publication No. BRH/DBE 70-7 (December, 1970).

8.   Terrill, James G., Jr. Statement before the House Committee on Interstate and Foreign Commerce, Subcommittee on Public Health and Welfare on H.R. 10729, August 14, 1967 (Serial No. 90-11), p. 18.

9.   Public Health Service, National Center for Radiological Health, Technical Service Branch, "A Pilot Survey for X-Radiation Emissions from Color Television Receivers in Pinnellas County, Florida, Rad. Health Data and Repts. 9:525-530 (October, 1968).

10.   _____, "Radiation Control," Congressional Quarterly (April 5, 1968), pp. 696-97.

11.   Radiological Health Program, Commonwealth of Puerto Rico
Department of Health, "Results of Survey of X-Radiation from
Color Television Receivers in the Metropolitan Area of San
Juan, Puerto Rico, 1969-1970," Rad. Health Data and Repts.
12:547-551 (November, 1971).

12.   Braestrup, C. B., and Mooney, R. T., "X-Ray Emissions
from Television Sets," Science 130:1071-1074 (October 23,
1959).

13.   National Council on Radiation Protection and Measurement
(NCRP), Interim Statement on "X-Ray Protection Standards for
Home Television Receivers" (February 23, 1968).

14.   Michaelson, Sol M. Statement before the House Committee
on Interstate and Foreign Commerce, Subcommittee on Public
Health and Welfare, 90th Congress, on H.R. 10729 (Serial No.
90-11), p. 453.

15.   Farquhar, W. A. Statement before the House Committee on
Interstate and Foreign Commerce, Subcommittee on Public Health
and Welfare, 90th Congress, on H.R. 10729 (Serial No. 90-11),
p. 55.

16.   Laser, David. Statement before the House Committee on
Interstate and Foreign Commerce, Subcommittee on Public Health
and Welfare, 90th Congress, on H.R. 10729 (Serial No. 90-11),
p. 383.

17.   Donnelly, Warren H., "Bushwhacking, Licensure, and
Senator Bartlett," Radiologic Technology 42:4, 248-257 (1971).

18.   _____, "Radiation Control," Congressional Quarterly
(Oct. 11, 1968), p. 2732.

19.   _____, "Radiation Control," Congressional Quarterly
(August 2, 1968), pp. 2056-2057.

20.   _____, "House-Weakened Radiation Control Bill Cleared,"
Congressional Quarterly (Nov. 25, 1968), pp. 2971, 2972, 2981.

21.   FRC, Background Material for the Development of Radiation
Protection Standards, Report No. 1, Washington, D.C.:
Government Printing Office (May 13, 1960).

22.  Morgan, K. Z., "Never Do Harm," Environment, Vol. 13, No. 1 (January-February, 1971), pp. 28-38.

23.  ICRP Committee, R. H. Mole, Chairman, "Radiosensitivity and Spatial Distribution of Dose," ICRP Publication No. 14, Pergamon Press, London (1969), p. 40.

24.  Terpilak, Michael S., Weaver, Charles L., and Wieder, Samuel, "Dose Assessment of Ionizing Radiation Exposure to the Population," Rad. Health Data and Repts. 12:171-188 (April, 1971).

25.  Gehan, Edmund A., "Relationship of Prenatal Irradiation to Death from Malignant Disease," Biometrics 28(1):239-245 (March, 1972).

26.  Graham, Dr. Saxon, National Cancer Institute Monograph (1966).

27.  _____, Editorial, British Medical Journal 4:xx (October 21, 1972).

28.  Diamond, Earl L., Schmerler, Helen, and Lilienfield, Abraham, "The Relationship of Intra-uterine Radiation to Subsequent Mortality and Development of Leukemia in Children," Amer. J. of Epidemiology 97(5):238-313 (May 1973).

29.  National Academy of Sciences, "The Biological Effects of Atomic Radiation," Report of the Committee on Genetic Effects of Atomic Radiation, Washington, D.C., 1956.

30.  Ramey, James T., "Radiation Standards -- Past, Present and Future," Atomic Energy Law Journal, Vol. 11, No. 1 (Spring, 1969), pp. 1-35.

31.  Bunce, L. A., and Sattler, F. W., "Radon-222 in Natural Gas," Rad. Health Data and Repts. 7:441-444 (August, 1966).

32.  Hickey, J. L. S., and Dampbell, S. C., "High Radium-226 Concentrations in Public Water Supplies," Public Health Reports 83:551-557 (July, 1968).

33.  Ferri, E. S., and Christiansen, H., "Lead-210 in Tobacco and Cigarette Smoke," Public Health Reports 82:828-832 (September, 1967).

34.  U.S. Congress, Joint Committee on Atomic Energy, "Summary Analysis of Hearings, May 27-29 and June 3-7, 1957, on the Nature of Radioactive Fallout and Its Effects on Man" (August, 1957).

35.  U.S. Congress, Joint Committee on Atomic Energy, "Fallout from Nuclear Weapons Tests," A Summary Analysis of Hearings May 5-8, 1969 (August, 1959).

36.  U.S. Congress, Joint Committee on Atomic Energy, "Radiation Protection Criteria and Standards: Their Basis and Use -- Summary Analysis of Hearings May 24, 25, 26, 31 and June 1, 2, 3, 1960" (October, 1960).

37.  Federal Radiation Council, "Background Material for the Development of Radiation Protection Standards," Report No. 1 (May 13, 1960).

38.  FRC, "Background Material for the Development of Radiation Protection Standards," Report No. 2 (September, 1961).

39.  Thompson, Dr. Paul C., Hearings before the Joint Committee on Atomic Energy, U.S. Congress, on Federal Radiation Council Protective Action Guides, June 29 and 30 (1965), p. 3.

40.  _____, Hearings before the Subcommittee on Air and Water Pollution, Committee on Public Works, United States Senate, on S. 4092 (August 5, 1969).

41.  Gofman, John W., and Tamplin, Arthur R., Hearings before the Subcommittee on Air and Water Pollution, Committee on Public Works, United States Senate, U.S. Congress, on S. 3042 (November 18, 1969).

42.  Letter from Robert H. Finch, Secretary of Health, Education and Welfare, to Senator Edmund S. Muskie, Chairman, Subcommittee on Air and Water Pollution, Committee on Public Works, U.S. Senate, on January 28, 1970 (Gofman, op. cit.).

43.  NAS-NRC, "Report of the Advisory Committee on the Biological Effects of Ionizing Radiation," Washington, D.C. (November, 1972).

44.  ICRP, "Recommendations of the International Commission on Radiological Protection," ICRP Publication No. 1, Pergamon Press, London (1959).

45.  Snow, Donald L., "Standards Needed in Controlling
Radiation Exposure to the Public," Amer. J. Pub. Hlth. 60:243-
248 (February 1970).

46.  Brodsky, A., "Balancing Benefits Versus Risk in the
Control of Consumer Items Containing Radioactive Material,"
Amer. J. Pub. Hlth. 55:1971-1992 (December, 1965).

47.  Morgan, K. Z., Hearings before the Joint Committee on
Atomic Energy, U.S. Congress, January 27-30, February 24-26,
1970, Part 2 (Vol. 1), pp. 1277-1301.

48.  DHEW, 1969 Annual Report to the Congress on the
Administration of the Radiation Control for Health and Safety
Act of 1968, Public Law 90-602 (April 1, 1970), BRH/OBD 70-3.

49.  Yao, K. T. S., and Jiles, M. M., "Effects of 2450 MHz
Microwave Radiation on Cultivated Rat Kangaroo Cells," US-DHEW,
PHS, CPEHS, ECA, Bureau of Radiological Health, Division of
Biological Effects, Rockville, Md. (November, 1969).

50.  American Conference of Governmental Industrial Hygienists,
"Threshold Limit Values of Physical Agents Adopted by ACGIH for
1970," p. 8, 1914 Broadway, Cincinnati, Ohio.

51.  Zaret, Milton M., Hearings before the Senate Committee on
Commerce, 93rd Congress, on Oversight of P.L. 90-602 (Marc h 9,
1973).

52.  Naval Medical Research Institute Research Project Report
NM001 056-13-02, Ibid.

53.  Michaelson, Prof. Sol M., Hearings before the House
Committee on Interstate and Foreign Commerce, Subcommittee on
Public Health and Welfare, 90th Congress, on H.R. 10729
(October 11, 1967), p. 453.

54.  _____, Hearings before the Senate Committee on Commerce,
93rd Congress, on Oversight of P.L. 90-602 (March 9, 1973).

55.  _____, "Human Exposure to Nonionizing Radiant Energy --
Potential Hazards Safety Standards," Proc. IEEE (April, 1972).

56.  Whitehead, Clay T., Hearings before the Senate Committee
on Commerce, 93rd Congress, on Oversight of P.L. 90-602
(March 9, 1973).

57. Harris, Jesse Y., "Electronic Products Inventory Study," USDHEW, PHS, CPEHS, ECA, Bureau of Radiological Health, Rockville, Maryland (September, 1969).

58. American National Standards Institute, "Safety Level of Electromagnetic Radiation with Respect to Personnel," C95.1 (1966).

59. Behling, Ulrich H., "Biological Effects of Radio and Low-Frequency Electromagnetic Radiation," Bureau of Radiological Health, Consumer Protection and Environmental Health Service, DHEW (April, 1969).

60. Smith, Stephen W., and Brown, David G., "Radiofrequency and Microwave Radiation Levels Resulting from Man-Made Sources in the Washington, D.C. area," DHEW, Public Health Service, Food and Drug Administration, Bureau of Radiological Health, DHEW Publication No. (FDA) 72-8015, BRH Publication No. DEP 72-5 (November 1971), 56 pp.

61. Moore, Wellington, Jr., "Biological Aspects of Microwave Radiation, A Review of Hazards," U.S. Department of Health, Education and Welfare (July, 1968).

62. Goncharove, N. N., et al., "Industrial Hygiene Problems of Working with Ultra Short-Wave Transmitters Used in Television and Radio Broadcasting," Translation - ATD, Report 66-125 (Sept. 27, 1966).

63. Kall, A. R., Final Technical report on research project to study radiation hazards caused by high power high frequency fields. United States Information Agency, Contract No. 1A-11651 (1968).

64. Michaelson, S. M., 1968, "Biological Effects of Microwaves: Future Research Directions," Special Panel Discussion, Symposium on Microwave Power, Boston, Massachusetts (1968), p. 12.

65. Susskind, C., Hearings before the Committee on Commerce, United States Senate, Ninetieth Congress, Second Session, on S. 2067, S. 3211, and H.R. 10790, Part 2 (Serial No. 90-49) (May, 1968), p. 722.

66. Slepicka, Z., "The Effects of Electromagnetic Radiation in the Meter Range in Workers at a Short-wave Transmitter," Pracov, Lek. 19:5-11 (1967). Supra note 57.

67.  Huzl, F., "Estimation of Workers Exposed to Meter and
Longer Electromagnetic Waves in the West-Bohemıa Region,"
Pracov, Lek. 18:100-103 (1966). Supra note 57.

68.  Drogichina, E. A., and Sadchikova, M. N., 1965, "Clinical
Syndromes Arising Under the Effect of Various Radio Frequency
Bands," Giglyena Truda i Professional' nyye Zaboleveniya
(Labor Hygiene and Occupational Diseases) 9:17-21, Moscow.
Supra note 57.

69.  Osipov, Yu, A., 1965, "The Health of Workers Exposed to
Radio-Frequency Radiation," in Gigiyena truda i vliyaniye na
rabotayuschikh elektromagnitnykh poley radiochastot
(Occupational Hygiene and the Effect of Radio-Frequency
Electromagnetic Fields on Workers), Leningrad, Izd. Meditsina
104:144. Supra note 57.

70.  Hazzard, DeWitt G., "Biological Effects of Visible and
Infrared Radiations," Bureau of Radiological Health, Consumer
Protection and Environmental Health Service, DHEW, Unpublished.
Supra note 57.

71.  Leach, William M., "Biological Aspects of Ultraviolet
Radiation, A Review of Hazards," Division of Biological Effects,
Bureau of Radiological Health, DHEW BRH/DBE 70-3 (September,
1970).

72.  Jagger, J., "Introduction to Research in Ultraviolet
Photobiology," Prentice-Hall, Englewood Cliffs, N.J. (1967),
p. 164.

73.  Blum, H. F., "Sunburn," in Hollaender, A. (ed.),
Radiation Biology, Vol. 2, McGraw-Hill, New York (1955),
pp. 487-528.

74.  Blum, H. F., "Ultraviolet Radiation and Cancer," in
Hollaender, A. (ed.), Radiation Biology, Vol. 2, McGraw-Hill,
New York (1955), pp. 529-559.

75.  Council on Physical Therapy, 1943, "Acceptance of
Ultraviolet Lamps for Disinfecting Purposes," J. Am. Med. Assn.
122:503-505 (1943).

76.  Council on Physical Medicine, 1948, "Acceptance of
Ultraviolet Lamps for Disinfecting Purposes," J. Am. Med. Assn.
137:1600-1603 (1948).

77.  Steinberg, E. B., "Ultrasonics in Industry," Proc. IEEE 53:1292 (October 1965).

78.  Hart, D., "Survey of Ultrasonics in Medicine," Presentation at Commercial Applications of Ultrasonic Symposium (February 6, 1969), New York, New York.

79.  Fred, R. K., et al., "Summary Report on the Biological Effects of 'Ultrasonic' Energy," USDHEW, PHS, CPEHS, ECA, Bureau of Radiological Health, Division of Biological Effects, Rockville, Maryland (May, 1969).

80.  Landau, Emanuel, "Are there ultrasonic dangers to the unborn?" Practical Radiology 1(6):27-31 (June, 1973).

81.  Lehmann, J. F., DeLateur, B. J., and Silverman, Dr. R., "Selective Hearing Effects of Ultrasound in Human Beings," Arch. Phys. Med. Rehabil. 47:331-339 (1966).

82.  Hill, C. R., and Eng, C., "The Possibility of Hazard in Medical and Industrial Applications of Ultrasound," Brit. J. Radiol. 41:561-569 (1968).

83.  Hawley, S. A., Macleod, R. M., and Dunn, F., "Degradation of DNA by Intense, Noncavitating Ultrasound," J. Acoust. Soc. Am. 35:1285-1287 (1963).

84.  Connolly, C. C., "The Action of Ultrasound from Shock Excited Transducer on the Fetus of the Mouse," British Acoustical Society Meeting (June 16, 1967).

85.  Berman, E., and Rosenstein, L., "Sound and Infrasound," BRH, DBE.

86.  Youmans, Harry D., Jr., "Biological Aspects of Magnetic Fields," Bureau of Radiological Health, Consumer Protection and Environmental Health Service, DHEW.

87.  DHEW, Federal Register 34:8952 (June 4, 1969).

88.  DHEW, PHS, "Regulations for the Administration and Enforcement of the Radiation Control for Health and Safety Act of 1968," BRH/OBD 71-1 (March, 1971).

89.  DHEW, Federal Register 35:8363-8365 (May 28, 1970).

90.  DHEW, Federal Register 36:18645 (September 18, 1971).

91.  Murphy, Emmet, Steward, H., Coppola, S., and Modine, N., "X-Ray Emission from Shunt Regulator Tubes for Color Television Receivers," MORP 67-1 National Center for Radiological Health, U.S. Public Health Service.

92.  National Council on Radiation Protection and Measurements (NCRP), Recommendations for Color TV Receivers With X-Radiation Emission, Radiology M3:22 (1960).

93.  Wyckoff, Dr. Harold O., "Status of the Review of the 1969 NCRP Recommendation," Conference on Detection and Measurement of X-Radiation from Color Television Receivers, Washington, D.C. (March 28 and 29, 1969).

94.  National Center for Radiological Health Technical Services Branch, "A Summary of the Washington, D.C. Metropolitan Area Survey of Color Television Receivers," Rad. Health Data and Repts. 9:531-538 (October, 1968).

95.  DHEW, "Performance Standard for Television Receivers," Federal Register, Vol. 34, No. 247 (December 25, 1969), pp. 2073-2074 and Vol. 36, p. 23523 (December 10, 1971).

96.  Becker, Seymour, "Results of a Follow-up Radiation Survey on Color Television Sets, Suffolk County, New York," Rad. Health Data and Repts. 12:457-458 (September, 1971).

97.  Properzio, William S., Woodcock, Ray C., and Heidersdorf, Sidney D., "X-Ray Emission from Cold-Cathode Gas Discharge Tubes Used for Educational Purposes" (February, 1970), BRH/DEP 70-1; DEP, BRH, EHS, PHS, DHEW.

98.  NCRPM, "Radiation Protection in Educational Institutions," Report No. 32 (1970).

99.  DHEW, Public Health Service, "Proposed Performance Standard -- Demonstration-Type -- Cold-Cathode Gas Discharge Tubes," Federal Register 35:21 (Friday, January 30, 1970).

100. DHEW, Public Health Service, "Demonstration-Type Cold-Cathode Gas Discharge Tubes," Federal Register 35:97, 7699 (Tuesday, May 19, 1970).

101. DHEW, Federal Register 36:23523 (December 10, 1971).

102. Frey, Jeffrey, and Bowers, Raymond, "What's Ahead for Microwaves," IEEE Spectrum 9:41-47 (March, 1972).

103. Meisels, Manfred, "Industry Warming to Microwave Power," Microwaves (May, 1968), pp. 10-17.

104. Eure, John A., et al., "Radiation Exposure from Industrial Microwave Applications," Amer. J. Pub. Hlth. 62:1573-1577 (December, 1972).

105. Bureau of Radiological Health, Division of Electronic Products: Survey of Selected Industrial Applications of Microwave Energy, U.S. Department of Health, Education and Welfare, Public Health Service Publication No. BRH/DEP 70-10 (May, 1970), 67 pp.

106. Restall, Charles J., M.D., et al., "A Microwave Blood Warmer: Preliminary Report, Anesthesia and Analgesia...Current Researches," Vol. 45, No. 5 (September-October, 1967), pp. 625-628. Supra note 57.

107. Van Dress, M. G., and Freund, W. H., "The Food Service Industry: Its Structure and Characteristics, 1966," USDA Statistical Bulletin No. 416 (February, 1968).

108. Walker, Gerald M., "Microwave oven safety at issue," Electronics 46:62-63 (March 29, 1973).

109. PHS, "Health Hazards of Microwave Ovens," Public Health Reports 85:425 (May, 1970).

110. Eden, W. M., "Microwave Oven Repair: Hazard Evaluation," Electronic Radiation and the Health Physicist -- Health Physics Society Fourth Annual Midyear Topical Symposium, BRH/DEP 70-26.

111. Seabron, LaVert C., and Coopersmith, Lewis W., "Results of the 1970 Microwave Oven Survey," USDHEW, Public Health Service, Food and Drug Administration, Bureau of Radiological Health, DHEW Publication No. (FDA) 72-8007, BRH Publication No. BRH/DEP 72-2 (August, 1971).

112. DHEW, "Proposed Performance Standards for Microwave Ovens," Federal Register 35:100, 7901-7902 (May 22, 1970).

113. DHEW, FDA, "Performance Standard for Microwave Ovens," Federal Register 35:194, 15642-15644 (October 6, 1970).

114. DHEW, FDA, Federal Register 36:23523 (December 10, 1971).

115. DHEW, FDA, "(Proposed) Performance Requirements to Improve the Reliability, Safety Interlock Systems on Microwave Ovens," Federal Register 38:67, 9027-9029 (Monday, April 9, 1973).

116. Edwards, Charles C., HEW NEWS 71-59, Friday, October 8, 1971.

117. Moeller, D. W., Terrill, J. G., and Ingraham, S. C., "Radiation Exposure in the United States," Public Health Reports 68:57-65 (January, 1953).

118. Fess, L. R., "Summary of Diagnostic X-Ray Statistics Relating Facilities, Equipment, and Personnel by Healing Arts Professions," Rad. Health Data and Repts. 10:379-380 (September, 1969).

119. Moeller, D. W., "Meeting Radiological Health Manpower Needs," Amer. J. Pub. Hlth. 61:1938-1946 (October, 1971).

120. DHEW, FDA, "Proposed Performance Standards for Diagnostic X-Ray Systems and Other Components," Federal Register 36:19607 (October 8, 1971).

121. DHEW, FDA, Federal Register 37:16461 (August 15, 1972).

122. DHEW, FDA, Federal Register 38:112, 15444-15446 (June 12, 1973).

123. Koch, E. I., "X-Ray Technologists and X-Ray Equipment Should be Regulated and Licensed," Congressional Record, Vol. 118, No. 133, Part 2 (August 17, 1972), H7919-7934.

124. Koch, E. I., "Introduction of H.R. 672, the X-Ray System Radiation Control Act of 1973," Congressional Record, Vol. 119, No. 1 (January 6, 1973), H77.

125. Koch, E. I., Hearings before the Committee on Commerce, U.S. Senate, on the Radiation Control for Health and Safety Act of 1968, on March 9, 1973.

126. Gordon, J. P., Zeiger, H. J., and Townes, C. H., "The Maser - New Type of Amplifier, Frequency Standard, and Spectrometer," Phys. Rev. 99:1264-1274 (1955).

127. Maiman, T. H., "Simulated Optical Radiation in Ruby," Nature 187:493-494 (August, 1960).

128. Eleccion, Marce, "The Family of Lasers: A Survey," IEEE Spectrum 9:3, 26-40 (March, 1972).

129. Lutz, Ann M. (Roberts), and Steward, Harold, "Trends in Laser Applications: Public Health Implications," Amer. J. Pub. Hlth. 61:2277-2281 (November, 1971).

130. Elion, H. A., "Laser Systems and Applications," Appendix 4, Pergamon Press, Oxford, 1967.

131. "Electronic Industry Association," R & D, System Sales (1965, 1966, 1967, First Half of 1968), May 15, 1969. Supra note 57.

132. Terrill, J. G., Jr., "Microwave, Lasers, and X-Rays -- Adverse Reactions Due to Occupational Exposures," Paper Presented at 1968 AMA Congress on Occupational Health, October 1, 1968.

133. American Conference of Governmental Industrial Hygienists (1968), "A Guide for Uniform Industrial Hygiene Codes or Regulations for Laser Installations," Laser Focus, Vol. 4 (October, 1968), p. 51.

134. David, T. P., and Mautner, W. J., "Helium-Neon Laser Effects on the Eye," U.S. Army Research and Development Command (April 2, 1969).

135. Eleccion, Marce, "Laser hazards: New standards of safety issued by the Bureau of Radiological Health mean laser costs may begin to rise," IEEE Spectrum 10(8):32-38 (August, 1973).

136. DHEW, PHS, FDA, BRH Bulletin, Vol. VI, No. 9 (Monday, May 15, 1972).

# 5

## RADIATION EXPOSURES FROM CONSUMER RADIOLOGIC SERVICES

Richard D. Grundy

CONTENTS

## Introduction

Radiologic technology is the science of applying ionizing radiation to human beings for diagnostic or therapeutic purposes. The attendant benefits from the use of radiation for medical and dental diagnosis and therapy are well recognized. Nevertheless, the safety and efficacy of current radiologic practices still remain a major public health issue, and the question must always be asked: Do current radiologic practices provide maximum benefit and minimum risk for the patient?

Currently, medical and dental exposures account for over 90 percent of all human exposures to manmade ionizing radiation. In addition, the patient's (i.e., the consumer's) "genetically significant exposure"* from medical diagnosis in the United States is much higher than those in other countries that have comparable levels of health care (Table 1). Consequently, the American consumer's exposure attendant to the provision of medical and dental radiologic services deserves special consideration. It is particularly important to consider the role of the radiologic-equipment operator in the United States.

The discussion in Chapter 4 was concerned with the regulation of radiation emissions from electronic products such as new X-ray equipment; however, the manner in which this equipment is operated can significantly affect its emission and, in turn, the consumer-patient's exposure.

This chapter is concerned with the role of the operators of medical and dental radiologic equipment in affecting consumer-patient exposures as well as voluntary programs, such as certification, and mandatory licensure, by which these

---

*The "genetically significant exposure" (dose) is defined as the gonad dose which, if received by every member of the population, would result in the same total genetic effect to the population as the sum of the individual doses actually received. This definition is based upon the following assumptions and considerations: (a) The relevant dose is the accumulated dose to the gonads; and (b) The individual gonad dose is weighted with a factor which takes into account future number of children expected of the irradiated individual compared with an average member of the population (in this connection, the fetus is treated as such an irradiated individual and not as the child of an irradiated parent). The genetically significant dose from medical procedures for the U.S. population (1964) was found to be 55 millirads per person per year. The genetically significant dose from dental procedures was well below 1 millirad (1).

Table 1  Genetically Significant Dose From Medical Diagnosis
In Various Advanced Countries (2, 3)

| Country | Exposure (millirem* per year, per capita) |
|---|---|
| United States | 55-95 |
| Japan (1958-1960) | 39 |
| Sweden (1955) | 38 |
| Switzerland (1957) | 22 |
| Great Britain (1957-1958) | 14 |
| New Zealand (1963) | 12 |
| Norway (1958) | 10 |

*See definition on p. 191.

individuals can demonstrate their proficiency. Such
demonstrated competence is not now required for employment.
A review is then presented of congressional interest in, and
the arguments for, mandatory State or federal licensure of
radiologic technologists, the principal operators of
radiologic equipment. The challenge is there. The issue is how
to most effectively deal with it.

The number of diagnostic tools has expanded from the use of
ionizing radiation, such as X rays, to encompass more
sophisticated techniques employing radiopharmaceuticals,
particle accelerators, and sources of nonionizing radiation
such as microwaves and ultrasonics. This proliferation of
sources has been accompanied by an increasing risk of
unnecessary radiation exposure. As noted in Chapter 4, the
National Council on Radiation Protection and Measurement
(NCRPM), the International Commission on Radiological
Protection (ICRP), and the Federal Radiation Council (the
functions of which are now a part of the Environmental
Protection Agency) have warned that, besides the benefits, any
exposure to such radiation must be assumed to carry with it
some risk of adverse public health effects.

This premise led the NAS-NRC Committee on the Biological
Effects of Ionizing Radiation (BEIR) to comment in 1972 on the
adequacy of current FRC radiation protection guides, which
notably do not apply to medical and dental exposures, stating
that

"The present guides of 170 mrem/yr grew out of an effort to balance societal needs against genetic risks. It appears that these needs can be met with far lower average exposures and lower genetic and somatic risk than permitted by the current (FRC) Radiation Protection Guide.... To this extent, the current Guide is unnecessarily high. The exposures from medical and dental uses should be subject to the same rationale. To the extent that such exposures can be reduced without impairing benefits, they are also unnecessarily high." (emphasis added) (4)

Commenting on the significance of such consumer radiation exposure, Dr. Donald Chadwick, former Executive Secretary to the FRC, remarked that

"Our knowledge of the biological effects of radiation has many gaps, but enough is known that practitioners of medicine, dentistry, and public health should make every feasible effort to prevent or reduce all unnecessary radiation exposure. The size of the population at risk and the possible consequences of failure to take appropriate action are too great." (5)

In order to place the attendant consumer risks in perspective, it is meaningful to note that in recent years the medical uses of radiation for diagnostic and therapeutic purposes has been increasing to a point where now more than half the population annually receives at least one diagnostic X-ray examination.

In 1964, this amounted to some 506 million diagnostic exposures during 50 million dental and 93 million medical visits (Table 2). By 1970, the use of medical X rays had increased by an additional 25 percent over 1964 (4, 7); some 129 million persons, or 63 percent of the population, received 210 million diagnostic radiologic examinations (or 68.5 examinations per 100 persons) (6). In the process, in 1970 alone, an estimated 8 million pregnant women and their unborn children were placed at risk (7).

The increased use of nuclear materials (e.g., radiopharmaceuticals) in the diagnosis or treatment of disease presents even newer risks and radiation protection challenges. In 1970 alone, some four million Americans were administered radiopharmaceuticals (4); in fact in 1971 roughly 25 percent of all hospital in-patients were exposed to radiopharmaceuticals for diagnosis or therapeutic reasons (4). Concurrently, the use of nonionizing radiation (e.g., microwaves and ultrasonics)

Table 2  Data From PHS 1964 and 1970 Exposure Studies (6)

|  | 1964 | 1970 |
|---|---|---|
| Persons X-rays (millions) | 108 | 129 |
| X-ray visits (millions) | 143 | 179 |
| Examinations (millions) | 173 | 210 |
| Films (millions) | 506 | 650 |
| Medical-hospital X-ray visits (millions) | 50.4 | 65.3 |
| (percent of visits) | 57.4 | 60.3 |
| Physician office X-ray visits (millions) | 23.3 | 28.0 |
| Dental office X-ray visits (millions) | 50.1 | 67.5 |
| Medical X-ray units (thousands) | 86 | -- |
| Radiologists (thousands) | 8.5 | -- |
| Medical practitioners (thousands) | 240 | -- |

for therapeutic purposes also has emerged as a significant medical tool, although often without medical supervision.

In recognition of the potential hazards the FDA's Bureau of Radiological Health undertook steps to reduce exposures not contributing to diagnosis and therapy. Evidence of success is observed in a decrease between 1964 and 1970 in man's annual "genetically significant exposure (dose)" despite a concurrent 10 percent per capita increase in the number of annual X-ray examinations (8).

A federal-State system -- the Nationwide Evaluation of X-Ray Trends (NEXT) -- also has been established to monitor the effectiveness of programs designed to reduce consumer X-ray exposures.

Radiologic practices, like many other extremely useful and even necessary technologic advances, can be misused through ignorance, neglect, carelessness, and lack of appropriate education and training; in this case, in the fundamentals of radiation protection. Current radiologic practices are, in part, the product of the "capacity fallacy," the trap of providing a service or product because it is possible to do so. As a result, consumer radiologic services or practices now are often performed at greater "benefit" to the dentist, the physician, or the hospital than to the patient.

A common misconception is that "it is easy to take X-ray pictures." In a categorical denial of this dangerous premise, it must be emphasized that, "It is not easy to make 'X-ray pictures'; it is easy to be a buttonpusher." (11)

Modern radiologic equipment utilizes many more automatic and fool-proof devices than during earlier periods. As noted in

Chapter 4, the approach being taken by the FDA in implementing
the Radiation Control for Health and Safety Act of 1968 (P.L.
90-602) is the establishment of equipment performance (or
emission) standards. However, as the subsequent discussion
highlights,

"An unqualified operator of radiologic equipment
inadvertently can overturn any benefits derived from equipment
performance standards established pursuant to P.L. 90-602;
the outcome is unnecessary consumer hazards. This is true
irrespective of whether the operator is a poorly trained
physician or radiologic technologist." (3)

For example, an incompetent operator can unwittingly expose
a patient to as much as 200 times the amount of radiation
associated with a competent or professional radiologic
procedure (9). An in-depth knowledge of radiologic procedures
is not enough, for each patient presents a unique body
configuration for which the operator must adjust his
procedures, even though a similar part of the body may have
been examined for the previous patient (9). In short, where
the operators of medical and dental radiologic equipment are
poorly qualified or trained there is no assurance that
procedures are performed well even with the best and most
foolproof of modern equipment.

Nevertheless, in only four states -- California, Kentucky,
New Jersey and New York -- are the operators of medical and
dental X-ray equipment licensed. Conversely, some 46 states do
not require demonstrated proficiency as a prerequisite to
performing medical radiologic services. In addition, no State
requires the operators of dental X-ray equipment or microwave
and ultrasonic diathermy equipment to have any training in
radiation protection or to demonstrate their competence in
any way.

In contrast, in all 50 States, school bus drivers must have
a special license. The present requirements for voluntary
certification by the American Registry of Radiologic
Technologists (ARRT) should be considered mandatory for
minimum requirements for employment.

Considering risks to the patient, the question logically
should be asked: Should even doctors in all instances be
allowed to prescribe radiologic services much less perform
them themselves? Under such an "extreme" policy, the exception
would be those instances where a physician or dentist has
appropriate education, training, and certification or licensure
in the proper uses of radiation and in radiation protection.

Obviously, this is a rather impractical policy; clearly, a physician should be allowed to order an X-ray examination where a fracture is suggested even though his knowledge of radiation protection is minimal. Thus the issue quickly becomes a matter of how to perform the actual examination for maximum diagnostic benefit and minimum radiation risk to the patient.

Moreover, a physician cannot assume that the benefits of a consumer radiologic procedure in the treatment or diagnosis of a disease will inherently outweigh the attendant patient risks. In short, for the physician prescribing or the person administering radiologic services, the challenge is a new concept of professionalism. Concern must not only be for the immediate medical or dental benefits from a radiograph, but also for the long-term consequences of radiologic services for the consumer and society at large. This represents a significant departure from the traditional perspective of physicians where the principal concern has emphasized the immediate medical benefits to an individual patient. This new perspective stems from the "new consumerism" movement which advocates a broad societal policy that seeks to augment the rights and powers of the consumer-patient in relation to the seller-physician and dentist.

When the patient is viewed as a consumer seeking a specialized health care service, application of the new consumerism dictates that the consumer benefits alone from a given radiologic service must be derived at minimum, not just acceptable, risk of adverse side-effects.

Clearly, there are instances where the anticipated benefits are so great and the needs so urgent that the non-specific and latent risks of induced leukemia, genetic damage, life shortening, and other long-term effects are inconsequential by comparison. Nevertheless, the adverse effects can be assumed higher than any expected benefits when the same radiologic procedures are performed on asymptomatic patients as a screening measure or for relatively trivial reasons.

Following the tenets of new consumerism, a physician or dentist prescribing radiologic procedures must pre-judge the demonstrable benefits on the basis of anticipated diagnostic finding or therapeutic benefits. The NCRPM emphasized this imperative when it stated that a "...risk is acceptable when it is at least compensated by demonstrable benefits" (10), and only then.

Unfortunately, performance of the benefits-cost calculus is less clear for the largest number of radiologic procedures which cannot be classified as either of the two mentioned extremes. The choice most often is between the value of life for its own sake and the value of a certain quality of life. Such determinations are often beyond the physician's personal wisdom (11).

## Current Radiologic Practices

Overview  The physician traditionally has been accepted by society as the prime mover in health care delivery. In this position he has been responsible for overseeing the quality of medical services generally. However, there now is a trend toward divestiture of physicians of supposed routine but specialized functions and services such as radiologic services.

An immediate benefit from this divestiture is a freeing of the physician to provide those medical services for which he is uniquely qualified; a potential long-term benefit is the provision of non-M.D. services by specialists, thus upgrading the overall quality of health care services.

Stemming from this divestiture, physicians now constitute only 9 percent of the individuals providing health care services (12). This compares with 35 percent in 1900 and an estimated 5 percent by 1975 (13, 14). Nevertheless, the physician generally retains ultimate responsibility for the diagnostic function and rightly so.

The American Medical Association (AMA), the American College of Radiology (ACR), and the American Hospital Association (AHA) have argued that the physician, by law, has the basic responsibility for exposing the consumer to potentially hazardous radiation -- no one else can bear this responsibility. Taking this position one step further, it is suggested that each physician knows best when to prescribe radiologic services in the sense that he either knows how to administer diagnosis or therapy himself or knows when the patient should be sent to someone else, and what qualifications that someone else should have. It is then concluded that the physician knows best how he can utilize the benefits of radiologic services at minimum risk to his patients.

On its surface, this premise appears valid; however, in practice it quickly changes due to conflicts and competing pressures on the physician.

While medical authorities generally accept the prudent rule that no amount of human exposure to radiation is so small as to be dismissed as harmless, medical authorities nevertheless also note that the physician never should be deterred by this risk when he is convinced that X-ray examination will produce needed information that could be crucial to a patient's welfare.

However, while physicians are trained in pharmacology to
understand immediate drug actions and reactions, they are not
always trained in fields which would enable them to judge the
long-term safety and effectiveness of radiologic services as
well as of many other medical devices they encounter and use
in their practice.

In performing a risk assessment, the physician or dentist
must be capable of weighing the immediate benefits to the
patient  against potential somatic (non-reproductive) effects
such as leukemia and cancer as well as genetic (reproductive)
hazards or inheritable changes affecting generations yet
unborn. The performance of such cost-benefit analyses is
impracticable for most physicians or dentists.

Thus, for any radiation protection policy to be even
partially effective it must be predicated on the elimination of
radiation exposure that does not contribute directly to the
diagnosis or therapy. Under such an approach, where no new
information can be provided, either because the clinical
manifestations of disease are confirmed or the diagnosis is
already completed, the utility of radiologic services is
questionable. When such examinations are prescribed purely for
confirmatory purposes, they represent an unnecessary risk as
well as expense for the consumer-patient.

Under the present system, however, the consumer has no
choice but to rely on his physician or dentist to decide
whether diagnostic or therapeutic radiologic services are
required. Yet, an examination of the competing pressures under
which the physician or dentist now must operate is quite
revealing. Only when these policies and practices and their
associated consumer risks are generally acknowledged will there
be sufficient incentive to foster improvements in the quality
of radiologic services.

First, a physician, even when well aware of the attendant
consumer risks of radiation, often is under sufficient pressure
of a malpractice suit to call for non-essential X-ray films for
his own protection (15, 16). Some physicians are so fearful of
malpractice suits that unnecessary X-ray films are ordered
solely to have visual proof available on the nature of an
injury in the event of a possible court action by a patient
(16, 17).

Discontinuance of this unfortunate practice will occur only
when it is generally agreed that a physician's discretion
should be limited to actions affecting the patient's interests
and radiologic services and should not be prescribed
exclusively for the physician's benefit as a defense against
malpractice suits. However, current pressures on the physician

are so great that correction of this situation may require his
specific protection by law. Otherwise even more law suits may
arise due to a patient's misconception of when radiologic
services should be prescribed.

Second, even when radiologic services are necessary,
insufficient care often is taken to avoid duplication. Dr.
John McClenahan has pointed out that

"Some interns and some chiefs reorder, by reflex, a series of
X-ray examinations when a patient enters their hospital even
though he may carry in his hands a set of films one week old
that establish his diagnosis unequivocally." (18)

Such consumer risks would be reduced if present practices
were modified to require that recent X-ray films not be repeated
unless there is a clear reason to question their results; and
present practices must be viewed with skepticism.

Another unfortunate reflex action occurs where head injuries
are involved. Although preliminary examinations may not
indicate a fracture, skull X-ray films frequently are ordered;
yet several studies (19, 20, 21) indicate that treatment often
is not significantly different as a result of the examinations.
In fact, these studies conclude that such examinations are
unwarranted because of their negligible significance (21), and
that 34 percent of all skull X-ray exams are simply performed
in anticipation of legal actions or insurance claims by
patients (20).

Because of this almost routine procedure, an estimated
$7,125 (19) to $7,650 (20) is spent on such examinations before
any information is obtained that alters the treatment of any
patient with a suspected head injury. Besides the questionable
risks to the consumer, such practices represent a major expense
for society. One study suggests that $25,500 to $37,800 is
spent on each bit of information that in any way altered the
course of treatment.

Third, there are the so-called "routine" and often "free"
chest X-ray examinations. Frequently as a patient enters the
doctor's office, he is automatically referred to the department
of radiology under the premise that "It's a 'ruling-out'
process. This is done under the premise that something not
found during the medical examination might be found in
radiology." (22)

Such routine mass X-ray examinations now are only justified
for specific population groups where there is a suspected high
incidence of disease; for example, for tuberculosis -- the
initial justification for the mobile X-ray units.

Likewise, there is questionable justification for routine X-ray examinations when hiring manual and certain other workers. Besides the debatable sensitivity of the lumbar X-ray exam in "detecting prodromal low-back disorders," the issue is whether the supposed benefits are actually realized by the employee who may be ill or by his employer who is alert to possible future litigation (18).

"Free" X-ray examinations sometimes are still offered and even advertised by chiropractors (6), although this is considered unethical by others in the chiropractic profession and discouraged by their State societies. Unfortunately, such "sales practices" are not subject to regulation (6), nor are they justification for loss of licensure.

Fourth, from an economic standpoint, an X-ray unit costs as much as $10,000 to $20,000 and this cost eventually must be recovered (23). Even an otherwise ethical physician in his office practice may be influenced by this capital expenditure.

Unfortunately, there are instances where doctors and dentists use their X-ray equipment for clearly financial motives (16, 22). Another incentive promoting questionable practices is Medicaid and other health programs which pay $15 to $25 per examination. In some ghetto clinics a patient even before seeing a doctor may have taken two chest X-ray films, a spinal X-ray film for the chiropractor, and two X-ray films of the feet for the podiatrist (22). Later, the same patient also may have a full set of 14 mouth X-ray films before seeing a dentist (16, 22). An extreme example is found in the case of one New York dentist with 17 X-ray machines in his two offices, who recently sued Medicaid for non-payment of over $300,000 in X-ray fees (22).

In summary, the four most common causes for unnecessary consumer-patient radiation exposure are (24):

- lack of training or inadequate training of the equipment operators;

- X-ray machines that do not comply with applicable standards;

- inadequate positive shielding for operators; and

- lack of concern of the operators for good radiation protection procedures.

These factors contribute to a generally recognized situation where both consumer-patients and operators are subjected to unnecessary exposure. Yet even with all its faults and the aforementioned competing pressures on the physician, our present system for providing radiologic services is too useful to modern health care delivery to be even partially abandoned.

In general, the consumer-patient assumes that radiologic examinations do not create a health hazard and that operators are licensed where required (24). Whether they also assume that licensure is requisite for employment is unclear.

Yet a 1972 survey in Suffolk County, New York, showed that many owners and operators do not even know whether their X-ray equipment is functioning according to regulatory requirements (24). Consequently, the patient, the doctor's office staff, and the operator often are unsuspectingly being exposed to unnecessary radiation (24).

Nature of Consumer Hazards  Thus unnecessary consumer hazards often accompany the benefits derived from the diagnostic and therapeutic uses of ionizing radiation. Such hazards usually arise out of inadequate or faulty professional judgment. Several extreme examples can be drawn from the lay press which attest to the lack of information or expertise that can occur among non-radiologists (23):

- A man had his legs amputated following third degree burns incurred during X-ray treatment for eczema;

- A woman's scalp was burned during a routine X-ray procedure, causing her to lose her hair; and

- A woman, age 28, received excessive radiation in the process of taking abdominal X-ray films, which brought on menopause.

Other hazards are found in the cases where a man undergoing X-ray treatment received an electrical shock that set his clothes on fire; and a woman was electrocuted when a doctor's nurse-technician inadvertently placed the patient in contact with either an exposed high-voltage wire or the terminal of the X-ray tube. These extreme cases, and others, demonstrate the immediate potential hazard to which a patient can be subjected by a non-professional operator.

Principal concern, however, is for long-term somatic effects including the risks of leukemia and other malignancies, and life-shortening, as well as genetic effects.

The attendant risks for society as a whole were estimated by the NAS-NRC BEIR Committee (14). For a general population exposure of 170 millirem per year (or 5 rem per 30-year reproduction generation), the estimated genetic effects in the first generation would amount to between 100 and 1,800 cases of serious, dominant diseases and defects annually (assuming 3.6 million births annually in the United States).

While this represents an incidence of only 0.05 percent in the first generation, after several generations this incidence rate could increase five-fold. This would amount to a total

incidence between 1,100 and 27,000 serious disabilities
annually at equilibrium or about 0.1 percent in the first
generation and about 0.75 percent at equilibrium (4).
    Then there are the somatic risks which the BEIR Committee
also predicted for the same average exposure of the U.S.
population (5 rems per 30 years). These could amount to roughly
3,000 to 15,000 cancer death annually, depending upon which
underlying assumptions prove to be correct, with the most
likely estimate being about 6,000 cancer deaths annually (4).
This represents an increase of about 2 percent in the
spontaneous cancer death rate, or an increase of about 0.3
percent in the overall death rate from all causes (4).
Conversely, for each 5 rems decrease in annual exposure there
is a reduction in the spontaneous cancer death rate of about
2 percent (or 6,000 cancer deaths annually). In addition, there
is an attendant reduction in genetic effects.
    The difficult problem is how to use these risk estimates as
a basis for radiation protection guidance. Whether a risk is
acceptable or not depends on whether it can be avoided, and to
the extent it cannot be avoided, how it compares with the risks
of alternative actions or inaction.
    Complicating the task, guidance for consumer radiologic
services, while based upon general population concerns, must
also be applicable to individual patient decisions; ultimately
the consumer still must rely on his physician's or dentist's
personal judgment as to whether such services should be
prescribed.
    At a minimum, the physician or dentist must be able to
identify those consumer-patients who have received previous
radiation exposures. Besides avoiding duplication within this
group, it also is possible to identify high risk groups or
individuals by virtue of their previous extensive exposure.
For such individuals special precautions should be taken to
avoid unnecessary additional exposures.
    Moreover, besides general population considerations and
this high risk group, there also exist high risk segments of
the population, such as pregnant women, and children, who
must be characterized as particularly susceptible to ionizing
radiation effects (25, 26, 27). The relative risk of juvenile
cancer is about 60 percent greater among those children whose
mothers were exposed than among those children whose mothers
were not exposed (28). Over the first ten to fifteen years of
life, this amounts to about one juvenile cancer death per
2,000 children prenatally exposed (29), in addition to genetic
hazards.

Concern for cancer in children led the ICRP to recommend (30) that, where practicable, for women of childbearing age, X-ray exposures to pelvic and abdominal regions should be administered only during the ten-day interval following the beginning of menstruation. Those professionals following this recommendation undoubtedly have prevented much misery and suffering, and have saved many thousands of lives of young children (3). And simple precaution against unnecessary exposure of unborn children is for women to advise their doctors of the date of their last menstrual period or whether there is reason to believe they are pregnant. When changing doctors or dentists, patients also may avoid unnecessary X-ray exposures by requesting that previous films be forwarded.

Despite these precautions, the benefit-cost calculus associated with exposing pregnant women still requires considerable personal wisdom on the part of physicians. For example, the risk of childhood cancer frequently must be weighed against a suspected hazard of mortality at birth or close to birth. While the first risk may be small the consequences may be more devastating than the hazards in the second instance.

Operator Hazards   Unfortunately, the hazards to radiologic personnel are frequently assumed to be part of their occupation. Radiation protection guidance, however, should be predicated on extreme pessimism with regard to potential adverse effects of any radiation exposure whenever or wherever delivered. Rigorous control and personnel monitoring techniques are required to reduce occupational exposures.

The potential operator hazards were revealed in a 1965 study comparing the causes of death for radiologists against other physicians who did not use X rays (31). It was revealed that among the radiologists who died between 50 and 60 years of age, there were 7.3 times as many leukemia deaths and 1.7 times as many deaths from other malignancies, cardiovascular and renal disease, and other causes of death (3, 31). Radiologists dying between 1935 and 1958 lived an average of four years less than other physicians.

The opponents of mandatory licensure of radiologic technologists are quick to reply that this situation has improved since 1965. They note that this life shortening (among radiologists compared to physicians in general) diminished steadily after World War II, and vanished entirely by 1960. This can be attributed, in part, to conformance with the ICRP's maximum permissible occupational exposure; but, more importantly, it may be due to the increased use of radiologic

technologists, rather than radiologists, to provide consumer
radiologic services. Whether such life-shortening effect may,
in part, simply have been transferred to the technologist is
unknown (4), for similar epidemiologic studies have not been
performed on this occupational group.

Depending on the type of installation, several steps can be
taken for adequate operator protection: "In the case of a
medical X-ray machine in a fixed location, the operator must be
provided with a shielded booth or equivalent (fixed floor
screen of adequate size), or the control may be in another room
and the exposure switch must be so located that when pressing
the exposure switch, the operator cannot look around the edge
of the wall of the booth at the patient. This is to avoid
exposure of the operator to scattered radiation. In the case
of mobile (bedside) equipment, the operator must have a long
cord (as for dental installations) and also be provided with
a protective apron." (32)

More importantly, if radiologic technologists are not
competent enough to avoid unnecessary exposure of themselves
then they also must be assumed to be incompetent in preventing
unnecessary consumer exposures.

Medical Diagnosis   Ideally, as aforementioned, any consumer-
patient radiation exposure should be based upon a rigorous
analysis of the attendant risks vs benefits; however, the
scientific data are only available to perform such evaluations
for society as a whole (Table 3). Difficulties inherent in the
application of this concept to individual exposures led the
ICRP, in 1965, to state:

"It is not yet possible to balance risks and benefits since it
requires a more quantitative appraisal of both the probable
biological damage and the probable benefits than is now
possible." (33)

Although benefit vs risk analysis for individual consumer-
patient exposures was viewed impractical by the ICRP, the
decision still must be made by each individual physician, on
a subjective basis. Clinical judgment is important in this
regard. Thus, a decision by a mature internist with a good
reputation or a doctor's doctor is preferable to that of a
fresh medical graduate.

Thus, prudence dictates that radiation protection practices
emphasize minimization of risk to each consumer, rather than
individual cost-benefit analyses. The objective must be to keep
the attendant radiation exposures as low as practicable. As

Table 3  Comparison of Consequences of X-ray Diagnostic Exposure
Presently Received by All U.S. Population and the Consequences
of a Continuous Exposure from All Nuclear Industries (4)

| Types of Radiation Damage | Consequences of Medical X-ray Diagnostic Exposure Presently Received by U.S. Population (deaths per year) | Consequences of Hypothetical Exposure of 0.85 mrem/year to U.S. Population from Nuclear Industries (deaths per year) |
|---|---|---|
| Genetic | 1,100 to 44,000 | 3 to 120 |
| Leukemia | 500 | 3 |
| Thyroid Cancer | | |
| Dental X rays | 16 to 160 | 0.2 to 2 |
| Thorax X rays | 2 to 20 | |
| Other cancer | 500 | 3 |
| Life shortening | 1,200 | 8.5 |
| Total deaths | 3,300 to 46,000 | 18 to 140 |

The hypothetical exposure from all nuclear industries is based
upon 5 percent of the FRC's general population guidance of an
allowed 170 mr/yr.

aforementioned, for pregnant women, special precautions also
must be taken.

As discussed in Chapter 4, the Radiation Control for Health
and Safety Act of 1968 (P.L. 90-602) provides for the FDA's
control over the quality of radiologic equipment and
accessories. Nevertheless, there still remains the need to
assure competent operations, with the operators falling into
four categories: physicians, radiologists, licensed or
certified radiologic technologists, and technicians. Other than
the radiologists, who are also physicians, certified or licensed
radiologic technologists are the only other operator class that
has demonstrated proficiency in radiation sciences. This is
accomplished through examination either by voluntary
certification boards such as the American Registry of
Radiologic Technologists (ARRT), or by one of the four
mandatory State licensure boards in California, Kentucky,
New Jersey, and New York.

Although the attendant consumer risks from current practices
are easily documented, the position of the ACR and the AMA is
that the administration of radiologic services such as X-ray
examinations should be governed by the general legal and
professional requirements imposed upon the practice of medicine.
Under this policy, certification or licensure of radiologic
technologists is deemed unnecessary, because the radiologist
or other physician is viewed as responsible for the proper
execution of the entire procedure and, in turn, the welfare
of all parties involved.

The following examination of this system in practice
suggests several significant public policy issues regarding
the qualifications of physicians to judge the attendant
consumer risks from present radiologic services.

In A Physician's Office  About 40 percent of all diagnostic
X-ray examinations are performed by physicians or under their
supervision. What does this mean for the consumer? For the ACR
estimates that a medical student in the united States on the
average receives only 4.4 hours of instruction on radiation
protection (34). While this may be sufficient to instill an
awareness of the hazard, it is unreasonable to assume that it
is sufficient to stimulate the sparing and efficient use or
prescribing of radiologic procedures. Further support for this
conclusion is found in the fact that only California requires
medical students to take instruction in radiation protection
and includes related questions on State Medical Board
examinations.

In recognition of this situation, the FDA's Bureau of
Radiological Health has initiated specialized systems for the
training of medical students in the diagnostic uses of X rays.
As of June 1973, such programs were being used in five
medical schools (8).

The position of the AMA remains that the physician is the
person best qualified to judge whether diagnostic X-ray
examinations should be prescribed. While there is no one else
better qualified to make this decision, there, nevertheless,
is considerable room for improvement.

Turning to the actual performance of consumer radiologic
services, more X-ray examinations are being performed by
non-radiologists than by radiologists (23). Thus, the consumer
risks are multiplied many times. For example, when abdominal
examinations are performed by physicians in their offices, the
consumer is subjected to twice the radiation risk when compared
to examinations performed by radiologists (35).

Another non-efficacious practice often occurs where a
physician's diagnostic examination workload is insufficient

to warrant the darkroom facilities required for radiologic
film procedures. Consequently, fluoroscopy is employed,
resulting in a greater X-ray exposure than would be required
for a comparable radiologic procedure (15). A photofluorographic
chest X-ray examination also exposes a patient's skin to 1,000
millirads or more, while a well-conducted full-plate chest
radiographic X-ray film procedure can be carried out at
exposures as low as 10 to 20 millirads (2).

Further compromising the quality of such examinations, a
1972 Suffolk County, New York, survey indicates that many
fluoroscopic units also have inadequate filtration, inadequate
shutters, or malfunctioning timers (24). In addition,
fluoroscopic X-ray rooms often are not darkened adequately;
therefore, to compensate, the milliamperage frequently is
increased producing more X rays and, in turn, more patient
exposure.

Current medical practices were characterized by Jack E.
Horsley, an attorney specializing in defending doctors in
malpractice suits, as follows:

"What it all boils down to is that to perform X-ray
procedures competently a physician must possess the necessary
skill and learning, and apply them with reasonable care. The
way things are today, it's not generally known whether a
doctor doing radiology work in his office is competent and
careful unless he's sued for malpractice and the court makes
a decision." (23)

The implication is that a doctor's competence is not always
measured by demonstrated proficiency but rather, in some
instances, by the lack of conviction for malpractice. Although
this further highlights the critical need to limit the
performance of radiologic services to specialists, the
interpretation of radiographs still should reside with the
physician or, preferably, a radiologist.

The principal reason this situation occurs in practice is
that in the majority of instances, the physician is a captive
of the manufacturer, both for installation of his equipment
and for the on-site training of himself and his assistant. In
addition, the physician depends on the manufacturer for
preventative maintenance, overhaul, and upgrading of his
equipment over its usable life, although this service is not
rendered automatically.

In turn, the manufacturer's position is that X-ray equipment
is sold as professional equipment on an installed basis. Where
training is provided on the customer's premises or in factory

training programs, the principal concern is for the performance
of equipment from the standpoint of the operator's rather than
the patient's safety.

A by-product of the current system is unnecessary consumer
radiation exposure. For example, nationally some 53 percent of
the units in general medical practitioners' offices in 1967
exhibited improper collimation (6); however, in 1970 a high
percentage of these medical units still were improperly
collimated, indicating the need for a major effort to correct
existing X-ray equipment deficiencies (35). There also were a
large number of X-ray facilities in which accessory patient or
operator shielding was lacking or inadequate or there was
infrequent use of personnel monitoring systems (35).

Further possible actions for reducing consumer and operator
radiation exposures are suggested. The USPHS (36) and the
American Public Health Association (37) have stated that the
consumer's "genetically significant exposure" from diagnostic
X-ray examinations could be reduced by more than two-thirds,
from 55 to 19 millirads, by simply collimating the X-ray beam
to the size of the film. Such collimators are available for
$400 to $2,000. Distribution of this cost over the 650 million
X-ray films taken in 1970, the physician's cost would amount to
only about one cent per film (6).

A 1969 USPHS survey of 5,263 medical X-ray facilities
concluded that a major effort was needed to accomplish this
reduction in unnecessary population and occupational exposure
(38). In addition to instances of improper collimation, there
was a high percentage of installations with inadequate
filtration, lack of accessory shielding, and absence of
manually reset cumulative timers on fluoroscopes, although
these deficiencies are easily corrected.

Some improvement was found between 1964 and 1970 in reducing
the "genetically significant exposure"; however, the USPHS
warned against interpreting their data optimistically. The
observed one-third decrease was due primarily to a reduction in
the gonadal exposure to males; the exposure to women of
childbearing age actually increased by 12 percent over the
same period (23).

The use and abuse of diagnostic X-ray examinations led Mr.
Van Farowe and Mr. Hahn, Chief and Health Physicist,
respectively, in the Radiation Section of the Michigan
Department of Public Health, to state:

"As in so many fields, the understanding of the effects of
radiation exposure has lagged far behind the technological
advances promoting its use. Learning the principles of X-ray

diagnosis alone does not qualify an individual to expose humans
to this potentially hazardous source of energy; a complete
orientation and complete awareness of responsibility to patient
and future generations are necessary to make such critical
judgments. Let this generation not be accused of neglecting
to exercise all possible control over radiation exposure with
such disregard that future generations are faced with an acute
problem. Foresight in this area by this generation may
eliminate future problems of a magnitude already experienced
by mankind through neglect in other areas affecting future
survival." (15)

In the United States, physicians, not radiologists, order
an estimated 99 percent of all medical X-ray examinations;
moreover, many of these same physicians represent an important
practical obstacle to effectively limiting exposures (39). The
less enlightened members of the profession do not consider it
in their ultimate best interest to assist health agencies in
reducing consumer exposures. Some even believe that the manner
in which their X-ray equipment is used is none of government's
business and that efforts by government agencies to improve
common radiologic practices constitute an unwarranted
interference with the practice of medicine (39). However,
change in this attitude is needed if the overall public
interest is to be achieved in the provision of radiologic
services.

Diagnosis By A Radiologist  The radiologist as a medical
specialist, generally, is directly or indirectly monitored by
hospital officials, specialist colleagues, the Joint Commission
on Accreditation of Hospitals, the city, and the State. The
skills of the physician who does not specialize in radiology
are rarely scrutinized in this area (23).

Radiologists are notably more careful than are
non-radiologists about limiting X-ray fields to the size of
films (36). This is due to several factors: (a) employment of
the radiologist or radiologic technician in a hospital or office
depends upon the steady performance of his equipment; (b)
usually the best professional equipment is both purchased and
maintained properly; (c) the equipment's radiation output is
calibrated frequently; and (d) it often is replaced or
supplemented as soon as better equipment becomes available.
The same cannot be said for many units in physicians' offices
which are often used intermittently over long periods of time.
However, as a result of expansion of State and local
regulations governing the inspection and regulation of X-ray

sources, in recent years there have been improvements in the
quality of many of these older units.

Fortunately, although not necessarily prescribed in
hospitals, about 60 percent of all diagnostic medical X-ray
examinations are performed in hospitals, either by radiologists
or by radiological technologists. Among the 7,000 hospitals in
the United States about 95 percent employ a staff radiologist.
Their radiologic departments also tend to employ certified
radiologic technologists where available. While it does not
necessarily follow that radiologic examinations performed in
other than hospitals are performed poorly, there are
indications that this is most likely the case. A 1964 USPHS
survey, however, indicated that many hospital X-ray units (21
percent) also were improperly collimated (6).

Although most radiologic services are performed in hospitals
under the supervision of a radiologist, some 99 percent of
these actually are ordered by general practitioners (39).
Consequently, at the time the examination is performed the
radiologist frequently possesses little understanding of the
need for examination or for the factors entering into the
physician's decision to prescribe the radiologic service. Thus,
the radiologist actually may be the individual who determines
whether, for example, a woman is pregnant. Moreover, at the
stage when a patient arrives on the radiologist's premises, it
frequently is past the time when many of such relevant questions
can be raised (39). An exception is the "professional"
radiologist who requires the requisite information in advance
from the prescribing physician.

In summary, serious policy questions can be raised regarding
the efficacy and validity of current radiologic practices that,
in effect, allow all physicians to prescribe virtually any
radiologic service even though they may not have demonstrated
their knowledge of proper procedures or of radiation protection.
Moreover, considering the attendant patient risks, to allow a
non-specialist to administer diagnostic and therapeutic
radiologic services is tantamount, according to Carson Kaulman,
M.D., "...to permitting surgery to be done by any M.D. who
has a scalpel." (23)

The Radiologic Technologist  In 1966, the National Advisory
Committee on Radiation (NACOR) estimated a need for some 15,000
new radiologists (40), all of whom have not been trained in the
interim period. Therefore, it is reasonable to assume that many
of their anticipated functions are now being served by less
qualified individuals (34).

For the most part the actual performance of consumer
radiologic services is now delegated to more than 100,000
full-time and 50,000 part-time X-ray equipment operators. For
the purpose of this discussion, "radiologic technologists" are
those allied health personnel who have demonstrated proficiency
by being certified by an organization such as the American
Registry of Radiologic Technologists (ARRT) which, in 1971,
included some 66,300 radiologic technologists among whom some
421 were radiation therapy technologists and 1,272 were nuclear
medicine technologists (41). Conversely, between one-half to
two-thirds of the operators of X-ray equipment have not
demonstrated their qualifications to perform these services
to the extent required for ARRT certification. These latter
individuals, who are scattered throughout the offices of
physicians and dentists, represent a significant potential
hazard to the consumer as well as to themselves.

An insight into the qualifications of the individuals who
perform X-ray examinations is provided by a North Dakota survey,
which revealed that only 51 percent of them were actually
certified by the ARRT (42). Among the non-certified operators,
some 76 percent had less than one year's training and for 74
percent, radiation protection was not even included in their
limited training (42). In other words, about 36 percent of the
individuals administering X-ray examinations to consumer-
patients had received no formal training in radiation
protection.

Looking to the future there is little sign of improvement.
The Department of Labor estimated that annual needs for new
radiologic technologists would average 7,700 until 1980 (43),
providing a very good employment outlook for both full-time
and part-time operators. This is due primarily to an expanded
use of radiologic services for the diagnosis and treatment of
disease.

An additional perspective is provided from an examination of
how radiologic technologists receive their training. In the
past, radiologic technology had emphasized on-the-job training,
the emphasis being on vocational education, with students
serving an apprenticeship (44).

The position of the ACR was to encourage the training of
radiologic technologists primarily in some 1,300 hospital-based
schools (45). However, these schools have generally suffered
from a lack of qualified educators and suitable facilities,
and usually exist in a totally non-academic environment (45).
In many instances, formal classroom and laboratory instruction
have been considered of secondary importance, and there often

has been no requirement for student radiologic technologists to
understand the underlying assumptions, advantages and
limitations of the radiologic procedures or equipment (44).

A further strain has been imposed on such training
institutions as the demand for increasingly more complex
medical services has grown. In the process many activities
considered peripheral to the diagnosis and treatment of
patients have been sacrificed by hospitals and clinics, often
including the teaching and supervision of students in the
paramedical sciences (44).

Consequently, such hospital-based training programs have
increasingly fallen behind in meeting new personnel needs.
Continued principal reliance on these training programs for
qualified paramedical professionals appears almost certain to
produce shortages at least as acute as those predicted for
physicians.

Training programs are thus migrating slowly into community
colleges and other educational institutions (44). This is not
without some potential difficulties, since clinical experience
often is unavailable at colleges and universities. However,
significant positive steps are being undertaken with FDA
support to overcome such difficulties in these programs (44).

Since the establishment of minimum training standards for
radiologic technologists in 1920, there has been a continuing
upgrading of formal and technical educational programs.
Between 1959 and 1969, AMA-approved radiologic technologist
training programs had increased three-fold from 456 to 1,270;
however, only 40 programs (3.6 percent) offered Associate in
Arts degrees and 11 programs (less than 1 percent) could lead
to a Bachelor of Sciences degree (46). For the 1968 to 1969
school year these schools graduated slightly less than 5,000
radiologic technologists, although between 1970 and 1975,
there is an estimated need for 52,000 qualified technologists
(46).

Potential For Improvement   Upon completion of a two year review
of scientific evidence on low level radiation effects in late
1972, the NAS-NRC BEIR Committee concluded that medical and
dental radiation can be used with far lower average exposures
and lower genetic and somatic risks. Current exposures were
considered unnecessarily high and capable of reduction without
impairing diagnostic benefits (4). The recommendation of the
BEIR Committee was that

"Medical radiation exposure can and should be reduced
considerably by limiting its use to clinically indicated

procedures utilizing efficient exposure techniques and optimal operation of radiation equipment." (4)

In the final analysis, however, solutions to this situation rest in the hands of physicians, radiologists, and in particular, radiologic technologists. The noted health physicist, Karl Z. Morgan, has observed that present radiologic practices result in 90 percent more consumer-patient exposure than is necessary because of carelessness or ignorance on the part of individuals performing radiologic services (2, 3). Medical diagnostic radiation exposures could realistically be reduced to less than 10 percent of their present levels without curtailment in the beneficial uses of diagnostic X rays (2, 3). Dr. Morgan has proposed various actions to reduce excessive consumer medical and dental radiation exposures (Table 4). Even taking many of these actions into account, due to the increased use of radiologic services, by the year 2000 the consumer's annual "genetically significant exposure" to ionizing radiation would still exceed 200 millirads (31).

Although the USPHS observed some improvement in the reduction of consumer radiation exposures between 1964 and 1970, the United States still lags behind such countries as England (17) where the laws are much stricter.

In general, British doctors order far less X-ray examinations than Americans (who have the highest per capita rate in the Western world), and duplication is rare (1, 2, 17). In 1964, the consumer's "genetically significant exposure" in England was only 14 millirads, compared to 55 millirads in the United States (3). Although our average annual "genetically significant exposure" had been reduced to 36 millirads by 1970, British authorities estimate theirs had been reduced to 2 millirads (17).

This reduced risk is accomplished without any loss in the overall quality of health care delivery. In England the overall infant mortality rate is lower and their life expectancy slightly greater than in the United States (14).

Looking to the future, further improvements can accrue from electronic radiography which may replace X-ray film or fluoroscopy for many examinations, at about 1 percent of exposure levels (17). Although this new technique still employs X rays, it does not rely on film. The image is converted into a television signal that is stored on a magnetic disk and then replayed over a television monitor. The principle is similar to that known as "stop-action," employed on television sport programs.

Table 4   Radiation Exposure -- Some Problems and Solutions (2)

| Problem | Remedial Action |
| --- | --- |
| 1. Some X-ray equipment is being imported into the United States which does not contain meters to indicate X-ray current and voltage. | 1. Prohibit import of such equipment. |
| 2. Only the State of California requires in medical schools education and training in X rays and their safe use and State Board examinations in these subjects. | 2. Bring about such programs in the remaining 49 States. |
| 3. Only New York, New Jersey, and California now require of X-ray technologists education, training and certification in X rays and their safe use. | 3. Bring about such programs in the remaining 47 States. |
| 4. Image intensifiers have made it possible to reduce dose to patient from fluoroscopic examinations by a factor of 100 or more. However, in many cases, this factor is lost completely because some radiologists now fail to use equipment properly. | 4. Gain this factor of 100 in patient dose reduction by properly directed educational programs (and, if necessary, inspection programs). |
| 5. There is a shortage of radiologists and properly qualified X-ray technologists. These shortages would perhaps decrease by taking suggested measures 2, 3, and 4 above. | 5. Intensify educational programs. Add the rank of senior X-ray technologist with a minimum of four years of special training. Permit these senior X-ray technologists to be completely responsible for |

Table 4 (cont.)

| Problem | Remedial Action |
|---|---|
| | care and operation of diagnostic X-ray equipment. This would upgrade the X-ray technologist profession and that of the radiologist. The radiologist could then concentrate on the more professional requirements of X-ray therapy, radiographic, interpretation, etc. |
| 6. Some medical institutions and doctors still require routine X-ray pelvic measurements in pregnancy cases. | 6. Strongly discourage such practice. |
| 7. In many medical and dental radiograms, the cross-sectional area of X-ray beam is two or more times the area of the film. | 7. Require use of proper diaphragm, cones, and collimators (including rectangular precision collimators and automatic collimators). |
| 8. Fluoroscopic equipment improperly used (e.g., to fluoroscope music students to follow progress in proper use of throat muscles or to inspect employees leaving a factory to discourage stealing tools, etc.). | 8. Prohibit such use. |

Inspection Programs  Significant improvement in current
radiologic practices also can be achieved through aggressive
State and local government inspection programs. Two notable
programs are those in New York City and Suffolk County, New
York. Since 1958, the New York City Department of Health has
routinely inspected medical and dental X-ray equipment (32).
Although their equipment standards are similar to those for
similar programs in other parts of the United States, the
unique feature of their program is that each "public health
sanitarian" is empowered to serve summons for Health Code
violations.

When the program was initiated in 1959, only 8 percent of
radiographic and fluoroscopic X-ray units in physicians' offices
were in compliance; however, this had improved to 20 percent
by 1963 and a notable 73 percent by 1966 (32). By comparison,
the frequence of compliance for hospital and clinic units had
increased from 54 percent in 1963 to 81 percent by 1966. These
improvements in equipment compliance were achieved only through
repeated follow-up inspections and instructions to operators
by the City's public health sanitarians. The difficult task
ahead is to overcome the remaining deficiencies.

When Suffolk County, New York, began its Radiation Control
Program in 1962, similar results were observed to those for
New York City -- about 25 percent of the X-ray units surveyed
met code requirements (24). After ten years of effort, their
1972 survey showed that 66 percent of the X-ray units within
their jurisdiction were in compliance with New York State
Ionizing Radiation Regulations.

Although some progress has been achieved toward reduction
of unnecessary consumer-patient radiation exposure, it was
concluded (24) that further significant reductions in
exposure could be accomplished without a decrease in the
number of examinations or the amount of diagnostic information,
if properly trained and licensed operators would (a) use fast
film, (b) maintain up-to-date techniques, and (c) routinely
have their X-ray machines inspected. More importantly, however,
was the observed need to educate the public to demand that
X-ray equipment and operators comply with applicable voluntary
as well as mandatory radiation protection guidance and
regulations.

What is disturbing is that these two programs found similar
initial compliance experience which most likely also exists in
those instances where there are no State or local inspection
programs. Under such circumstances, it must be assumed that
consumer-patients are being subjected to significant
unnecessary overexposures.

An Obsolete Technology  The mobile chest X-ray van serves as an
example of an obsolete institutional technology, whose original
and limited value in the screening for tuberculosis no longer
exists. Yet, for economic and often emotional reasons such
mobile units are still being sponsored by some public groups,
local tuberculosis associations, and private companies (47).

Among health departments, the tuberculin skin test is now
the generally preferred, although not universally adopted,
case-finding method for tuberculosis. It also is the least
expensive method. Where X-ray screening methods are still
warranted, due to a high incidence of tuberculosis in population
groups at high risk, the preferable approach is routine chest
examinations of hospital admissions.

However, many teachers, food-handlers, and barbers are still
told that their legal requirement for licensure can only be
met by a chest X-ray examination. Such X-ray programs should be
conducted in conjunction with tuberculin skin tests and only
then where follow-up treatment services are available. In
summary, the reasons for discontinuance of mobile X-ray units
are as follows (48):

- Generally, the equipment is obsolete, exposing people to as
much as ten times the radiation received from standard 14 by
17 inch X-ray exposures;

- The X-ray scattering that occurs often exposes people
standing in line and even those passing near the van;

- The units find very few active cases of tuberculosis and
then at large cost. For example, in Denver between 1965 and
1970 more than 100,000 chest X rays were given to find 15 active
TB cases at a cost of $8,115 each; and

- The individuals least likely to have TB are subjected to
needless radiation exposure.

Discontinuance of this screening practice was recommended
by the USPHS in 1965 when the statement was made that

"Mass chest X-ray programs should not be given to all
population groups but instead should be focused on groups
within communities where the incidence of tuberculosis is
known to be high." (49)

It took seven years, however, before the National
Tuberculosis and Respiratory Disease Association (TB-RD), a
long-time promoter of such examinations, in 1972 expressed the
opinion that local TB associations

"...should no longer conduct chest X-ray screening programs.
Community X-ray surveys using mobile or portable X-ray units
among general population groups are not productive as a
screening procedure for pulmonary diseases and should be
eliminated...(and) TB-RD associations should no longer conduct
chest X-ray screening programs." (48)

Concurrently, this position was endorsed on February 18,
1972, by the USPHS in cooperation with the ACR and the American
College of Chest Physicians (50). This change in position was
due in large part to the efforts of the FDA's Bureau of
Radiological Health (49).

Although many health authorities were initially reluctant
to begin the massive campaign to re-educate the consumer to
the advantages of the tuberculin skin test, it is now the
preferred initial screening method for tuberculosis.
Nevertheless, in this regard, there still remains some
reluctance among health officials, in many instances the same
individual in whom the consumer has also placed responsibility
for his radiation protection.

Dental X-ray Usage Dental radiography is an indispensable
diagnostic tool in modern medicine, although unavoidably
accompanied by certain recognized health hazards. Thus, every
precaution is warranted to reduce unnecessary radiation
exposures which endanger the eyes, the facial area, and the
thyroid (51), to the absolute minimum compatible with the
diagnostic objective. Nevertheless, similar criticisms and
concerns to those made for medical X-ray examination practices
are appropriate with respect to the efficacy of dental
radiologic services.

In 1964, about 46 million consumers, or one-quarter of the
U.S. population, were administered dental X-ray examinations,
and 12 percent of this group received more than one examination
during the year (36). The frequency of dental visits was higher
among women than among men, and about three times as high
among white persons than for non-whites.

Annually, some 54 million dental X-ray examinations are
performed using 226 million films. Some 99 percent of these
are "periapical projections," used primarily to study the root
of the tooth and the surrounding structures, and "bitewing
projections," used primarily to detect caries between molar
teeth (52).

Involved are over 100,500 dental X-ray units (53), being
operated by about 89,000 dentists and their 130,000 dental
assistants. In his training, a dental student typically

receives 70 hours of instruction in radiology and the dental hygienist, 55 hours (54). However, the fraction of these times devoted to radiation protection is unknown.

In an attempt to improve dental X-ray instruction, the FDA's Bureau of Radiological Health, in 1973, developed a pilot program for training radiology teachers for dental auxiliary schools (8). Although only a beginning, this program offers promise of improved radiation protection.

Turning to the quality of dental radiologic equipment, a 1964 USPHS survey revealed that some 27 percent of all dental X-ray units inspected were not in full compliance with applicable State regulations (52). In New York City, there was an observed increase between 1960 and 1966 in the dental X-ray units in compliance with applicable standards from 47 percent to 89 percent (32).

The 1972 Suffolk County survey was not as encouraging; only about 75 percent of the X-ray units were in compliance (24). This is more consistent with the 1964 national results. First, following inspection some dentists actually removed dental collimators (24). The reason given by dentists to their dental assistants was that the accurate positioning of the X-ray tube head before taking the radiograph is time consuming (24).

The second observation was that some dentists use conventional X-ray units to perform cephalometric examinations (24). However, a different collimating device should be used for such examinations since they require a larger X-ray beam at a greater distance.

There also is an apparent need for a continuing program of resurveys, emphasizing the use of high-speed (fast) film and maximum developing techniques (55). In Alameda County, California, survey revealed that some 27 percent of the offices were using slow or intermediate films. Moreover, these offices were responsible for 45 percent of the total consumer exposure at the cone-tip (55). A change to faster film reduced their exposure by 54 percent. However, nationally in 1964, only 42 percent of the films used could be classified as fast (52).

Another common practice in dentistry is to overexpose and underdevelop radiologic film. This practice obviously must be accompanied by patient overexposure (52).

The 1964 USPHS survey also indicated that for more than one-half of the dental radiographs taken the beam size is three or more times the actual area of the film. This situation existed although devices were and are available which provide for precision collimation of the dental X-ray beams to the film's size.

Since the 1950s, there has been a reduction in dental radiation exposures, due to the efforts of the USPHS and the ADA. This is attributed largely to the use of more sensitive film and improved X-ray equipment. The ADA also has promoted five methods for limiting the radiation exposures of consumer-patients (52):

- limitation of X-ray beam size to that required to expose the film;

- insertion of metal filters to remove unnecessary radiation from the X-ray film;

- use of higher kilovoltage;

- use of higher speed or more sensitive film; and

- limitation, as mentioned, of the frequency and extent of radiation examinations consistent with good practice.

More recently, the ADA has advocated that, "Radiologic examinations should not be used as an automatic part of every periodic or routine dental examination." (4)

The FDA's Bureau of Radiologic Health had delineated five other activities which offer potential for further improvement (52):

- development of a uniform standard with criteria which specify the use of dental X-ray equipment and operational procedures that produce a minimum amount of patient radiation for a given examination;

- extension of minimum standards of all States to include required special instruction of dentists and auxiliary personnel;

- continued surveys, documentation, and corrective follow-up of the physical characteristics of X-ray equipment by State and federal agencies to minimize radiation exposure from dental radiography;

- further clarification of dose estimates either by physical measurements or suitable mathematical models; and

- a survey of trends in dental public health that may affect the frequency and number of X-ray examinations required to maintain good dental health.

At issue is the apparent failure of many dentists to heed the aforementioned admonition from their own Association. The obvious conclusion is that the area for greatest reduction of unnecessary dental X-ray exposure is with regard to technique and judgment (55). This would require that dentists be better educated and motivated to (1) take only those X-ray films necessary for proper diagnosis, (2) use the fastest film available, (3) develop films properly in suitable darkrooms, and (4) interpret them with the aid of proper equipment (55). An alternative remedy would be to prohibit by regulation the manufacture and sale of "slow" X-ray film.

An area for future improvement is in the use of dental tomography. This technique reduces a patient's exposure from the 9,940 mr now associated with a 14-film full-mouth examination to about 800 to 900 mr, or some 90 percent, while furnishing the same diagnostic information (10).

Adequate protection against potential operator hazards from dental radiologic equipment can be achieved merely by having the exposure switch at the end of a sufficiently long electrical cord and the room so arranged that the operator may always be at least 6 feet away from the patient and from the tube head and the useful beam (32).

Radiation Therapy   There are two additional radiologic procedures which represent possibilities for excessive consumer-patient exposures. These are external radiotherapy, commonly referred to as radiation therapy; and the more significant, and more recent, internal administration of radiopharmaceuticals, commonly referred to as nuclear medicine. Both these specialties rely on ionizing radiation for diagnosis or treatment. Many of the newer radiopharmaceuticals must be controlled from the standpoint of both their radiotoxicity and their physical, chemical, or pharmacologic toxicity (11). During 1970 alone, some four million Americans were administered radioactive materials for medical reasons, and in 1971 roughly 25 percent of all hospital patients were exposed to such materials.

Considering the risks of nuclear medicine, the need for its prudent use is apparent. Many physicians follow the commendable posture that the performance of external radiotherapy and nuclear medical procedures should be restricted to three classes of patients: (a) those with known or clinically suspected disease that could result in major disability, morbidity, or death; (b) those on whom all indicated non-radiation testing or treatment has been performed or ruled out due to a risk of adverse effects equivalent to that from radiation exposure; or (c) those who are expected to clearly benefit from the use of this therapy.

External Radiotherapy   External radiotherapy is used in the treatment of both non-malignant and malignant conditions; yet,

entirely different issues of benefit are involved. Where
patients are suffering from malignant conditions their life
expectancy is usually shorter than for the general population
and, in turn, they have fewer, if any, children (56). Where
treatment is for non-malignant diseases, such as skin diseases,
the consequences of the disease itself are not as severe;
thus, the issues of unnecessary radiation exposure is
considerably more important.

Several different radiation sources are used in therapy,
ranging from conventional X-ray therapy; to sealed isotopes
(for instances, radium and strontium-90 plaques), which are
applied to the surface of the skin; to teletherapy equipment
employing radioactive cobalt and cesium; and, more recently,
to proton beam therapy.

In general, teletherapy is restricted to the treatment of
cancer, an average series being about 12 administrations per
patient (1). In fact, some 157,000 consumer-patients were
treated in 1966 alone for cancer with teletherapy equipment
(1).

The resultant annual average per capita exposure in the
United States from external radiotherapy is from 12 to 20
millirems (1). Although these exposures are much lower than
those due to diagnostic uses of radiation, their significance
cannot be discounted. Also, as unnecessary diagnostic X-ray
exposures are reduced, the significance of consumer exposures
from external radiotherapy will become more important.

Here also at issue is the insufficient number of fully
trained radiotherapist technologists to meet the manpower
needs of even existing radiotherapy departments (57), where
available, qualified radiotherapy technologists are often
foreign-trained and working in the United States only on a
temporary basis. In fact, there were only 421 radiation therapy
technologists in 1971 who were certified by the ARRT (41).
With the advent of very sophisticated external radiotherapy
techniques (e.g., proton beam therapy), this shortage is of
increasing concern.

Nuclear Medicine   From an uncertain beginning in the 1940s,
nuclear medicine achieved status as a medical specialty in
1971 with the creation of the American Board of Nuclear
Medicine. Specialists in nuclear medicine must obtain a license
to perform their specialty from the Federal Government.

Why has organized medicine accepted federal regulation of
nuclear medicine while opposing similar controls over other
radiologic practices? There is inferential evidence that the
fear of radiation contamination was sufficiently widespread in
the profession to overcome the traditional fears of federalized
medicine (58).

From the beginning the physicians generally cooperated with the AEC in controlling the practice of nuclear medicine and at times added more stringent controls of their own (58). Yet these same physicians seemed relatively less concerned about consumer radiation exposures from X rays and radium, which are not regulated.

Certification as a nuclear medicine technologist is currently available from two registries: the ARRT and the American Society of Medical Technologists (ASMT). However, discussions have been initiated toward eventually combining these two voluntary registries.

"Nuclear medicine" usually refers to the internal administration of radioactive materials for diagnostic and therapeutic purposes. The materials themselves are generally designated as radiopharmaceuticals.

Perhaps the most well-known nuclear medicine procedure is the treatment of thyrotoxicosis using radioactive iodine. Previously, surgery, drug therapy, or a combination of both methods were used. Associated with surgical procedures is a small and persistent mortality as well as a low frequency of paralysis of vocal cords (58). Nevertheless, drug therapy should not necessarily be considered safer than surgery (58). The principal consumer-patient hazard from radioactive iodine procedures is the risk of leukemia.

Many nuclear medicine practitioners believe the benefits from their procedures are inherently great enough to justify the associated risks (58). A principal justification for this position is that radiation safety programs are required by the Federal Government (58).

Nevertheless, there is no evidence that the advent of nuclear medicine has lowered the incidence of any disease; rather, the principal benefit is to the physician by improving his ability to diagnose and treat disease (58). This is not meant to imply there are no consumer benefits.

While it is alleged that nuclear medicine procedures frequently facilitate medical diagnosis at lower risks to a patient than for conventional procedures (63), the full long-term risks from nuclear medicine procedures for the consumer-patient and for the person administering the procedures are largely unknown. Nevertheless, the frequency of administration has grown rapidly from 400,000 for 1959 to an estimated 1,500,000 by 1966, and an indicated 8 million in 1970 for either treatment or diagnosis (1).

On the basis of this trend there could be an estimated 20 million administrations by 1980 (69). In fact, radiopharmaceutical sales have increased from $53 million in

1969 to an estimated $83 million for 1970 (59) and are still growing.

Accompanying this trend is an increasing potential for unnecessary consumer radiation exposure. In 1970, the annual genetically significant exposure from nuclear medicine procedures was an estimated 0.5 millirads; under current growth patterns this could exceed 2 millirads by 1980 (1).

Based upon these projections, there also will be a need for 15,000 to 20,000 nuclear medicine technologists by 1980 (46). However, in 1971, there were only 1,272 nuclear medicine technologists in the United States who were certified by the ARRT (41). Moreover, there already is an existing need for nuclear medicine physicists, health physicists, and radiation safety officers for hospitals with extensive nuclear medicine programs.

Proponents of nuclear medicine also are prone to point to the alleged safety record associated with the AEC's regulation of nuclear medicine (58). However, what is not generally recognized is that the AEC's 2,800 medical licensees are not required to report accidental overexposures of patients due to diagnostic or therapeutic procedures. Moreover, AEC inspectors during routine inspections are not required to determine whether accidental exposures have occurred. Therefore, no statistics are available on the incidence of over-exposure to patients among the physicians licensed by the AEC.

Nevertheless, over the 11-year period ending April, 1972, there were 20 reported excessive administrations of radiopharmaceuticals; the actual number is probably much larger considering the estimated annual number of administrations of radiopharmaceuticals. Although it is the AEC's opinion that the number of excessive administrations has not been substantial (60), they have no records to support this opinion. Under current policies the licensed physician, not the AEC, also has complete control over the qualifications of his nuclear medicine technicians. Moreover, the AEC does not impose any minimum standards for assisting technicians, nor does the AEC require records as the bases for making determinations on the qualification of such individuals.

Commenting on the quality of radiation practices in hospitals, an AEC investigator observed in April 1969 that

"The hazard...(at the hospital), in our opinion, as in several other medical programs, lies not so much in the potential for the overexposure of the hospital personnel, but in the possible over- or misadministration of isotopes to

patients due to a lack of supervision and control of the
technicians." (60)

Earlier, in August 1968, the same investigator, at another
hospital, commented that

"It must also be realized that authorized users as a
practical matter do not and probably cannot exercise any real
personal supervision over many of the activities being carried
on in a radioisotope laboratory with an active program....
This being true, it appears the Commission has a responsibility
for obtaining assurance from the hospital or clinic that these
individuals are competent and that operating procedures are
promulgated for them to observe...." (60).

In summary, the primary responsibility for administration
of radiopharmaceuticals rests with the doctor performing the
procedure; however, the ultimate responsibility rests with
the hospital to insure that the nuclear medicine department is
staffed with personnel competent to perform or supervise the
prescribed services. However, as pointed out by an AEC
investigator,

"...each license stipulates that byproduct material shall be
used by or under the supervision of named doctors. Over the
years, however, the phrase 'under the supervision of' has
received the broadest possible interpretation. A medical
licensee is rarely, if ever, cited for noncompliance with
that license condition even under such circumstances as are
described in this case." (60)

Consequently, an AEC investigator, in October 1970, found
a licensed nuclear medicine program that was not even being
supervised by a physician. Inspection revealed that
radiopharmaceuticals were being administered to patients by
medical assistants without direct medical supervision. Moreover,
diagnostic tests were actually being interpreted by other than
a physician. Noting numerous other items of noncompliance with
AEC regulations, the same AEC inspector wrote:

"Administratively, the most significant item concerned the
routine human use of byproduct material (diagnostic
radiopharmaceuticals) by...(a non-medical doctor) and little
or no involvement of the authorized M.D.s in the diagnostic
byproduct material program." (60)

Six months after the above finding the AEC issued a notice
of 13 alleged violations to the facility. After eight months
there still was only a part-time physician supervising the
nuclear medicine department. It took 11 months before a
full-time physician assumed control and supervision.
Nevertheless, in August, 1972, almost 2 years after the
initial inspection, the licensees were still in disagreement
with the AEC's finding that radiopharmaceuticals had been used
without proper supervision. This case study represents an
extreme example of the consequences of divestiture of what
could have been in the past considered the physician's routine
medical services.

Upon completion of a review of the AEC's licensing programs
in 1972, the GAO concluded that the AEC should improve its
regulatory control over the handling of radioactive materials
by medical licensees and pharmaceutical suppliers (60). The
GAO recommended further that the control over the shipment
and use of such radioactive materials should be strengthened
by (60):

- defining in its medical licenses or regulations the
activities that may be delegated by physicians and those
that may not;

- requiring that physicians determine whether technicians have
been properly trained to perform their duties and keep records
showing the basis for such determinations;

- establishing a specific requirement that suppliers verify
that transferees are authorized to receive the quantity or
type of materials being shipped and provide guidance as to
acceptable methods of verification; and

- requiring medical licensees to report to AEC all known
misadministrations of radioactive materials to patients so
that AEC can determine the causes and whether adequate
corrective actions were taken by the licensee.

With respect to the recommendation that medical licensees
be required to report all known misadministration of
radioactive materials, the AEC alleged that it was necessary
to study the situation because of "accepted medical ethics"
surrounding the physician-patient relationship and the possible
consequences of Government's interjecting itself into this
relationship.

Even though nuclear medicine is federally regulated by the
AEC, it is clear that there is considerable room for
improvement. In fact, one might ask whether the AEC's regulation
of nuclear medicine is control in name only. Thus, the FDA's

regulation of radiopharmaceuticals as drugs may prove
beneficial (61).

Ultrasonics      The use of ultrasonic radiation in medical
diagnosis and physiotherapy is rapidly growing and is expected
to approach that of X rays (67). Applications include
diathermy and such medical studies as intracranial pulsation;
visualization of ventricular structures in children or
localization of tumors; fetal cephalometry; and visualization
of ligaments.

Although the total population at risk is unknown, the number
of people exposed annually to ultrasonic diathermy alone could
easily increase from the 1970 figure of 2 million to more than
110 million by 1976 (62). These consumer-patient services, in
1970, were being provided at some 3,000 medical ultrasonic
installations (63); however, growth patterns suggested the
existence of some 10,000 installations in 1972 (64), and an
expected 175,000 medical installations by 1975 (62).

Eventually, equipment performance or emission standards
will be promulgated pursuant to P.L. 90-602 (see Chapter 4);
however, the actual operators of the equipment do not have
to demonstrate their proficiency or knowledge of the attendant
risks. Also, it is clear that the public health risks from the
uses of ultrasound in medicine and diathermy have not been
adequately evaluated (65). Thus, risk estimates for neither
individual exposures nor general population effects can now
be made.

While some observed cause-effect relationships are
consistent with existing theory, certain cases cannot be
explained (62). There is ample justification for proceeding
with caution before ultrasound receives widespread application
in medicine. However, ultrasound already is widely used for
in utero diagnostic procedures, although available knowledge
of the attendant risks reveals an impressive, and almost total,
lack of studies of long-term effects on the fetus exposed in
utero (65). Nevertheless, such procedures are alleged to be
relatively safe compared to ionizing radiation procedures (66).
Even stronger claims have been made "...that the benefits of
diagnostic ultrasound far outweigh any risk that can be
estimated at present." (67)

In contrast, it also has been pointed out that even if one
were to accept the view that the benefits of diagnostic
ultrasound as used in obstetrics far outweigh the risk, itself
debatable, one also must ask whether the procedure itself is
being performed with minimum risk to the patient and whether
the operator is qualified to even make such a judgment (65).

Unfortunately, issues of risks cannot be settled by casual observations of practicing physicians. While available evidence indicates that intensities employed in diagnostic procedures in the hands of a trained operator do not seem hazardous (64), this conclusion is not based on long-term epidemiologic evidence.

In summary, the safety of ultrasound cannot be guaranteed simply because there are minimal short-term overt effects (62). Moreover, ultrasound of more intense therapeutic intensities can be hazardous even in the hands of trained technicians. Consequently, ultrasonics should always be used with extreme caution. Nevertheless, the attendant risks must be viewed as justified where lack of treatment presents a high risk to a patient; for example, in the case of brain tumors.

Concern is for the burgeoning use of ultrasonics in medicine with only minimal commensurate knowledge on the part of the average physician of the attendant consumer-patient hazards. It is quite simple, for example, to construct a theoretical case for possible damage resulting from ultrasonic exposure of a fetus in the early stages of development (69). In short, the public health effects of ultrasound could represent a significant radiation protection issue, which must be dealt with before, rather than after, the fact.

Diathermy   An entirely new consumer-patient radiologic service is the emerging widespread use of diathermy in medical and dental practices (67). There were an estimated 15,000 microwave and 15,000 shortwave installations in operation in 1972 (68).

The major factor contributing to unnecessary consumer exposures is the lack of qualifications of the individuals providing such services.

Microwave   Some 2 million people are treated annually with microwave (radiofrequency) diathermy by non-physicians (63). In the process, an additional 60,000 people may be occupationally exposed in physicians' offices and clinics (67).

Although microwave diathermy does not represent a hazard comparable to that from medical X-ray usage, possible acute effects from excessive exposures include the latent formation of cataracts where the eye is directly exposed; death following hyperthermia after whole-body radiation; and testicular damage (62).

For example, the susceptibility of the eye to the production of cataracts is witnessed in the case where a 38-year-old man who, following microwave diathermy treatment for strained neck muscles, developed bilateral posterior subcapsular cataracts (60). There also is ample evidence (62) of subtle effects from microwave exposures to support the regulation of consumer product sources for protection of the public health from their possible hazards (70).

Here, also, experience highlights the fact that medical practitioners, as well as the non-physician operator employing microwave diathermy, are often unaware of the potential hazards and, therefore, are not alert to possible adverse radiation related sequelae.

## Regulation of Operators

Overview  At issue through the previous discussion are the qualifications of the individuals providing consumer radiologic services. In turn, this issue can be viewed as characteristic of the broader policy issue as to whether all health care personnel should be required to demonstrate their proficiency. During the 92nd Congress (1971 to 1972), such legislation required all health care personnel to demonstrate their competence as a condition for extension of federal health care assistance. As expected, this issue followed the establishment of the federal Medicare and Medicaid programs.

An obvious factor in the provision of health care services is qualified health manpower. Two controls are absolutely essential: first, control over admission to the profession; and, second, control over the educational curriculum. Other factors include wages and working conditions, location and standards of health facilities, and administrative and organizational patterns. Licensure is intended to assure better quality health care services; however, if improperly implemented it also could create obstacles rather than contribute to sound solutions.

The radiologic technologist is just one of some 200 different paramedical or allied health specialists. Each of these specialties is directly affected by the sudden emergence of public concern for proficiency testing as a means for screening individuals entering them.

In November 1970, the Congress, in amendments to the Allied Health Act, directed the DHEW Secretary to conduct a study of the need for regulation of allied health personnel. Immediately, the AMA and the AHA called for a nationwide moratorium on licensure of any additional health occupations; however, the moratorium did not apply to hiring. This holding action was intended to provide time to develop long-term solutions. However, it has been alleged (69) that the AHA has failed to commit itself to the expenditure of funds, or assumption of a leadership role to help assure that the time

will be used to the advantage of health professions and the
health care system. Thus, specific licensure proposals still
remain to be acted on. It is clear, however, that licensure
overlaps the whole issue of the role of government in health
care delivery and, in turn, the "health care revolution."

The 1971 DHEW report on Licensure and Related Health
Personnel Credentialing (70) endorsed the AHA-AMA
recommendation for a moratorium on licensure. An additional
two-year stay was suggested so a master plan could be developed
for regulation of health personnel. However, the Report also
provides opportunity for still further extension of the
two-year moratorium; meanwhile, the hiring, often of
non-certified or -licensed health care personnel, continues.

Thus, as a society, we continue to require licensure of
doctors and dentists as medical practitioners but not their
assistants. At issue is not government interference but how
best to provide a partnership between the physician and the
allied health specialist for maximum benefits to the
consumer-patient.

What is frequently omitted from discussions of this issue
is the reality that the qualifications of almost two-thirds
of presently practicing radiologic technicians are unknown.
Moreover, a moratorium on licensure of radiologic technologists
negates the obvious potential benefits to be gained in reducing
excessive radiation exposures, considering that possibly
one-half of the X-ray examinations are being performed by
non-certified technologists. In short, protection of the public
has been deferred for the duration of the moratorium.

If all parties, including the AMA, the AHA, and the ACR,
are indeed serious about upgrading the quality of paramedical
services, a more consumer oriented approach would be a
complementary moratorium on the hiring of non-certified
technicians.

In the future, the consumer-patients' interests would be
further protected if physicians, as a condition of keeping
their licensure, were required to employ only properly trained
and licensed paramedical personnel. This could be judged by
successful graduation from an accredited school or by
appropriate certification.

Initiating Events  The debate over mandatory certification or
licensure of radiologic technologists has permeated medical
care circles for many years. Thirty years ago, in a January
1942 editorial, in the X-Ray Technician, James A. Morgan
stated:

"The reason why 'X-ray pictures' are not easy to make is the
fact that well qualified radiologists have set their standard
of judgment so high that technicians must have more than a
cursory knowledge of technical factors and use every means at
their disposal to produce the best possible radiograph....
However, until organized medicine lends the strength of its
numbers and recognition to the technicians.... When the medical
profession supports the existence and efforts of the American
Registry of X-Ray Technicians, and when the licensees of this
Board are recognized by the hospital associations, then the
fallacy that 'X-ray pictures' are easy to make will soon
dissipate." (71)

More recently, the National Advisory Committee on Radiation
reported in 1966 to the Surgeon General that:

"It will become increasingly difficult to increase the
effectiveness with which radiologic services are delivered to
the public. The establishment of minimum legal standards of
education, training, and experience for such technologists
appears to be necessary to bring this about." (40)

In 1966, DHEW Secretary John W. Gardner also created the
Task Force on Environmental Health and Related Problems,
charged with recommending Department goals, priorities, and
strategy to cope with environmental threats to man's health
and welfare. One of the Task Force's conclusions, in June,
1967, was that "...radiation hazards, in spite of the amount
of public sensitivity to the subject during the past quarter
century, are still in need of improved control.... Clearly
more protection is needed." (72) There was little doubt on
the part of the Task Force that

"...even with widespread concern about the danger of X rays,
many Americans are overexposed in diagnostic and therapeutic
practice.
  Consequently, the Task Force recommended that all persons
using X-ray equipment should be licensed to do so, after
fulfilling written examinations as to their competency. To use
X rays with optimal efficiency and, at the same time, reduce
patient exposure to a minimum, it will be necessary that:
(1) all equipment meet recommended standards; (2) the most
advanced techniques are employed by competent operators; and
(3) X rays are used efficiently, effectively, and judiciously
to promote the maximum benefit with minimum risk." (72)

The same year, in October 1967, the Surgeon General's
Medical X-Ray Advisory Committee on Public Health
Considerations in Medical Diagnostic Radiation also recommended:

"...that the prime consideration should be the total public
health interest and that the stage has been reached when
mandatory requirements of examination, training, and experience
are appropriate." (73)

This opinion was expressed by the Committee despite the
fact that "the voluntary procedures of certification by the
American Registry of Radiologic Technologists (ARRT) set a
generally high level of such assurance" (73) that medical X-ray
equipment operators are knowledgeable and competent. The
Committee held no brief for licensure per se, but rather
recognized that licensure, in many instances, may be the best
mechanism for assuring minimum proficiency.

The NAS-NRC BEIR Committee commented in 1972 that it is
precisely because medical radiation exposure can and should be
reduced considerably by limiting its use to clinically
indicated procedures utilizing efficient exposure techniques
and optimal operation of radiation equipment, that consideration
should be given to the following (4):

- Restriction of the use of radiation for public health survey
purposes, unless there is a reasonable probability of
significant detection of disease;

- Inspection and licensing of radiation and ancillary
equipment; and

- Appropriate training and certification of involved personnel.
Gonad shielding (especially shielding the testes) is strongly
recommended as a simple and highly efficient way to reduce the
"Genetically Significant Dose."

The BEIR Committee emphasized that

"Medical exposures are not under control or guidance by
regulation or law at present. The use of ionizing radiation in
medicine is of tremendous value but it is essential to reduce
exposures since this can be accomplished without loss of
benefit and at relatively low cost. The aim is not only to
reduce the radiation exposure to the individual but also to
have procedures carried out with maximum efficiency so that
there can be a continuing increase in medical benefits
accompanied by a minimum radiation exposure." (4)

Congressional Interest  In 1957, the Congress considered
legislation bearing on the qualifications of radiation workers.
At that time, the Joint Committee on Atomic Energy was
concerning itself with State control of certain manmade
radioactive materials. The Atomic Energy Act of 1954 thus was
amended authorizing the AEC to enter into agreements with
individual States to turn such control over to them. Under
such agreements, conditions are specified for the operators
who use licensed sources.

The years later, in 1967, congressional interest in the
qualifications of the operators of radiation equipment was
spurred by the 1966 recommendation of the National Advisory
Committee on Radiation (NACOR) that the USPHS

"...initiate drafting and setting of standards for
qualifications of persons who operate X-ray equipment...." (40)

About this same time, the 90th Congress was actively
considering the Radiation Control for Health and Safety Act,
H.R. 10790 and S. 2067. The thrust of that legislation was to
control radiation emissions from electronic products through
federal performance standards (see Chapter 4). At the time of
the NACOR recommendation, in 1968, both House and Senate
legislative committees were actively engaged in hearings.
However, Rep. John Jarman's Subcommittee on Public Health and
Welfare notably limited their considerations to unnecessary
consumer radiation exposures resulting from excessive emission
from medical and dental X-ray equipment itself. The
qualifications of the operators of this same equipment were
not dealt with in the report of the House Committee on
Interstate and Foreign Commerce (74).

Senator Bartlett's Initial Leadership  On the other hand, the
Senate Commerce Committee, under the leadership of Sen. Edward
L. Bartlett (D.-Alaska), immediately took an active interest
in the qualifications of the operators of electronic equipment
beginning with the first day of the Committee's hearings on
August 28, 1967. This difference in the scope of Senate and
House legislation was to play a significant role at the
subsequent House-Senate conference.

At later hearings in May, 1968, the Senate Commerce Committee
commenced an in-depth investigation of consumer radiation
hazards. By this time, three different bills for the regulation
of electronic products were pending before the Committee (see
Chapter 4); yet none of these measures concerned themselves
directly with the qualifications of the operators. Rather,

federal licensure of radiologic technologists was being
supported separately by Sen. Bartlett.
　　During this period, the position of the American Society
of Radiologic Technologists (ASRT) in the Senate was

"...that the interests of this nation, as well as that of
medicine and the individual patient, will be best served if
basic minimum federal standards are set for all those operators
applying ionizing radiation for other purposes." (75)

　　The ASRT considered federal minimum standards necessary and
desirable to (75):

- prevent a proliferation of standards throughout the country;

- aid the States unable to mount their own programs; and

- aid in providing a more consistent and constant protection
to the public from unnecessary exposure to ionizing radiation.

　　Significantly, the ASRT did not endorse federal mandatory
licensure; rather their support was for federal minimum
standards equivalent, at least, to those required for
certification by the American Registry of Radiologic
Technologists (ARRT).
　　On the other hand, the ARRT in 1968 issued a position
statement opposing state licensure in response to a model
bill then proposed by the ACR (75). Later, in 1969, the basis
for the ARRT's opposition was simply stated (75):

- The minimum standards were not described; and

- The Registry is committed to support nothing less than the
ARRT's standards.

　　The ARRT noted that support of unknown standards would be
in direct violation of their bylaws (75).
　　However, when the Senate later passed H.R. 10790, it became
politically necessary for the ASRT to support licensure. For
through the efforts of Sen. Bartlett, such authority was
contained in the Senate version of H.R. 10790 and the House
passed bill did not contain any provisions dealing with
licensure. Later, when this provision was dropped from the
final bill (P.L. 90-602) at the House-Senate Conference,
Senator Bartlett commented:

"...it makes no sense to set performance standards for
equipment without attempting to ensure that the operators of
the equipment are trained to use it correctly." (75)

The one relevant feature that survived was a report to the Congress on measures to assure consistent and effective control of radiation hazards.

1970 Report To The Congress   When the report was subsequently transmitted to the Congress in August, 1970, eight months late, one of the recommendations of the Secretary of Health, Education and Welfare was that

"The Public Health Service should vigorously promote licensure or certification of users of radiation sources in the healing arts. Licensure or certification should be uniformly applied at federal and State levels. Full use should be made of model regulations to assure compatibility between states." (75)

Consistent with this recommendation, the DHEW Secretary in October, 1970 exercised his authority under the Radiation Control for Health and Safety Act of 1968 "...to make such recommendations as he considers appropriate to promote reduction in consumer radiation exposure." The FDA's Bureau of Radiological Health issued model legislation to aid states in establishing minimum education and training standards for the operators of medical and dental radiologic equipment, and the users of radioactive materials (76).

Under the model law, a State could require certification of competence by all users of ionizing radiation for the diagnosis or treatment of disease, including physicians and dentists. However, a former ASRT President, Leslie Wilson, characterized the FDA model State legislation as putting "...the stamp of dignity to lowered standards and poorer quality of patient care (77)," when compared to the ARRT's requirements for certification.

The 91st And 92nd Congresses   During the Second Session of the 91st Congress, in June 1970, the issue of regulation of consumer radiologic services was revived by Sen. Jennings Randolph (D.-W. Va.). This interest stemmed from November, 1969 testimony before his Committee on Public Works from Drs. John W. Gofman and Arthur R. Tamplin on, "Federal Radiation Council Guidelines for Radiation Exposure of the Population-at-Large -- Protection or Disaster." (78)

Sen. Randolph's bill, S. 3973, provided for federal minimum standards for the training and mandatory State licensure of radiologic technologists (79, 80). Written as an amendment to the Public Health Services Act, the measure was thus referred to the Committee on Labor and Public Welfare and, in turn, to Sen. Edward Kennedy's Subcommittee on Health.

The previous month, on May 20, 1970, Richard A. Olden, then
Chairman of the ASRT's Committee on Legislation, had testified
before the same Subcommittee in support of the Allied Health
Professions Assistance Act. Sen. Kennedy's subcommittee was
informed that there was a general shortage of radiologic
technologists due in part to the rather high educational
requirements (81). Moreover, this situation was considered
poor, being further compounded by the fact that employment in
the field is not dependent upon any training in radiologic
technology (81). Thus, poorly qualified operators were being
hired to fulfill manpower shortages. Consequently, he
reiterated the ASRT's dedication to the formulation of
national minimum standards for training and employment of the
operators of medical X-ray equipment.

Subsequently, Sen. Randolph's bill died in 1970 without any
action being taken by the Subcommittee; however, he reintroduced
a similar measure in the 92nd Congress, S. 426, on January 28,
1971 (82). By this time, the number of cosponsors had risen
to include Senators Robert Byrd (D.-W. Va.); Peter H. Dominick
(R.-Colo.); Mike Gravel (D.-Alaska); Philip A. Hart (D.-Mich.);
Vance Hartke (D.-Ind.); Jacob K. Javits (R.-N.Y.); Thomas J.
McIntyre (D.-N.H.); Walter F. Mondale (D.-Mich.); Frank E.
Moss (D.-Utah); Edmund S. Muskie (D.-Me.); Gaylord Nelson (D.-
Wisc.); James B. Pearson (R.-Kan.); Claiborne Pell (D.-R.I.);
Hugh Scott (R.-Pa.); Ted Stevens (R.-Alaska); and Harrison A.
Williams (D.-N.J.).

Sixteen months later, on May 15, 1972, representatives of
the ASRT again testified before Sen. Kennedy's Subcommittee
on Health on related legislation, S. 3327, which provided
continuing support of schools and students of allied health
professions (83). Despite their expressed support for S. 426,
the Subcommittee did not take up active consideration of the
bill during the 92nd Congress, either.

However, during the 92nd Congress, support was forthcoming
in the House of Representatives when on August 17, 1972, Rep.
Edward I. Koch (D.-N.Y.) introduced H.R. 16249 (84, 85).
Representative Koch reintroduced his measure in the 93rd
Congress (91).

The 93rd Congress (1973)  Not to be deterred, Sen. Randolph
returned to the 93rd Congress to reintroduce his bill the
third time as S. 667, cosponsored by Senators Robert Byrd;
Peter H. Dominick; Birch Bayh; Mike Gravel; Philip Hart; Jacob
Javits; Walter F. Mondale; Frank E. Moss; Edmund S. Muskie;
Hugh Scott; Ted Stevens; and Harrison A. Williams.

Consequently, essentially identical bills again resided
before both Houses of the 93rd Congress (1973-1974), providing

the DHEW Secretary with authority to issue criteria and minimum
standards for the accreditation of institutions that train
radiologic technologists, and for State licensure of such
technologists. In establishing these criteria and federal
minimum standards, the DHEW Secretary would be required to
consult with State health departments and with appropriate
professional organizations (87).

The principal difference between the two proposals lies in
the Senate bill, which provides a mandatory, as opposed to
discretionary, requirement that the federal minimum standards
for the training and mandatory State licensure distinguish
between

- senior radiologic technologists;

- medical radiologic technologists;

- dental radiologic technologists;

- radiation therapy technologists;

- nuclear medicine technologists;

- photo-roentgen technologists; and

- technologists-in-training.

This distinction is intended to provide a hierarchy for
upward career mobility, with a functional description for each
specialty. The efforts of the ASRT and the ACR in this regard
(88) were particularly useful in developing this distinction.
However, the last two categories under S. 667 require
supervision by a radiologist, or a more senior licensed
technologist.

As envisioned, the "senior radiologic technologist" would
be required to have the equivalent of four years of prescribed
education and training before licensure. Eventually, such a
technologist might achieve sufficient status that he could be
placed in charge of a radiologic facility, without the
presently required direct medical supervision. This distinction
also is intended to provide a professional goal that could
serve as an incentive for technologists to pursue studies to
extend their competence.

For the purpose of promoting State rather than federal
licensure,  encouragement is given to the preferential
establishment of State programs. However, should a State fail
to adopt appropriate standards within two years of enactment
that meet the DHEW standards for accreditation of educational
institutions and for licensure of technologists, the federal
minimum standards would automatically become the standards
for that State.

In order to avoid duplication of licensure efforts, the
DHEW Secretary also would be authorized to certify appropriate
federal and State professional licensing organizations, such
as the ARRT, ASMT, or ARCRT, to assume a role as the federal
agent for the purpose of issuing licenses. The objective here
is to create a federal program which builds and expands on
existing voluntary certification programs rather than
duplicates or detracts from this existing effort.

Two issues still remain to be resolved: first, the
"grandfather" provisions affecting the current operators of
radiologic equipment. One option would be to accept valid
certification by the ARRT or the equivalent as fulfilling
federal minimum standards for licensure. Employed, but
noncertified, operators, in turn, might be classified as
"technologists-in-training" for one year, pending demonstration
of their proficiency by examination for this position or a
higher status of licensure.

Throughout this period, Sen. Randolph's bill was pending
before Sen. Kennedy's Subcommittee on Health. However, Sen.
John V. Tunney (D.-Calif.) actively entered the scene in March
1973, chairing 3 days of oversight hearings on the "electronic
products" act (P.L. 90-602) before the Senate Commerce
Committee (89). At the time, testimony was received in support
of S. 667 from Sen. Randolph; Rep. Koch; Mrs. Polly Story,
president-elect of the ASRT; and Dr. Karl Z. Morgan.

Subsequently, Sen. Tunney expressed interest to Sen.
Randolph in arranging for S. 667 to be referred to the Commerce
Committee for their eventual action. An attempt was then made
by Sen. Randolph to satisfy this request by his contacting
Senator Kennedy, since it offered promise for early legislative
action. However, Sen. Kennedy refused to waive jurisdiction,
writing Sen. Randolph that

"...this measure addresses a critically important health policy
area...the Health Subcommittee has become increasingly
concerned regarding the quality of medical services in America.
To a very considerable extent the quality or lack thereof of
those services is attributable to the competence and compassion
of the health manpower who deliver these services." (90)

He added

"The Subcommittee...has as its highest priority item the
complete recodification and restructuring of the entire (Public
Health Services) Act in anticipation of national health
insurance.... I believe this effort is the best forum to

consider and take testimony on the provisions of S. 667....
I believe it will be possible to legislate in this area." (90)

Meanwhile, Rep. Koch's bill remained on the calendar of
Rep. Paul G. Roger's Interstate and Foreign Commerce
Subcommittee on Public Health and Environment.

Throughout these discussions, concern has been expressed
that legislation might be enacted that would downgrade the
position of the radiologic technologist (91). While this could
occur, the objective of the licensure is to assure
professionalism through force of law. Legislation would only
point the way; achievement of this objective will require the
efforts and cooperation of the medical profession as well as
the radiologic technologist himself. The public policy issue,
as cogently expressed by Sen. Randolph, is:

"...assuring that the consumer, in this case the medical care
patient, is receiving the most efficacious medical services
that modern science is capable of delivering." (87)

Meanwhile, although both the physician and the radiologic
technologist have as their common prime goal the welfare of
the consumer-patient, there nevertheless continues a tug-of-war
between these two groups over licensure, with the helpless
victim of the struggle being the consumer-patient.

Epilogue
It is ironic that medical licensure laws were enacted over 100
years ago to protect the consumer against incompetent and
unethical medical practitioners; yet, these same 19th century
laws now serve as a straightjacket on the delivery of health
care services in the quantity and quality the consumer needs
and, rightly, expects to receive (92). In this regard, the
following observation by Surgeon General Leroy Burney is
appropriate:

"In law the suspect is innocent until his guilt is proven
beyond reasonable doubt. In the protection of human health
such absolute proof often comes late.... To wait for it is to
invite disaster, or to suffer unnecessarily through long
periods of time." (93)

Admittedly, regulation represents a departure from the
previously accepted sanctity of the doctor-patient relationship.
However, many of the previous merits of this philosophy have
been largely negated by a shortage of medical practitioners,

leading to a divestiture by the physician of many specialized
health care services, such as radiologic services.

However, this divestiture now presents an opportunity to
also improve the overall quality of health care delivery in
both degree and scope. Nevertheless, this goal will be
facilitated only through an effective partnership between all
members of the health care team.

Where a licensed radiologic technologist is on the scene
both the physician and his patients obtain the benefits of his
expertise. Paradoxically, where the physician's assistant is
untrained there is no assurance to the physician or the
consumer-patient that the radiologic procedures are being
performed well even with the best and most fool-proof of
modern equipment.

A frequently expressed argument against mandatory licensure
is an alleged critical manpower shortage in radiologic
technology. Actually affected, however, are those poorly
qualified "operators" who might be eliminated from the
employment picture. In the process the quality of consumer
radiologic services might actually be improved. Moreover,
acceptance of lesser qualifications for operators than
generally acknowledged as desirable under the guise of a
manpower shortage only serves to put the seal of official
dignity on an already poor situation (77).

A deep public disaffection has emerged regarding the quality
of health care services generally. The proper criterion for
consumer acceptance is broad societal efficacy -- concern for
the relationship between the quality of these services and the
social priorities of our times. Moreover, we also live in a
new age of "participatory democracy," and of "new consumerism,"
where the public demands accountability from all segments of
society -- the medical care professions are certainly not
exempt.

The task ahead is one of providing new methods of health
care delivery and new practices in manpower utilization which
deliver improved quality of health care, in both degree and
scope, to the consumer-patient.

For the foreseeable future, consumer exposure to ionizing
radiation from diagnostic and therapeutic uses will, hopefully,
continue to be comparable to those from natural background.
This prompted the BEIR Committee to state:

"The use of ionizing radiation in medicine is of tremendous
value but it is essential to reduce exposures since this can
be accomplished without loss of benefit and at relatively low
cost. The aim is not only to reduce the radiation exposure to

the individual but also to have procedures carried out with
maximum efficiency so that there can be a continuing increase
in medical benefits accompanied by a minimum radiation
exposure." (4)

In recognition of the public health implications from
current radiologic practices in the United States and the
slow response toward improvement, the aforementioned regulatory
response has been advocated by several expert committees and
public health officials. The suggested elements of such a
program include requirements that:

- each owner or operator of radiologic equipment should be
required to demonstrate by certification or licensure their
competence in the operation of such equipment and their
knowledge in radiation protection;

- this requirement also should extend to public health
personnel who inspect such equipment;

- there should be routine inspection and licensing of
radiation and ancillary equipment;

- no new radiologic equipment should be installed unless the
owner and/or intended operators show evidence of certification
or licensure;

- plans for new or relocated facilities should be reviewed by
a regulatory agency;

- radiologic equipment should be registered with and new and
relocated equipment inspected by a regulatory agency;

- where violations exist, operations of radiologic equipment
should be suspended until violations are corrected and
reinspected; and

- there should be routine inspections and calibrations of
radiologic equipment by certified or licensed radiation
specialists.

Whether such a national program is ever realized or not,
the overshadowing question still remains: What are the
qualifications of the individuals, whether physicians or
radiologic technologists, providing these services? A detailed
examination of the current situation leads to several
conclusions:

- If unnecessary consumer radiation exposures are to be
successfully reduced, it is essential to improve the judgment
of physicians requesting radiologic services (35);

- The operators of medical and dental radiologic equipment should be motivated to minimize human exposure from diagnostic X ray through persuasion, education, and training, "including material on radiation protection in the long-term or formal education of users" (35, 38); and

- The operators of microwave, and particularly ultrasonic diathermy equipment, should be motivated similarly to consider the attendant potential hazards to the consumer and operator alike.

In recognition of the need to further upgrade the quality of consumer radiologic services, the 1972 Conference of Radiation Control Program Directors also recommended that (94):

- in addition to carrying out programs to assess healing arts and industrial uses of X rays, the (FDA) Bureau of Radiological Health should initiate studies of the efficacy of specific X-ray examinations;

- the FDA should bring all non-agreement radioactive materials (naturally occurring and accelerator-produced materials) under the Federal Hazardous Substances Act and a standard procedure for evaluation of radioactive material hazards; and

- regarding radiopharmaceutical controls, a joint task force of State and federal agencies should be established as soon as possible to develop an interagency communications program to review and evaluate regulatory controls, to plan regional training sessions, and to investigate the possibility of joint compliance activities.

Looking to the future, there also is considerable merit to recording consumer radiation exposures. Such a system would contain all relevant information on dates of previous exposure, type of examination, reason, shielding employed, estimated exposure dose, and, for women, pertinent details of pregnancy (95).

In summary, throughout this discussion, concern has been for the right of the consumer-patient to expect and to receive the most efficacious radiologic services from modern medical sciences -- the overriding goal being to obtain the desired diagnostic information at the lowest practical radiation exposure. The essentiality of this objective is reinforced by the Surgeon General's opinion that

"In almost every medical situation when a physician feels there is a reasonable expectation of receiving information...

that would affect the medical care of an individual patient, potential radiation hazard is not a consideration." (96)

Moreover, while it is possible to teach someone, in a short period of time, to perform radiologic services, it is <u>not</u> possible to teach them respect for warranted and essential radiation protection safeguards in any brief period of a few days, weeks, and even months.

Until consumer radiologic services are routinely capable of providing the maximum amount of interpretive diagnostic information with the least -- not just an acceptable -- risk, the consumer-patient is being subjected to an excessive and unnecessary hazard, and the radiologic services are non-efficacious.

<u>Acknowledgments</u>
The author would like to express his deep appreciation for the assistance lent by Dr. Catherine Wingate of the Office of Radiation Programs, Environmental Protection Agency, Washington, D.C.; Dr. Richard C. Riley, Division of Radiological Sciences, The University of Kansas Medical Center, Kansas City, Kansas; and Dr. Robert M. Albrecht, Epidemiologic Studies Branch, Division of Biological Effects, Bureau of Radiological Health, F.D.A., Washington, D.C. in the review of this chapter. The views and opinions expressed herein are those of the author alone.

References

1. Terpilak, Michael S., Weaver, Charles L., and Wieder, Samuel, "Dose Assessment of Ionizing Radiation on Exposure to the Population," Rad. Health Data and Repts. 12:171-188 (April, 1971).

2. Morgan, K. Z., "Never Do Harm," Environment 13:28-38 (January-February, 1971).

3. Morgan, K. Z., "The Need for Radiation Protection," Radiologic Technology 44:385-395 (1973).

4. National Academy of Sciences - National Research Council, "The Effects on Populations of Exposure of Low Levels and Ionizing Radiation," Report of the Advisory Committee on the Biological Effects of Ionizing Radiations, Division of Medical Sciences, Washington, D.C. (1972).

5. Chadwick, Dr. Donald, Address, Congress of Environmental Health, Chicago, Ill. (1969).

6. Terrill, James G., Jr., "Cost Benefit Estimates in the Major Sources of Radiation Exposure," AJPH 62:1008-1013 (July, 1972).

7. Malsky, Stanley, J., Ph.D., Hayt, David, M.D., Gould, Lawrence, M.D., Blatt, Charles, M.D., Simon, Donald, F., Ms., and Roswit, Bernard, M.D., "Radiation Exposure to Staff Cardiologist vs. Senior Resident Cardiologist and Patients During Cardiac Catheterization," Rad. Health Data and Repts. 13:387-91 (July, 1972).

8. DeVore, Robert T., "Diagnostic X-Rays: How Safe Are They?" FDA Consumer 7:6, 4-7 (June, 1973).

9. Morgan, James A., Editorial, "A Prevalent Fallacy," The X-Ray Technician (January, 1942).

10. National Council on Radiation Protection and Measurement, Report No. 39, Washington, D.C. (1969).

11. Adelstein, S. James, "The Risk: Benefit Ratio in Nuclear Medicine," Hospital Practice 8:141-149 (January, 1973).

12. Shryock, Richard, "Medical Licensing in America, 1650-1969," Johns Hopkins Press, Baltimore, Md. (1967).

13. Vincent, C. S., "The Plight of Radiologic Technology: Quantity and Quality," Radiologic Technology 43:75-79 (1971).

14. Moore, Frederick, J., "Physicians Delegate to Aides," Allied Med. Educ. Newsl. 3:6 (April, 1970).

15. Hahn, Dennis R., and Van Farowe, Donald E., "Misuse and Abuse of Diagnostic X-Rays," AJPH 60:250-254 (February, 1970).

16. Griffiths, J., and Ballantine, R., "Silent Slaughter," Henry Regnery Company, Chicago (1973).

17. Hope, Marjorie, and Young, James, "X-Ray Hazards -- And How to Avoid Them," Woman's Day, May, 1972, pp. 90-174, 176.

18. McClenahan, Dr. John, "Wasted X-Ray," Penn. Medicine 72:107-108 (November, 1969); also reprinted in Radiology 96:453-456 (August, 1970).

19. Roberts, F., and Snopfner, C. E., "Plain Skull Roentgenograms in Children with Head Trauma," American J. Roentgen. 114:230-234 (1972).

20. Bell, R. S., and Loop, J. W., "The Utility and Futility of Radiographic Skull Examination for Trauma," New Eng. J. Med. 284:231-239 (1971).

21. Harwood-Nash, D. C., Hendrick, E. B., and Hudson, A. R., "The Significance of Skull Fractures in Children: A Study of 1,187 Patients," Radiology 101:151-155 (1971).

22. Warshopky, Fred, "Warning: X-Rays May Be Dangerous to Your Health," Readers Digest, August 1972, pp. 173-177. Condensed from Family Health (August, 1972).

23. Kaulman, Carson, "There Ought to be a Law Against X-Ray Bunglers!" Medical Economics, October 23, 1972, pp. 83-87.

24. Becker, Seymour, "Results of a Survey of Diagnostic and Therapeutic X-Ray Machines, Suffolk County, N.Y., 1972," Rad. Health Data and Repts. 14:397-400 (July, 1973).

25. U.S. AEC, Division of Biology and Medicine, "Prenatal X-Ray and Childhood Neoplasmas," TID-12383 (April 1, 1961).

26. MacMahon, Brian, "X-Ray Exposure and Malignancy," J. of Amer. Med. Assn. 183:721 (1963).

27. Stewart, Alice, and Kneale, G. W., "Radiation Dose Effects in Relation to Obstetric X-Rays and Childhood Cancers," Lancet (June 6, 1970), p. 1185.

28. Graham, Dr. Saxon, National Cancer Institute Monograph (1966).

29. Gehan, Edmund A., "Relationship of Prenatal Irradiation to Death from Malignant Disease," Biometrics 28(1):239-245 (March, 1972).

30. ICRP, "Publication No. 6: Recommendations of the International Commission on Radiological Protection," New York, Pergamon Press (1964).

31. Seltser, R., and Sartwell, P. E., American Journal of Epidemiology 81 (1965).

32. Blatz, Hanson and Lynch, Daniel E., "Improvement in New York City X-Ray Installations During the First Seven Years of a Radiation Control Program," Rad. Health Data and Repts. 10: 89-92 (March, 1969).

33. ICRP, Recommendations of the International Commission on Radiological Protection (Adopted September 17, 1965), ICRP Publication No. 9, Pergamon Press (1966).

34. Raventos, Antolin, Statement before the House Committee on Interstate and Foreign Commerce, Subcommittee on Public Health and Welfare, 90th Congress, on H.R. 10729 (October 11, 1967).

35. Fess, L. R., McDowell, R. B., Jameson, W. R., and Alcox, R. W., "Results of 33,911 X-Ray Protection Surveys of Facilities with Medical or Dental Diagnostic X-Ray Equipment, Fiscal Years 1961-1968," Rad. Health Data and Repts. 11:581-612 (November, 1970).

36. Gitlin, J. N., and Lawrence, P. S., "Population Exposure to X-Rays, U.S. 1964," Public Health Service Publication No. 1519.

37. APHA, Conference Report on Radiological Health, Public Health Reports 83:229-231 (March, 1968).

38. Bureau of Radiological Health, "Preliminary Results of Surveys of 5,263 Medical X-Ray Facilities, 1962-1967," Rad. Health Data and Repts. 10  (June, 1969).

39. Blatz, Hanson, "New Directions -- States," in 3rd Annual National Conference on Radiation Control, Scottsdale, Arizona, May 2-6, 1971, DHEW Publication No. 72-8021.

40. National Advisory Committee on Radiation, "Protecting and Improving Health Through the Radiological Sciences," Report to the Surgeon General, USPHS (April, 1966).

41. Lange, Walter H., "Report of the Senior Technologist Trustee, American Registry of Radiologic Technologists, 1970-1971," Radiologic Technology 43:240-244 (1970).

42. Kraeger, James A., and Christianson, Gene A., "Survey Results of the Use of X-Rays in the Healing Art Specialties in North Dakota, 1964-1968," Radiologic Technology 42:161-174 (1970).

43. Department of Labor, "Occupational Outlook Handbook in Brief," 1972-1973 edition.

44. Hendee, W. R., "Changing Patterns in the Training of Radiologic Technologist: A Case Report," Radiologic Technologist 42:392-400 (1971).

45. Koenig, G. F., "Restructuring the Education of Radiologic Technologists," Radiologic Technology 43:127-129 (1971).

46. Tolan, Marjorie, "Invitational Manpower Conference on Allied Health Professions Assistants," Radiologic Technology 42:94-97 (1970).

47. Nelson, Bryce, "Mobile TB X-Ray Units: An Obsolete Technology Lingers," Science 174:1114-15 (December 10, 1971).

48. National Tuberculosis and Respiratory Disease Association, "Mass Chest X-Ray Screening -- An Idea Whose Time Has Gone," Bulletin 57:9 (October, 1971).

49. "What About Radiation? Mass Chest X-Ray Programs," USPHS Pub. 1196 (February, 1965).

50. Cole, William S., "Chest X-Rays," Science 175:563 (August 18, 1972).

51. Gileadi, Michael, "Joint Dental Radiation Survey in Puerto Rico, 1968," Rad. Health Data and Repts. 14(6):333-396 (June, 1973).

52. Bureau of Radiological Health, "Diagnostic Dental X-Rays and the Patient -- An Overview," Rad. Health Data and Repts. 10:1-50 (January, 1970).

53. National Center for Radiological Health, Compliance and Control Branch. Report of State and Local Radiological Health Programs for Fiscal Year, 1967, PHS CCB-68-2 (July, 1968).

54. Richards, Dr. Albert G., Statement before the House Committee on Interstate and Foreign Commerce, Subcommittee on Public Health and Welfare, 90th Congress, on H.R. 10729 (Serial No. 90-11).

55. Rosenthal, Robert B., and Malcolm, James C., "Results of a Program Directed Toward Reduction of Dental X-Ray Exposure," Rad. Health Data and Repts. 11:109-115 (March, 1970).

56. Report of the United Nations Scientific Committee on the Effects of Atomic Radiation, Supplement 16 (A/5216), United Nations, New York, p. 20 (1962).

57. Pearce, Colleen, and Webster, John H., M.C., "Radiation Therapy Technology: Problems and Progress," Radiologic Technology 43:1-6 (1972).

58. Johnson, Phillip C., "Benefits and Risks in Nuclear Medicine," AJPH 62:1568-72 (December, 1972).

59. Moeller, Dade W., "Meeting Radiological Health Manpower Needs," AJPH 61:1928-46 (October, 1946).

60. General Accounting Office, "Problems of the Atomic Energy Commission Associated with the Regulation of Users of Radioactive Material for Industrial, Commercial, Medical, and Related Purposes," Report No. B-16405 (August 18, 1972).

61. Edwards, C. C., "Proposal Regarding New-Drug Applications Requirements," Federal Register 36:1274 (January 27, 1971).

62. Villforth, John C., Response to letter from Senator Warren G. Magnuson, February, 1973, hearings before the Committee on Commerce, U.S. Senate, an oversight of the Radiation Control for Health and Safety Act of 1968.

63. Harris, Jesse Y., "Electronic Products Inventory Study," USDHEW, PHS, CPEHS, ECA, Bureau of Radiological Health, Rockville, Maryland (September, 1969).

64. Hart, D., "Survey of Ultrasonics in Medicine," Presentation at Commercial Applications of Ultrasonics Symposium, February 6, 1969, New York.

65. Landau, Emanuel, "Are There Ultrasonic Dangers to the Unborn?" Practical Radiology 1(6):27-31 (June, 1973).

66. Lele, P. P., "Application of Ultrasound in Medicine," New England Journal of Medicine 286:1317-18 (1972).

67. Lele, P. P., "No Chromosomal Damage from Ultrasound," New England Journal of Medicine 287:254 (1972).

68. Department of Health, Education and Welfare, "Annual Report on the Administration of the Radiation Control for Health and Safety Act of 1968," May 20, 1971 (H. Doc. 92-113).

69. Mead, G. G., "Washington Dateline," Radiologic Technology, Vol. 43:94-95 (1972).

70. DHEW, "Report of Licensure and Related Health Personnel Credentialling" (August 17, 1971), U.S. Government Printing Office, Washington, D.C. 20402 Stock No. 1720-0034.

71. Morgan, James A., "A Prevalent Fallacy," The X-Ray Technician, January, 1942, reprinted in Radiologic Technology 42:213 (1972).

72. Ron M. Linton, "A Strategy for a Livable Environment," A Report to the Secretary of Health, Education and Welfare by the Task Force on Environmental Health and Related Problems (June, 1967).

73. PHS, DHEW, Report of the Medical Advisory Committee (to the Surgeon General, USPHS) on "Public Health Considerations in Medical Diagnostic Radiology (X-Rays)" (October, 1967).

74. U.S. Congress, House of Representatives, Report to Accompany H.R. 10790 (H. Rept. No. 90-1166), March 12, 1968.

75. Donnelly, Warren H., "Bushwhacking, Licensure, and Senator Bartlett," Radiologic Technology 42:248-58 (1971).

76. DHEW, PHS, "Model Legislation for Uses of Ionizing Radiation in the Healing Arts," BRH/ORO 70-8 (October, 1970).

77. Wilson, Leslie, R. T., "President's Address: No More Tears," Radiologic Technology 43:226-29 (1972).

78. Gofman, John W., and Tamplin, Arthur R., Hearings before the Subcommittee on Air and Water Pollution, Committee on Public Works, United States Senate, U.S. Congress, on S. 3042, November 18, 1969.

79. Randolph, Senator Jennings, "S. 3973 -- Introduction of the Radiation Health and Safety Act of 1970," Congressional Record, Vol. 116, No. 99 (June 16, 1970), pp. S. 9046-48.

80. Randolph, Senator Jennings, "Senate Bill 3973," Radiologic Technology 42:104-7 (1971).

81. Olden, Richard A., Statement before the Subcommittee on Health, Committee on Labor and Public Welfare, United States Senate, May 20, 1970, reprinted in Radiologic Technology 42: 35-37 (1971).

82. Randolph, Senator Jennings, "S. 426 -- Introduction of t e Radiation Health and Safety Act of 1971," Congressional Record, Vol. 117 (January 28, 1971), pp. S. 443-45.

83. Mead, George G., "Washington Dateline: May 16, 1972 -- Society Testifies for S. 3327," Radiologic Technology 43:38-42 (1972).

84. Koch, E. I., "X-Ray Technologists and X-Ray Equipment Should Be Regulated and Licensed," Congressional Record, Vol. 118, No. 133, Part 2 (August 17, 1972), H. 7919-7934.

85. Mead, George G., "Washington Dateline: September 10, 1972," Radiologic Technology 43:158-61 (1972).

86. Koch, E. I., H.R. 673, Congressional Record, Vol. 119, No. 1 (January 6, 1973), H. 77.

87. Randolph, Senator Jennings, "Radiation Health and Safety Act of 1973," Congressional Record, Vol. 119, No. 17 (January 31, 1973).

88. Randolph, Senator Jennings, "Job Descriptions for Diagnostic X-Ray, Radiation Therapy, and Nuclear Medicine Technologists," Radiologic Technology 43:27-42 (1972).

89. U.S. Congress. Senate. Committee on Commerce. Hearings on Public Law 90-602, March 8, 9, and 12, 1973 (Serial No. 93-24).

90. Kennedy, Senator Edward M., letter of July 12, 1973, to Senator Jennings Randolph.

91. Tolan, John J., "Comments on Recent Proposals for Regulatory Control of X-Ray Exposures," Radiologic Technology 40:124-34 (1969).

92. Roemer, Ruth, "Legal Regulation of Health Manpower in the 1970's," HSMHA Health Reports 86:1053-64 (December, 1971).

93. Burney, Surgeon General Leroy, Address to 1958 National Air Pollution Conference.

94. DHEW, PHS, FDA, "BRH Bulletin," Vol. VI, No. 9 (Monday, May 15, 1972).

95. Eason, Charles F., and Brooks, Barbara G., "Should Medical Radiation Exposure Be Recorded?" AJPH 62:1189-93 (September, 1972).

96. USDHEW, "X-Ray Examinations...A Guide to Good Practice," Washington, D.C., U.S. Govt. Printing Office, 5505-003 (1971).